W34

Unwin Critical Library
GENERAL EDITOR: CLAUDE RAWSON

MADAME BOVARY

MADAME BOVARY

Rosemary Lloyd

London
UNWIN HYMAN
Boston   Sydney   Wellington

Published by the Academic Division of

Unwin Hyman Ltd
15/17 Broadwick Street, London W1V 1FP, UK

Unwin Hyman Inc.,
8 Winchester Place, Winchester, Mass. 01890, USA

Allen & Unwin (Australia) Ltd,
8 Napier Street, North Sydney, NSW 2060, Australia

Allen & Unwin (New Zealand) Ltd in association with the
Port Nicholson Press Ltd,
Compusales Building, 75 Ghuznee Street, Wellington 1, New Zealand

First published in 1990

British Library Cataloguing in Publication Data
Lloyd, R.
  Madame Bovary. – (Unwin critical library)
  1. Fiction in French. Flaubert, Gustave. Madame
  Bovary-Critical Studies
  I. Title
  843′.8

  ISBN 0–04–800084–1

Library of Congress Cataloging in Publication Data
Lloyd, R.
  Madame Bovary / Rosemary Lloyd.
  p. cm. — (Unwin critical library)
  Includes bibliographical references.
  ISBN 0–04–800084–1
  1. Flaubert, Gustave, 1821–1880. Madame Bovary. I. Title.
II. Series.
PQ2246.M3L5 1989
843′ .8—dc20

Typeset in Bembo by Gecko Limited, Bicester, Oxon
and printed in Great Britain by Billing and Sons, London and
Worcester

For Penny

CONTENTS

GENERAL EDITOR'S PREFACE

Each volume in this series is devoted to a single major text. It is intended for serious students and teachers of literature, and for knowledgeable non-academic readers. It aims to provide a scholarly introduction and a stimulus to critical thought and discussion.

Individual volumes will naturally differ from one another in arrangement and emphasis, but each will normally begin with information on a work's literary and intellectual background, and other guidance designed to help the reader to an informed understanding. This is followed by an extended critical discussion of the work itself, and each contributor in the series has been encouraged to present in these sections his own reading of the work, whether or not this is controversial, rather than to attempt a mere consensus. Some volumes, including those on *Paradise Lost* and *Ulysses*, vary somewhat from the more usual pattern by entering into substantive critical discussion at the outset, and allowing the necessary background material to emerge at the points where it is felt to arise from the argument in the most useful and relevant way. Each volume also contains a historical survey of the work's critical reputation, including an account of the principal lines of approach and areas of controversy, and a selective (but detailed) bibliography.

The hope is that the volumes in this series will be among those which a university teacher would normally recommend for any serious study of a particular text, and that they will also be among the essential secondary texts to be consulted in some scholarly investigations. But the experienced and informed non-academic reader has also been in our minds, and one of our aims has been to provide him or her with reliable and stimulating works of reference and guidance, embodying the present state of knowledge and opinion in a conveniently accessible form.

C.J.R.
University of Warwick,
December 1979

PREFACE

The text used in this study is C. Gothot-Mersch's edition, first published by Garnier in 1971. Page references to this edition are placed immediately after quotations. The translations are my own: I have aimed for accuracy rather than beauty in these renderings of Flaubert's texts and drafts.

Abbreviations used in the notes are as follows:

Corr = Flaubert's correspondence in the Pléiade edition. Since this edition has so far only reached the year 1858, letters written after that date are referred to by the date of composition.

Ebauches = *Madame Bovary, Ebauches et Fragments inédits*, 2 vols (Paris: Louis Conard, 1936)

MBNV = *Madame Bovary, nouvelle version*, ed. J. Pommier and G. Leleu (Paris: José Corti, 1949)

I should like to record here my gratitude to my New Hall colleagues for many fascinating lunchtime discussions during the period when I was working on this book; to Alison Fairlie, for the helpful and stimulating remarks she made on an earlier version of this study; and to my husband, Paul, for everything.

CHAPTER 1

Overture

Roughly one-third of the way through *Madame Bovary*, we come across the story of la Guérine. At this point in the novel, Emma Bovary, unhappily married and physically unsatisfied, disappointed by the apparently unbridgeable gap between her expectations of life and her experience of life, lacks as yet the courage and the opportunity to take a lover. Her despair assumes both a physical and an emotional form, beyond the understanding of either her doctor husband or the village priest and it prompts her maid, Félicité, to recount the following tale:

> —Ah! oui, reprenait Félicité, vous êtes justement comme la Guérine, la fille au père Guérin, le pêcheur du Pollet, que j'ai connue à Dieppe, avant de venir chez vous. Elle était si triste, si triste, qu'à la voir debout sur le seuil de sa maison, elle vous faisait l'effet d'un drap d'enterrement tendu devant la porte. Son mal, à ce qu'il paraît, était une manière de brouillard qu'elle avait dans la tête, et les médecins n'y pouvaient rien, ni le curé non plus. Quand ça la prenait trop fort, elle s'en allait toute seule sur le bord de la mer, si bien que le lieutenant de la douane, en faisant sa tournée, souvent la trouvait étendue à plat ventre et pleurant sur les galets. Puis, après son mariage, ça lui a passé, dit-on.
> —Mais, moi, reprenait Emma, c'est après le mariage que ça m'est venu (112).[1]

Among the many narratives nested in *Madame Bovary*, this one has particular significance. Related by a woman, to a woman, about a woman, it is presented, by its narrator, as offering a mirror of Emma's condition: 'Vous êtes justement comme la Guérine', and although Emma signals a difference ('Mais moi, c'est après mon mariage que ça m'est venu'), it is a difference of time, not of emotion. The text's narrative voice is deafeningly silent here: Félicité is allowed to tell the tale in her own words, and Emma's remarks herald the end of the chapter. Apparently no ironic comment, explicit or implicit, nor any hint of how to read this brief passage is given to us. Yet it raises several questions about the ways in which we respond to stories: on a most basic level they are seen as paradigms, allowing for substitutions (Emma for la Guérine, 'after marriage' for 'before marriage'), reflections of universal truth, which the hearer may apply to her own situation. Of course Emma is encouraged to do so, not merely by Félicité's opening statement, but also because the heroine has sought help from the same sources as she herself has, the doctor and the priest, those who minister to the body and those who minister to the soul. For both women, moreover, the source of the sickness is sexual, and its nature seems incapable of being expressed in language. Félicité suggests a parallel with fog, but wraps that simile around with 'so it seems' and 'a sort of'. Emma's own desire to confide in another person is shown to founder both on the social fact of there being no one else of her class and age in the village, and on the difficulties inherent in giving expression to emotions as fleeting and changeable as clouds.

The whole question of how individuals use language, which is so central to the novel, is also raised here, in the way in which Flaubert explores the possibilities of conveying peasant diction in direct speech, drawing on the simplicity and intensity of the images – the comparison between la Guérine and a shroud, the picture of her lying flat on her stomach on the pebbles – and the forms of emphasis – the repetition of 'si triste' – to offer parallels with Emma's own sufferings, which are usually expressed in the more analytical and polished language of *style indirect libre*. Equally important is the visual side to the story: however much Emma's response to reality is conditioned by her reading, it is also very much a product of engravings and paintings, and a study of the pictures conjured up by her imagination indicates the extent to which she is most touched by that which she can most clearly visualize. Flaubert's desire to explore such psychological realities and to indicate how different individuals react under similar circumstances is evident not only in the novel itself but also in remarks in his letters, where, for example, he reflects that the first version of his *Education sentimentale* needs a chapter revealing 'pourquoi telle action a amené ce résultat dans ce personnage plutôt que telle autre'[2] and insists that *Madame Bovary* represents the entirety of his psychological knowledge, the 'somme de [sa] science psychologique'.[3]

For the reader of Flaubert's novel the temptation to proceed to a substitution of Emma for la Guérine is intensified by the fact that both women bear names that reveal, not their personal identity, but their relationship to a man: Madame Bovary and la Guérine. Indeed, the tale indicates very clearly the extent to which identity is a product of social position, since la Guérine is defined by her relationship to a family group, and her father is identified by his function in society, that of fisherman in a particular village. Throughout *Madame Bovary* Flaubert explores the importance of social forces on the shaping of individuals and clearly relishes the opportunity of capturing and analysing forms of behaviour and thought that typify French society at the time in which he was writing.

Félicité's simile, moreover, pulls into sudden sharp focus the many links between love and death that the novel suggests: 'elle vous faisait l'effet d'un drap d'enterrement'. Emma's response is not to reject the similarity suggested, but to point instead to minor differences. But here, too, suggestions of death are present, for if la Guérine could move from one situation to another by marriage, Emma is in a position from which there is no exit other than death, her own or that of her husband. Moreover, the fact that marriage solved la Guérine's problem is only indirectly attested, by an unidentified 'on' (in 'dit-on'). The traditional fairy-tale ending of 'they married and lived happily ever after' is not provided directly by Félicité, and is in any case ironically subverted, since the habitual tag is replaced by a mere negation: 'something left her after her marriage', and is undermined by Emma's gloss on her own marriage. And if we assume that for *ça* can be substituted 'le brouillard', we fall into a further trap. Can la Guérine's situation be substituted for Emma's when Emma is so demonstrably not 'justement comme la Guérine'?

One final ironic detail should be mentioned: Félicité's passing reference to the sea-shore, which Emma finds so romantic in literature and imagination, but which here serves only as a grim background to la Guérine's melancholy. No golden beach or setting sun here, only the cobbles of a rocky and decidedly unromantic shore. Indeed, throughout the novel Flaubert systematically refuses Emma the surroundings, relationships and experiences her reading had led her to expect from life.

It is the assumptions about the contract between story and life that Flaubert's irony sets out to unravel, since it is precisely her simplistically mimetic and analogical reading that leads Emma astray. Questions concerning difference, similarity and substitution lie at the heart of *Madame Bovary*, although it will be my contention in what follows that Flaubert does not necessarily reject or deny the possibility and indeed the pleasure of mimesis. One of the major challenges of responding to the novel is posed by the very richness of the text, for Flaubert habitually operates on at least three levels: the exploration of social patterns of behaviour, the psychological analysis of an individual's development, and the narratological experiments with the point of view adopted, the different forms of language employed and the presentation of time and space. What this study of *Madame Bovary* attempts to do is to focus on some of the questions the text raises, while remaining aware that concentrating on separate issues always leads to a sense that the other elements involved also call for analysis.

Notes: Chapter 1

1 'Ah! yes', continued Félicité, 'You're just like la Guérine, the daughter of old Guérin, the fisherman of Le Pollet. I knew her at Dieppe before I came to work for you. She was so sad, so very sad, that if you saw her standing at the entrance to her house, you'd think she was a shroud spread out in front of the doorway. What she was suffering from, so it seems, was a sort of fog in her head, and the doctors couldn't do a thing about it, nor the priest either. When it was particularly bad, she'd go off all alone to the sea shore, and the customs officer, when he was doing his rounds, often used to find her lying flat on her stomach and crying on the pebbles. Then, after her marriage, they say it left her.'
'But', replied Emma, 'In my case, it was after my marriage that it came to me.'
2 Corr, II, 30: 'why a certain action produced that particular result in a certain character, rather than any other action'.
3 Corr, II, 124.

CHAPTER 2

Preparing the way

Aussitôt, cependant, apparaît Flaubert
(Robbe-Grillet: *Le Miroir qui revient*)

The decade in which Flaubert produced *Madame Bovary*, and particularly the year 1857 in which the volume was first published, were especially rich in the history of Western literature. Although the death of Balzac in 1850 heralded a brief eclipse for the novel form, these ten years saw a remarkable proliferation of poetic publications, and a lively and wide-ranging aesthetical debate concerning the possibilities of prosodic forms and the interrelationship of truth, beauty and morality. In the world of the visual arts, Realism was taking over from Romanticism as the dominant mode, with the leading Realist painter, Courbet, questioning traditional assumptions about what was acceptable subject-matter for art, and exploring ways in which art could present the humdrum and banal. The publication in volume form of Baudelaire's *Les Fleurs du mal* and of Flaubert's *Madame Bovary* marked a significant turning point both in poetry and in prose fiction, calling into question modes of writing and bringing into sharp focus the problematics of language. *Madame Bovary*, despite the hostile reception given it by certain critics, has come to be seen as a vital testing ground for theories of narrative, and Flaubert, through the sophistication of his techniques, the sardonic force of his social criticism and the acuity of his psychological insights, remains one of the most challenging and demanding of all prose writers.

Much of the novel is, to varying extents, a response to the main literary movements of the age. Romanticism, after the débâcle of Hugo's *Les Burgraves* in 1843, was on the wane, although its enthusiasm for the macabre, the emphasis it placed on the individual and on emotions, and several other of its more easily assimilable commonplaces continued to be current coin among the reading public. With the defeat of republican ideals after the revolution of 1848 and Napoléon III's coup d'état and declaration of empire in 1852, many writers had turned away from political involvement in the age, but some, mainly novelists, adopted and revised the techniques of Balzac to create what they saw as a mimetic representation of reality. One further movement should be mentioned here, if only for the revulsion it aroused in Flaubert, as in Baudelaire: the now justly-forgotten school of good sense, which promoted the ideals of the bourgeoisie, the double standards of its morality and above all the moral value it conferred on material wealth.

The years in which Flaubert was working on his novel were ones of comparative stability for France, seeing the country's increasing industrialization and a continuing movement away from traditional sources of wealth and social status towards a hierarchy based on money created by industry or the stock exchange. Noticeable, too, was the rise in power of the press. Once the cost of producing newspapers had been transferred from the consumer to the advertisers, the increase in sales and in the number of newspapers produced was immense and, as part of a bid to attract and hold readers to a particular periodical, the practice of including a serialized novel was also becoming increasingly common. Predictably, the government sought to control such power by a series of frequently draconian legislative measures, using the power of censorship not merely to curtail what were seen as infringements of public morality but also to force opposition papers to temper their political attacks. Flaubert's decision to publish his novel first through a periodical carried therefore the risk of censorship both from the editor and from the government, and his association with the often controversial but highly influential *Revue de Paris* may well have meant that the accusations of offending public sensibilities were, as he himself claimed, merely a front to enable an attack on the paper itself.[1]

Born in 1821 in Rouen, Flaubert was the fifth of six children, three of whom died in infancy. Gustave's older brother, Achille, became, like his father, a successful doctor: the youngest child, Caroline, was to die of puerperal fever at the age of twenty-one.

Gustave himself embarked on a law course, but suffered an attack of what might have been epilepsy in 1844 and henceforth lived with his mother, apart from various voyages in France and abroad. He had in fact been writing since his early teens, creating a weekly magazine in 1834–35, to which he gave the ironic title 'Art et Progrès', parodying bourgeois assumptions about the role of art in a way which points forward to much of his later work. In 1837 he published a short story, 'Bibliomanie', in a Rouen literary journal, *Le Colibri*, and in a spirit of buffoonery that presages *Bouvard et Pécuchet*,[2] he wrote a 'Leçon d'histoire naturelle, genre commis'. Indeed, the strongly marked links between the juvenilia and his later writing indicate the extent to which he had already formulated his central concerns, and had begun to refine his main techniques, from a remarkably early age. Certainly the complexity of his character, with its surges of Romantic lyricism counterbalanced by a desire to reveal the everyday reality of existence, is clearly reflected in the variety of subject matter to be found in his early writing. With *Smarh*, completed in 1839, Flaubert traced out a first version of the work to which he most frequently returned, *La Tentation de Saint-Antoine*, and revealed that side of his nature which was 'épris de *gueulades*, de lyrisme, de grands vols d'aigle, de toutes les sonorités de la phrase et des sommets de l'idée'.[3] *Un parfum à sentir* and *Passion et Vertu*, however, reflect the other 'bonhomme distinct' that made up his literary personality, the one 'qui fouille et creuse le vrai tant qu'il peut, qui aime à accuser le petit fait aussi puissamment que le grand, qui voudrait vous faire sentir presque *matériellement* les choses qu'il reproduit'.[4]

These early works reveal just how deeply ingrained in Flaubert's character are the preoccupations both with subject matter and with style that underpin *Madame Bovary*. From a very early stage Flaubert was clearly fascinated by the individual's power of self-delusion and the way in which the need for an existence of intensity and coherence could drive even the more mediocre individuals to acts of violence and self-destruction. Moreover, this image of a possible life vastly different from the quotidian is presented, both in the juvenilia and in the later novels, as a product primarily of language. Stylistically, too, these works, for all their immaturity, already reveal some of the techniques of Flaubert's later novels, particularly the ability

to convey sounds and light, and the characteristic nature of his
imagery. A somewhat self-mocking authorial comment at the
end of *Un parfum à sentir*, moreover, offers a sidelight on the
young Flaubert's image of writing, which helps to set in context
a study of the works of that period:

> Vous ne savez peut-être quel plaisir c'est: composer!
> Ecrire, oh! écrire, c'est s'emparer du monde, de ses
> préjugés, de ses vertus et le résumer dans un livre; c'est
> sentir sa pensée naître, grandir, vivre, se dresser debout
> sur son piédestal, et y rester toujours.
> Je viens donc d'achever ce livre étrange, bizarre,
> incompréhensible.[5]

Passion et Vertu, completed in December 1837, shows the young
Flaubert already concerned to explore 'cette route immense de
la passion, qui commence avec un sourire et qui ne finit que sur
une tombe'.[6] The theme itself is, of course, a familiar element
of Romanticism, particularly that of the later Romantics, but
Flaubert's treatment of it suggests, even at this early stage,
the deflating irony that marks *Madame Bovary*. Like Rodolphe,
Ernest, for instance, is presented to us from the outset as offering
little in common with the typical Romantic hero: 'loin d'être une
de ces âmes d'exception comme il y en a dans les livres et dans
les drames, c'était un cœur sec, un esprit juste, et par-dessus tout
cela, un chimiste'.[7] The science of seduction practised by Ernest
will be that of Rodolphe, but it is conveyed in the early work
with even greater cynicism through the concision with which it
is elucidated:

> Mais maintenant un homme s'avance vers une femme, il
> la lorgne, il la trouve bien, il en fait le pari avec ses amis;
> est-elle mariée, la farce n'en sera que meilleure.
> Alors il s'introduit chez elle, il lui prête des romans, la
> mène au spectacle, il a surtout soin de faire quelque
> chose d'étonnant, de ridicule, enfin d'étrange; . . . c'est
> une cruauté d'anatomiste, mais on a fait des progrès dans
> les sciences et il y a des gens qui dissèquent un cœur comme
> un cadavre. [8]

Just as Rodolphe's awareness of Emma's dissatisfaction with her
married life led to the conclusion: 'ça bâille après l'amour,

comme une carpe après l'eau sur une table de cuisine. Avec trois mots de galanterie, cela vous adorerait' (134),[9] so Ernest, as brutally but more concisely, concluded on the basis of Mazza's love of poetry, the sea and Byron: 'C'est une sotte, je l'aurai'.[10] Similarly, too, the way in which Rodolphe's seduction of Emma during their afternoon ostensibly spent riding reveals a pattern of brusqueness, followed by apparently platonic adoration leading to the act of love, traces a pattern already established in that Ernest, when Mazza visits him in his room, claiming that she wants the relationship to end, begins by locking the door, then feigns adoration before proceeding to the 'voluptés qui brûlent'.[11] Mazza's convictions and responses, moreover, herald those of Emma, particularly in her tendency to perceive the external world as an extension of her own emotions and in her recurrent dissatisfaction with the limitations and disappointments of existence: like Emma, Mazza wonders if, 'derrière la volupté, il n'y en avait pas une plus grande encore, ni après le plaisir une plus vaste jouissance'.[12]

Similarities of character, moreover, are increased by a preoccupation with light and sound, and by the presence of certain images that recur in the later novel. The problem of conveying in language the quality of the light shed by a lamp clearly intrigues Flaubert even at this early stage, although his solution in adolescence is markedly more influenced by Romanticism than that of his later works: 'la lampe brûlait et jetait au plafond un disque lumineux qui tremblait en vacillant sur lui-même, comme l'œil d'un damné qui vous regarde'.[13] Equally, the emotive importance of sound, which will add so much to the evocation of Emma's boredom, is seized on in *Passion et Vertu* as a means of conveying Mazza's desires and fears:

> elle resta longtemps, jusqu'au jour, à écouter les heures qui sonnaient à toutes les cloches, à entendre tous les bruits de la nuit, la pluie qui tombe et bat les murs, et les vents qui soufflent et tourbillonnent dans les ténèbres, les vitres qui tremblent, le bois du lit qui criait à tous les mouvements qu'elle lui donnait en se retournant sur ses matelas.[14]

Even certain recurrent images of *Madame Bovary*, that of wine as a symbol of human temperament, for instance, or that of the

circle to indicate the way in which the individual longing for the
exceptional finds herself locked into the banal, can be discovered
in prototype form in *Passion et Vertu*.[15]

Novembre, which Flaubert wrote in 1842, also points forward to
the later works, particularly in the vision of humanity it expresses
and in its exploration of the power of language to dominate the
mind. Indeed, Flaubert was to affirm to Louise Colet in 1853:
'J'ai relu *Novembre*, mercredi, par curiosité. J'étais bien le même
particulier il y a onze ans qu'aujourd'hui.'[16] Mankind offers
the first-person narrator of *Novembre* the image of a 'surface
mouvante de méchants, de lâches, d'idiots et de laids',[17] while
the very word *maîtresse* is sufficient to incite long ecstasy,[18] and
the term 'adultery' carries with it an intense evocative charge:

> il y eut dès lors pour moi un mot qui sembla beau entre
> les mots humains: adultère. Une douceur exquise plane
> vaguement sur lui. Une magie singulière l'embaume;
> toutes les histoires qu'on raconte, tous les livres qu'on
> lit, tous les gestes qu'on fait le disent et le commentent
> éternellement pour le cœur du jeune homme, il s'en
> abreuve à plaisir, il y trouve une poésie suprême, mêlée
> de malédiction et de volupté.[19]

Emma, and Léon, too, both reveal a similar tendency to
embroider a vision of reality on the deceptive web of words.

The first version of Flaubert's novel *L'Education sentimentale*,
written between 1843 and 1845 (a period during which he
suffered the fit that led him to abandon his law course and
devote himself to writing), allowed him, particularly through his
character Jules, to explore and refine his philosophy of art, but
it also contains much which more specifically points forward to
Madame Bovary. The complex interrelationships between art and
life, between language and experience, between the individual
and society, which are so vital to the later novel, are also
central here. The scene depicting the first meeting between
Emma and Léon and showing in particular their artistic and
literary preferences offers many parallels with the description
of a conversation between Henry and Mme Renaud, in which
they speak of the great delight of being borne away by a genius's
dream, on some golden cloud, beyond the known worlds[20] and

where Flaubert conveys the essence of what they have said in the
elliptical list-form that he so frequently uses for purposes both of
ironic mockery and nostalgic longing:

> ils parlèrent ensemble des histoires d'amour fameuses au
> théâtre, des élégies les plus tendres; ils aspirèrent en pensée
> la douceur des nuits étoilées, le parfum des fleurs d'été; ils
> se dirent les livres qui les avaient fait pleurer, ceux qui les
> avaient fait rêver, que sais-je encore? ils devisèrent sur le
> malheur de la vie et sur les soleils couchants.[21]

The characteristically sardonic juxtaposition of the final sentence
quoted above marks this passage as unmistakably Flaubertian.
The same episode reveals the extent to which he is already
collecting the *idées reçues* with which his later work is studded:
'L'Allemand, à qui on demanda son avis [sur la musique],
répondit qu'il ne se connaissait pas en musique, ce qui sembla
drôle, les Allemands devant être musiciens'.[22] The degree to
which the individual's ability to savour an experience is shaped
by reading is a further point already present in this youthful
work: 'Henry se reprochait de ne pas sentir les exagérations
magnifiques qu'il avait lues dans les livres, et chaque jour
cependant il lui arrivait au cœur d'inexprimables sensations
qu'il n'avait jamais rêvées.'[23] Jules, too, turns to literature as
a means of making sense of life: 'Pour trouver quelque chose
d'analogue à ce qui se passait dans son âme, il chercha, dans
les poètes et dans les romanciers, une situation semblable à
la sienne, un caractère comme le sien; . . . il croyait que
rien n'approchait de sa douleur, que toutes les autres étaient
bornées, que la sienne seule était infinie'.[24] Indeed, Jules, whose
nature is described as nervous and feminine,[25] seems to present
an example of bovarysme *avant la lettre*, when we are told
that 'ce qui le rendait à plaindre, c'est qu'il ne savait bien
distinguer ce qui est de ce qui devrait être'.[26] Moreover, the
images of enclosure and restriction that convey Emma's sense
of the stifling nature of everyday existence are also very much
present in the first version of *L'Education sentimentale*. Having
asserted, for example, that Henry and Emilie were happy because
they believed themselves to be so, since happiness depends only
on the idea one has of it, Flaubert adds an image in which
the allusion to birds is typical of *Madame Bovary* even if the

complexity of its comparisons is such that it runs counter to the greater sobriety of the later novel:

> le bonheur est de même, cage plus ou moins large pour des bêtes petites ou grandes; le milan étoufferait dans celle où le serin vole à l'aise, et d'autres, où l'on enferme les vautours, feraient mourir les lions; mais que les barreaux soient resserrés ou élargis, il arrive un jour où l'on se trouve tout haletant sur le bord, regardant le ciel et rêvant l'espace sans limites.[27]

A further example of such images is provided by the description of the minor character Alvarès, who, in a simile Flaubert is to use in reference to Charles, is depicted as constantly turning, like a merry-go-round horse, around an unchanging obsession.[28] Jules's response to this perennial and universal problem is that of a determined artist: 'si chaque passion, si chaque idée dominante de la vie est un cercle où nous tournons pour en voir la circonférence et l'étendue, il ne faut pas y rester enfermé, mais se mettre en dehors.'[29] This solution is, of course, denied both to Emma, since she is 'de tempérament plus sentimentale qu'artiste' (37–38) and to the hero of the final version of *L'Education sentimentale*, Frédéric Moreau, the man who possessed all weaknesses.

The early novel also points forwards to *Madame Bovary* in several of its scenes, notably that which immediately follows Emilie's declaration of love, and that of the waltz. In the first of these, Henry, who resembles Emma in his need of external proof that he exists, gazes at his reflection in a mirror, and just as Emma repeats to herself, not that she is in love, but that she has a lover, so Henry thinks: 'Elle l'aimait! il s'aimait lui-même, il était grand, il était magnifique, il dominait tout.'[30] Strong parallels also exist between the depiction of the Vaubyessard ball and the waltz in the *pension*. Henry, watching Emilie dance, finds that each time she passes him 'sa robe lui effleurait les jambes, le satin soyeux s'accrochait presque au drap de son pantalon, et il attendait qu'elle repassât devant lui, avec une anxiété infinie'.[31] The description of Emma's waltz with the *vicomte* contains several similar elements: 'en passant auprès des portes, la robe d'Emma, par le bas, s'ériflait au pantalon; leurs jambes entraient l'une dans l'autre; il baissait ses regards vers elle, elle levait les siens vers lui; une torpeur la prenait, elle s'arrêta.' (54)[32] And just as Emma, after the ball, gazes out of the window into the surrounding darkness until dawn, so Henry watches the day break through his window and finds that 'quoique le bal l'eût ennuyé, il le regrettait déjà et y rêvait comme à une chose ancienne'.[33]

Certain characters in the first version of *L'Education sentimentale* can also be seen as prototypes of those in *Madame Bovary*. Nowhere is this more obvious than in the depiction of Henry Gosselin's father, whose tastes and whose predilection for clichés portend those of Homais. Like Homais, he admires equally Voltaire and Rousseau; detests priests, but believes in the necessity of religion for the masses; sentimental and kindly, he refuses to give a penny to a beggar until he has assured himself that the man is not lazy; in favour of the theories of progress and equality, he would be deeply shocked if his grocer did not pay him the respect he considers due from an inferior. Homais's extraordinary command of the *idée reçue* is also adumbrated in M. Gosselin: 'il avait ses idées faites sur tous les sujets possibles: pour lui toute jeune fille était *pure*, tout jeune homme était un *farceur*, tout mari un *cocu*, tout pauvre un *voleur*, tout gendarme un *brutal*, et toute campagne *délicieuse*'.[34] Here, moreover, Flaubert can be seen using italics to isolate the spoken words, forcing the reader to perceive them as alien to the narrator's discourse. And both men, of course, 'regard[ent] certaines choses élevées comme des niaiseries, mais en prenant au sérieux bien plus de bouffonnes, à commencer par [eux-mêmes]'.[35] As we have seen, several characteristics of Emma are explored in Henry, but there are also comparisons to be made with Emilie, who shares her curious taste for vinegar (59), and who also combines tendencies which Flaubert designates as masculine with her more feminine behaviour: 'il se mêlait à la douceur de sa caresse une sorte de force contenue, de virilité cachée, qui faisait qu'elle subjuguait, enchantait'.[36]

If the first version of *L'Education sentimentale* can be seen as a testing ground for certain expressions, situations and characters that are further developed in *Madame Bovary*, we can already detect in it – and indeed in earlier works as well – the seeds of Flaubert's later experimentation with the possibilities of a variety of narrative voices and the complexities of *style indirect libre*. The movement between the third-person narration of Henry's adventures, with occasional interventions by an undefined first-person narrator, and Jules's letters, written, of course, in the first person, suggests that Flaubert is trying out certain possibilities and testing the limitations of traditional narrative positions. Equally, the reader is aware of a flexing of muscles in the use of conversations, reported speech ('il se mit à raconter enfin toutes les déceptions de la journée')[37] and, far more rarely, indirect reported speech, such as accompanies the description of Henry's response when Emilie tells him she loves him: 'il était grand, il était magnifique, il dominait tout'.[38]

After the completion of this work, Flaubert did not embark on another full-length novel until 1848, when he started work on *La Tentation de Saint-Antoine*. In the interval he saw his sister enter into what he considered to be an unsuitable marriage, suffered the deaths of his father, his sister and his close friend Le Poittevin, and experienced an intense and sometimes stormy love affair with Louise Colet. Although that affair came to an end in August 1848, the two remained in contact and by 1851 they were lovers once again. The letters he exchanged with her until they finally separated in 1854 contain illuminating information about his views on literature, his approach to writing, and above all the problems he encountered while working on *Madame Bovary*.

On 12 September 1849, Flaubert completed the first version of *La Tentation de Saint-Antoine*, which was to undergo numerous revisions until he finally published it in 1874. According to Maxime Du Camp, whose *Souvenirs littéraires* provide an entertaining although far from entirely accurate account of his friendship with the novelist in the years when Flaubert was unknown to the general public, *La Tentation* was read to Du Camp and Flaubert's close friend Louis Bouilhet[39] in a four-day non-stop session that left his friends in consternation. They advised him to abandon a project they considered completely unmarketable and to turn instead to giving an account of contemporary existence. Flaubert, well aware, as we have seen, of the duality of his literary persona, seems to have acknowledged a degree of accuracy in this response and abandoned the project temporarily, setting off for Egypt with Du Camp, a gifted photographer as well as a writer. During their journey, Flaubert, in addition to gathering together documentation on which he would draw both for further versions of *La Tentation* and for *Salammbô*, began formulating a more 'realistic' work, at first conceived as a Flemish novel in which he would trace the destiny of a young woman who would lead an uneventful life in the provinces, finding escape only in religious mysticism. Returning through Greece and Italy, Flaubert settled back into his old working patterns at Croisset in June 1851 and on 19 September of that year announced that he was beginning work on *Madame Bovary*. The Flemish novel was set aside, to reappear in greatly altered form as *Un cœur simple*, but to recur to some degree in all his novels, while Flaubert drew inspiration, on a superficial level, from accounts of the life and death of a Normandy woman, Delphine Couturier, wife of an 'officier de santé' called Delamare. He also appears to have made use of the diaries of Louise Pradier, whom he knew personally and whose amorous adventures and financial embarrassments seem to have suggested certain aspects of Emma's experiences.[40] The publication and analysis of the journal of 'Mme Ludovica', in other words Louise Pradier,[41] reveals that, although both her sexual adventures and her financial predicaments may have provided Flaubert with certain elements of his heroine, the crudeness of expression and the lack of any sense of intellectual questioning make her mémoires at most a very basic starting point for Flaubert's narrative and psychological experiments. The relationship between Flaubert and a further possible source of inspiration for Emma, his mistress Louise Colet, has also been explored in considerable detail.[42] Yet whatever anecdotal parallels there may be, the complexity of Flaubert's analysis and the irony of his perception clearly stem not from specific sources but rather from his awareness of the behaviour, convictions and modes of thought of his contemporaries. This awareness has, of course, been moulded by his reading and offers a subtle blend of acceptance of certain contemporary beliefs (particularly, perhaps, in regard to the nature of women) and an ironic and at times cynical rejection of the convictions of the age.

During the five years from 1851, Flaubert worked with almost fanatical intensity on his novel, staving off as far as possible the attentions of Louise Colet by writing her long, intricately argued letters in which he explores the problems encountered and the exhilaration experienced in creating *Madame Bovary*. On 30 April

1856 he completed the novel and by 1 June was already writing
to Bouilhet that the manuscript had been sent to Du Camp,
currently editor of the periodical *La Revue de Paris*, confessing:
'j'ai *maintenant* grand envie de me voir imprimé et le plus
promptement possible.'[43] Yet his energy was such, at least where
writing was concerned, that he was already revising *La Tentation*,
with the result that the *Revue de Paris* published *Madame Bovary*
in serial form between October and December, while fragments
of *La Tentation* appeared in December and January in the highly
considered periodical *L'Artiste*. Du Camp's fears of censorship,
which had led him to insist on various cuts to *Madame Bovary*,
proved only too justified: both Flaubert and the editors of *La
Revue de Paris* were accused of offences to public morality and
religion, and were brought to trial on 29 January and 7 February
1857. The prosecuting attorney, Ernest Pinard, alleged that not
only were the descriptions of adultery more seductive than those
of Emma's death, but also that no character in the novel was in a
position to condemn her and that therein lay the work's greatest
offence:

> il n'y a pas dans le livre un personnage qui puisse la
> condamner. Si vous y trouvez un personnage sage, si vous
> y trouvez un seul principe en vertu duquel l'adultère soit
> stigmatisé, j'ai tort. Donc, si dans tout le livre il n'y a pas
> un personnage qui puisse lui faire courber la tête, s'il n'y a
> pas une idée, une ligne en vertu de laquelle l'adultère soit
> flétri, c'est moi qui ai raison, le livre est immoral![44]

Despite this impassioned pleading, Flaubert and the editors of
the *Revue de Paris* were acquitted and the novel was published
by Michel Lévy in April 1857.

There were to be several further editions of *Madame Bovary*
during Flaubert's lifetime, some of them undergoing substantial
revision. As C. Gothot-Mersch points out, in her appendix to the
Garnier edition of 1971, although the 1857 text was reprinted in
1862, 1866 and 1868, Flaubert had already introduced more than
60 corrections into an edition of 1858, and in 1862 Lévy produced
a revised text containing no fewer than 208 corrections. A
new edition with 127 corrections appeared in 1869, with the
Charpentier edition of 1873 introducing a further 168 variants
and being described as the 'édition définitive'. Although, in 1874,

Lemerre published a *Madame Bovary* containing 263 variants on the text of 1858, the Charpentier version continues to be regarded as the definitive text which modern editions reproduce.[45] This continuing desire to perfect his work is typical of Flaubert, indicating the extent to which the narrative and stylistic aims he set himself – and his friends – in his letters were not mere theory but an integral part of his novelistic practice.

The response of critics during the 130 years since its first appearance reveals not only how central the novel has been in forming the aesthetic and narrative ideals of readers of our own time, but also in shaping the works of a wide variety of writers, for whom the encounter with Flaubert proved decisive.[46] Nevertheless, the hostility with which many of its first readers responded to it cannot lightly be dismissed. There can be no doubt that *Madame Bovary* touched many raw nerves and that, if the issue of adultery was given such prominence in attacks on the novel, although the text consistently makes these illicit affairs as debasing as any overtly moralistic work would depict them, the reason lies in the fact that the contemporary reader's expectations of social structures were threatened by a novel that constantly, if insidiously, undermines them, and which refuses to portray sexual transactions as part of the accepted commercial fabric. Adultery in *Madame Bovary* is merely the most easily attackable of a series of metaphors questioning the image the bourgeois reader – particularly the male bourgeois reader – had of himself, his society, his aspirations. The hostile critics who reviewed the book when it first appeared were, without any exception that I have found, male: for female response we are limited to such private comments as those in the letters of readers who, like Mlle Leroyer de Chantepie, wrote to Flaubert to affirm that he had told their personal story. The reason why male readers should have felt so affronted, and why female readers felt they needed a man to speak for them, can be understood only by considering the novel's social and intellectual background.

NOTES: CHAPTER 2

1 On the position and nature of the periodical press in Flaubert's day see C. Bellanger (ed), *Histoire générale de la presse française* (Paris: Presses

universitaires de France, 1969), II. For a brief summary see my *Baudelaire's Literary Criticism* (Cambridge: Cambridge University Press, 1981), pp. 5–6.

2 For a list of Flaubert's main publications see Bibliography, section IV.

3 Corr, II, 30: 'in love with bellows, lyricism, the great flights of the eagle, all the sounds of the sentence and the heights of thought'.

4 ibid.: 'who excavates and burrows into the real to the best of his ability, who loves emphasizing the small fact just as powerfully as the great one, who'd like to make you feel almost *materially* the things he's reproducing'.

5 *Œuvres de jeunesse*, I, p. 107: 'perhaps you don't know what a joy composing is! To write! Oh, to write means to seize hold of the world, of its prejudices and its virtues, and sum it all up in a book; it means feeling one's thoughts come to life, grow, live, stand up on a pedestal and stay there for ever. So I've just finished this strange, weird, incomprehensible book'.

6 *Bibliomanie*, (Paris: Jean-Cyrille Godefroy, 1982) p. 242: 'the vast route of passion, which begins with a smile and ends only on a tomb'.

7 ibid, p. 229: 'far from being one of those exceptional souls, the sort one finds in novels and plays, he was cold-hearted, clear-sighted, and worst of all, a chemist'.

8 ibid, p. 260: 'But nowadays a man approaches a woman, sizes her up, finds her acceptable, makes a bet about her with his friends and if she's married, the joke will be all the better for it. Then he introduces himself into her home, lends her novels, takes her to plays, and in particular is careful to turn her into something astonishing, ridiculous, bizarre, in a word ... his is the cruelty of an anatomist, but we've made progress in the sciences, and there are people who dissect a heart as they would a corpse'.

9 'she'll be gasping for love as a carp gasps for water when it lies on the kitchen table. Three sweet nothings and she'd adore you'.

10 ibid, p. 231: 'she's a fool, I'll have her'.

11 ibid, p. 237: 'the pleasures that burn'.

12 ibid, p. 273: 'behind sensual delight there were not an even greater delight, after pleasure, a vaster pleasure still'.

Among the many similarities between this early work and *Madame Bovary*, we might note the eagerness with which Mazza devours the poison, just as Emma swallows the arsenic with apparent greed; the exploration of her body in the final passages, which offers clear parallels with the scene in which the priest anoints Emma's body; and Ernest's parting letter, in which Flaubert has yielded to buffoonery in the concluding formula: 'je vous embrasse' (I embrace you). Rodolphe at least is granted the grace to reject 'votre tout dévoué' (Your entirely devoted) (209).

13 ibid, p. 234: 'the lamp was burning, projecting on the ceiling a luminous disk that trembled as it oscillated around itself, like the eye of a damned soul looking at you'.

14 ibid, p. 234: 'she remained for a long time, until daybreak, listening to all the bells sound the hours, the noises of the night, the rain as it fell and beat against the walls, the wind whistling and whirling in the darkness, the window panes trembling, the wooden bed that groaned at every movement she made as she tossed about on the mattress'.

15 ibid, pp. 239, 251.

16 Corr, II, p. 459: 'I reread *Novembre* on Wednesday, out of curiosity. I really was the same individual eleven years ago as I am today.'

17 *Novembre*, p. 78: 'a moving surface of wickedness, cowardice, stupidity and ugliness'.

18 ibid, p. 67.

19 ibid, p. 86: 'there was henceforth a word which to my eyes seemed beautiful in human language: the word "adultery". An exquisite sweetness floats vaguely over it. A curious magic embalms it; all the stories one recounts, all the books one reads, all the gestures one performs express it and comment on it eternally for a young man's heart, he drinks it in to his heart's content and he finds in it a supreme poetry, mingled with curses and pleasures'.

20 *L'Education sentimentale*, first version (Paris: Garnier-Flammarion, 1980), p. 78.

21 ibid, p. 78: 'they then spoke together of love stories made famous on the stage, the most tender of elegies; in imagination they breathed in the mildness of starry nights, the perfume of summer flowers; they told each other of the books that had made them .cry, those that had made them dream, and goodness knows what else. They spoke of life's unhappiness and of sunsets'.

22 ibid, p. 78: 'the German, who was asked for his opinion [on music] replied that he knew nothing about music, which seemed funny since Germans ought to be musicians'.
Compare the scene where Emma and Léon, who have just met, talk about their response to music (84–85).

23 ibid, p. 160: 'Henry reproached himself for failing to feel the magnificent exaggerations he had read about in books, and yet every day his heart experienced inexpressible sensations of which he had never dreamt.'

24 ibid, p. 176: 'to find something similar to what was happening in his soul, he sought among the poets and novelists for a situation similar to his own, a character like himself; ... he believed that no sorrow was equal to his, that all others were limited, that his alone was infinite'.

25 ibid, p. 139.

26 ibid, p. 139: 'what made him pitiable, was his incapacity to distinguish what is from what ought to be'.

27 ibid, p. 157: 'happiness is the same, a cage of greater or lesser size, for bigger or smaller animals; the kite would stifle in a cage in which the canary flies with ease, and others, in which vultures are contained, would kill lions; but whether the bars are close together or wide apart, a day comes when one finds oneself gasping on the edge, gazing at the sky and dreaming of limitless space.'

28 ibid, pp. 171–2.

29 ibid. p. 265: 'if every passion, if every dominant idea in life is a circle in which we turn about, seeing its circumference and its extent, the important thing is not to stay locked away inside but to get out'.

30 *L'Education sentimentale*, first version, p. 100: 'she loved him! he loved himself, he was tall, magnificent, he dominated everything'. For the role of narcissism and the mirror see pp. 116–17.

31 *L'Education sentimentale*, first version, pp. 121–22: 'her dress brushed his legs, the silky satin almost clung to the material of his trousers and he waited for her to pass by him again, with infinite anxiety'.

32 'as she passed by the doors, the hem of Emma's dress clung to his trousers; their legs intertwined, he looked down at her, she looked up at him. A torpor seized her and she stopped.'

33 ibid, p. 123: 'although the ball had bored him, he already regretted that it was over and mused about it as if it were something from long ago'.

34 ibid, p. 218: 'he had fixed ideas on all possible subjects: for him every young girl was *pure*, all young men were *jokers*, every husband a *cuckold*, anyone

who was poor was a thief, every policeman a *brute* and every countryside
delicious'.

35 ibid: 'consider certain lofty matters to be mere jokes, but take seriously many
which are more ridiculous, starting with themselves'.

36 ibid, p. 215: 'mingled with the sweetness of her caress was a kind of
controlled strength, a hidden virility, which enabled her to subjugate and
enchant'.

37 ibid., p. 129: 'finally he set about recounting all the disappointments of
his day'.

38 ibid., p. 100: 'he was great, he was magnificent, he dominated everything'.

39 Flaubert first met Bouilhet when they were boys in 1834. He published
Bouilhet's poems, *Dernières Chansons*, after the latter's death, and prefaced
them with a statement about his own views on literature and art.

40 For a detailed study of this see C. Gothot-Mersch, *La Genèse de Madame
Bovary*.

41 See J. Pommier and G. Leleu, 'Du nouveau sur *Madame Bovary*', *Revue
d'histoire littéraire de la France*, 1947, pp. 211–44. See also D. Siler, *Flaubert
and Louise Pradier*, which includes the text of the *Mémoires de Madame Ludovica*
(Paris: Archives des lettres modernes, no. 145, 1973).

42 See, for example, J. F. Jackson, *Louise Colet et ses amis littéraires* (New Haven,
Conn.: Yale University Press, 1937).

43 Corr, II, 613: 'I *now* have a great desire to see myself in print, and as
promptly as possible.'

44 Reproduced in *Madame Bovary* (Paris: Folio, 1972), p. 499: 'there is in the
book not one character capable of condemning her. If you find a virtuous
character or a single principle on the basis of which adultery is stigmatized,
then I am wrong. Therefore, if, in the entire book there is not a single
character who can make her hang her head in shame, if there is not an
idea, not a line on the basis of which adultery is covered with disgrace,
then it is I who am right, the book is immoral!'

45 For details see *Madame Bovary* (Paris: Garnier, 1971), pp. 359–64.

46 See *Magazine littéraire* (février 1988), for a recent account of such
influences.

CHAPTER 3

The intellectual and social background

On ne peut malheureusement s'abstraire de son époque.
(Flaubert, 24 November 1853)

Flaubert's letters bristle with outbursts of disgust directed at the age and the society he lives in: its stupidity, its mediocrity, its materialistic values, the moral and intellectual impoverishment of the aristocracy, the baseness of the peasants, the overriding hypocrisy and *bêtise* of the middle classes. All of these are the object of an implacable hatred, fueled and intensified by the realization that he himself was unalterably formed by that society and that age. His *Dictionnaire des idées reçues* offers hilarious perspectives on his image of the age, but reveals, too, a kind of mirror of Flaubert's own mind. As Du Bos points out, 'si Flaubert a poursuivi d'une haine si tenace la bêtise telle qu'elle se manifeste dans certaines façons de parler, c'est qu'il avait eu dans une appréciable mesure à combattre celles-ci chez lui-même'.[1] The endless repetition of cliché the novel's characters produce is at once repellent and fascinating, indicative both of intellectual laziness and the inescapable force of society's shaping power. The whole structure of *Madame Bovary* is sustained by a presentation of social forces aimed at revealing the inevitability of the central characters' actions. As classical tragedy depicts characters whose fatal flaw makes them the playthings of social and psychological forces over which they can exert no control, so the resolutely secular world set before us pins its characters down under a net of beliefs and expectations instilled in them by all the means society has at its disposal for making its citizens conform. Indeed, *Madame Bovary* draws much of its resonance and depth from its evocation of contemporary convictions and codes of behaviour. It is not too schematic to claim that at the diegetic level the novel draws largely on three main currents of thought: the sentimentalism prevalent in the eighteenth century, which leads into the Romanticism of the 1820s to 1840s; the analytical explorations of love that develop, in part, from other eighteenth-century writers; and the pragmatism of bourgeois thought, which had grown increasingly dominant since the 1830 revolution. The first current finds its clearest exposition in Emma and Léon; the second in Rodolphe; the third in Homais and, most destructively, in Lheureux, yet it is part of the complexity and subtlety of Flaubert's vision that each of these characters, with the exception of the single-minded Lheureux, also reveals tendencies associated with the other currents.

VERSIONS OF LOVE:
SENTIMENT AND CYNICISM

Mme de Staël, whose *De L'Allemagne* was to have such an influence on Romantic writers, sums up the temptations of sentimental novels in her important chapter entitled 'Des Romans'. According to her:

> la foule des romans d'amour publiés en Allemagne a fait tourner un peu en plaisanterie les clairs de la lune, les harpes qui retentissent le soir dans la vallée, enfin tous les moyens connus de bercer doucement l'âme; mais néanmoins il y a en nous une disposition naturelle qui se plaît à ces faciles lectures; c'est au génie à s'emparer de cette disposition qu'on voudrait encore combattre.[2]

Few writers have drawn attention so perceptively to the attraction of 'ces faciles lectures', to which Emma turns with such enthusiasm. Equally suggestive in the context of *Madame Bovary* is Mme de Staël's assertion that 'l'esprit humain est maintenant bien moins avide des événements même les mieux combinés que des observations sur ce qui se passe dans le cœur'.[3] In summing up the results of this change of attitude in the reading public, she points to the role played by the publication of *Werther* and concludes:

Werther avait tellement mis en vogue les sentiments
exaltés, que presque personne n'eût osé se montrer sec et
froid, quand même on aurait eu ce caractère naturellement.
De là cet *enthousiasme obligé* pour la lune, les forêts, la
campagne et la solitude; de là ces maux de nerfs, ces sons
de voix maniérés, ces regards qui veulent être vus, tout cet
appareil enfin de la sensibilité (original emphasis).[4]

This rigmarole of *sensibilité* may well incur a degree of mockery
from Mme de Staël for its lack of spontaneity, but she herself
indicates the way in which works of art conveying love are
explored as a means of interpreting or widening the reader's
own experience:

quelle magie le langage de l'amour n'emprunte-t-il pas de
la poésie et des beaux-arts! qu'il est beau d'aimer par le
cœur et par la pensée! de varier ainsi de mille manières un
sentiment qu'un seul mot peut exprimer, mais pour lequel
toutes les paroles du monde ne sont encore que misère!
de se pénétrer des chefs-d'œuvres de l'imagination, qui
relèvent tous de l'amour, et de trouver, dans les merveilles
de la nature et du génie, quelques expressions de plus pour
révéler son propre cœur![5]

The conviction that in literature and art can be found keys to the
understanding of the individual's emotions is of course deeply
rooted in Western culture and given cogency and credence
by such comments as these. What is at issue here is not
the location in a specific work or tradition of the approach
to reading epitomized by Emma and Léon, but merely an
indication of the extent to which it was current coin and the
degree to which the sentimentalism of the age encouraged
the unbridled expression of such emotions in the name of
spontaneity. French Romanticism itself, drawing freely on the
literary and philosophical judgements of Mme de Staël, was
also to foreground the individual, rather than society, and to
convey passionate love as the primary saving grace. But *De
L'Allemagne* is also illuminating in its exploration of mediocrity,
stupidity and folly, particularly as they are revealed in that vital
French activity, conversation. The degree to which Homais is
representative is suggested by Mme de Staël's affirmation that 'il

y a sur chaque sujet tant de phrases faites en France, qu'un sot,
avec leur secours, parle quelque temps assez bien, et ressemble
même momentanément à un homme d'esprit'.[6] Curiously, and
probably entirely coincidentally, this statement is followed by
a story in which a guest at a masked ball, passing in front
of a mirror, cannot be certain which of the reflected masked
figures is himself, and so resorts to nodding at the mirror to
locate his own reflection. The great cliché-monger, Homais, in
a discarded scenario, seeks confirmation that he exists by gazing
at his reflection in the glass jars of his pharmacy and is filled
with fear at the thought that he might merely be the product of
a writer's imagination.

Flaubert's recommendation to Louise Colet, in a letter written
in June 1853, that one must show the classicists that one is more
classical than they are, and make the Romantics grow pale with
rage by going beyond their own intentions,[7] has clearly been
put into practice in *Madame Bovary*, where Emma's imagination
offers an amalgam of Romantic clichés. Again it is typical of
Flaubert that he is able to show both the random and ridiculous
nature of these clichés, and to indicate why they should exert
such a strong attraction. It is also typical of him that from a
very early stage in his depiction of Emma he indicates the
extent to which her basic conventionality makes her resemble
both Homais and Rodolphe: he describes her as incapable of
understanding anything she herself does not feel or of believing
in anything which does not assume conventional forms (45).

Drawing on both German and English Romanticism, but
nevertheless creating a movement distinctly French, the
central figures of French Romanticism – Chateaubriand,
Hugo, Lamartine, Vigny, Musset, Desbordes-Valmore and,
later, Gautier, Nerval and Borel – created an ideal of a
special individual, deeply moved by nature, attracted both to
the sublime and the grotesque, tormented by longings for an
existence more intense than that of reality, longings that aroused
guilt and melancholia, an individual who both represented what
was finest in human nature and who was rejected by the mass
of man.

Our first real inkling of Emma's Romantic yearnings comes at
the point when the novel's central focus begins to switch from
Charles to Emma herself, when we are told that she longs to

marry at midnight in the light of blazing torches, an ideal that
founders, of course, on her father's blank incomprehension.
At first, her longing for an existence other than that which
inevitably awaits a woman of her class married to a country
officier de santé is revealed through brief indications – the desire
to add a fish pond to the garden at Tostes, and, perhaps, the
coquettish tearing off of flowers and greenery with her teeth as
Charles sets out for work in the morning (35). But the fabric of
her dream world gradually becomes clearer as Flaubert reveals
the role of the convent in shaping her imagination. The image
of the convent education is in itself an aspect of the sentimental
and Romantic novel that Flaubert may well be parodying here:
Marie d'Agoult, for instance, in her confessional novel, *Nélida*,
first published in 1846, speaks of the convent's 'charme solennel
qui attire et séduit les imaginations vives' and evokes at some
length the 'poésie du cloître'.[8] Other typical Romantic elements
in Emma's imagination are her conviction that happiness can be
found only elsewhere (Flaubert's inclusion of lemon trees in that
ailleurs is, of course, a parodic allusion to Goethe's poem 'Kennst
du das Land' and all its progeny); her image of the ideal man
of whom she demands, as she puts it in tribute to Hugo and
countless others: 'un cœur de poète sous une forme d'ange,
lyre aux cordes d'airain' (289);[9] her expectation that love will
be something sublime, a continuous state of exaltation that can
be attained with the aid of moonlight and music (45, 167); and,
eventually, a tendency to Orientalism and to the more macabre
depictions of the frenetic side of Romanticism. Throughout, her
imagination is marked, not by a tendency to use such images
as the basis for a creative and original recasting of reality, but
rather by a compulsion to copy, exemplified by the affectation
of dressing like a man and smoking cigars that reflects one of the
myths surrounding George Sand.

It is this refusal to see the world through other than Romantic
glasses that leads her to detect no incongruity in Rodolphe's
complaints of unhappiness and existential despair during the
comices agricoles, even when her common sense tells her that his
wealth and his gender nevertheless offer him a relatively agree-
able existence. His tormented soul's passage – 'ne savez-vous
pas qu'il y a des âmes sans cesse tourmentées? Il leur faut tour à
tour le rêve et l'action, les passions les plus pures, les jouissances

les plus furieuses' (147)[10] – moves her because, for all its banality, it calls to mind such a host of Romantic heroes, from Goethe's Werther to Mme de Staël's Oswald, from Byron's Manfred to Maturin's Melmoth. Equally, his assertion of two moralities (148) encounters memories of numerous heroes and heroines who conceive themselves and their desires to be superior to the rest of existence – Raymon in George Sand's *Indiana*, most of Stendhal's heroes, Lovelace in *Clarissa* and so forth. Even his assertion that 'ces attractions irrésistibles tiraient leur cause de quelque existence antérieure' (153)[11] recalls Romantic interest in metempsychosis, taken up for instance in Gautier's 'Affinités secrètes', first published in January 1849:

> De là naissent ces sympathies
> Aux impérieuses douceurs,
> Par qui les âmes averties
> Partout se reconnaissent sœurs.[12]

My argument here is not, of course, that Rodolphe is himself Romantic in nature, but rather that his experience of a certain type of contemporary woman has provided him with the stock phrases and attitudes she most longs for.

The Romantic tendencies of Emma's nature are thrown into further relief by those of Léon, which Flaubert tends to reveal with a rather coarser brush than he uses for his heroine. Léon's conviction that natural beauty elevates the soul, the escapist nature of his reading, and his belief that the aim of art is to arouse the reader's emotions are all part of the Romantic canon, but because Flaubert makes Léon express these ideas with the hesitancy of the spoken language he lays bare the degree to which they are debased by the self-centredness of Léon's character and the limitations of his intelligence. Elsewhere, too, he reveals with subtle cruelty the extent to which Léon is guided by fashion rather than conviction: the suggestion of Madeleine as a name for Emma's baby, together with his gift to Emma of a cactus plant, both stem from a desire to be in fashion, while the decoration he imagines for his room in Paris is an evident parody of the wilder side of Romanticism evoked in Borel's *Champavert* or Gautier's tales of the *Jeunes-France*, for instance: 'deux fleurets en sautoir, avec une tête de mort et la guitare au-dessus' (121).[13]

The mockery of Romanticism, however, is not just thematic: it is also stylistic, resulting from the manipulation of quotations, their insertion into a banal or incongruous context, as in Léon's superficial and ultimately ironic profession of admiration for the grave as a fine and quiet place (239), for instance, or from the parodic use of Romantic techniques: Hugo's delight in locking together the physical and the metaphysical, for example, is wickedly ridiculed in the sentence conveying Léon's admiration of Emma for 'l'exaltation de son âme et les dentelles de sa jupe' (271).[14]

While Emma's imagination is stocked with the basic themes of sentimental and Romantic fiction, Rodolphe's attitude both to women and to love reflects another contemporary current, which is also found in much of the literature of the time. Here, too, the influence of aspects of eighteenth-century thought can also be perceived. The libertinage of Laclos's *Les Liaisons dangereuses* may well, as is often argued, merely convey an aspect of Laclos's own mentality, rather than represent a social reality, yet its effect on subsequent generations was profound. While Rodolphe, in a minor and banalized manner, carries into the nineteenth century something of the tradition of the roué, *Madame Bovary* as a whole offers a parody of a genre more typical of the nineteenth century: the confessional novel. The opening passages, with their suggestion of a first-person narration, hint at the kind of framework frequently used in this kind of writing, while Rodolphe's response to love is an ironic putting into practice of several beliefs expressed in Constant's *Adolphe* and Musset's *Confessions d'un enfant du siècle*. Constant's depiction of an eighteenth-century response to sexual relations with women – 'cela leur fait si peu de mal et à nous tant de plaisir' – and Musset's affirmation that after the collapse of the Napoleonic Empire 'l'amour était traité comme la gloire et la religion; c'était une illusion ancienne'[15] offer revealing parallels to Rodolphe's down-to-earth and physical approach to his relationship with Emma. The refusal to elevate his emotions, the cynicism with which he corrupts her, the way in which, from the first, he has conceived of the relationship as short-term, provide the novel with a counterpart to Emma's heady blend of etherealized and erotic love, and add to the numerous carefully orchestrated tensions in the work. Moreover, just as we find in

Léon a more straightforward parody of Romantic convictions, allowing indirect comment on Emma's more complex beliefs, so Rodolphe's approach to love is shadowed by the coarser version provided by Charles's father. The shifts from sympathy to irony, the presentation of both romanticized love and cynical eroticism, and the narrative's ability to reflect both Emma's expectations and Rodolphe's manipulations also suggest that Flaubert is, in his own way, adding to the numerous analytical studies, or, to use the contemporary term, physiologies, of love. Indeed, Mme de Staël, de Villers, Fourier, Chateaubriand and others established such a vogue for detailed analyses of sexuality that P. Moreau affirms: 'le romantisme ne s'est jamais lassé de dresser une Carte de Tendre ou de Volupté'.[16] In particular, both Stendhal and Balzac produced theoretical depictions of love and, since Flaubert uses *Madame Bovary* to dissect the human heart, there is good reason to suspect that the novel, in offering a kind of working out of his own varied and complex responses to the subject, is defining itself against this particular background.

Stendhal's *De l'amour*, the first version of which was published in 1822, is only one of many attempts made in the first decades of the nineteenth century to depict and define a new form of eroticism. For Stendhal, love is the great affair of human existence, the only one worth pursuing. Like Flaubert, Stendhal stresses the role of reading in forming an individual's expectations of love: 'les idées de roman vous prenant à la gorge, on croit être amoureux et mélancolique'.[17] Stendhal's theory of 'cristallization', according to which the beloved assumes all the images of perfection the lover has ever formulated, his assertion that nothing so favours the birth of love as a mixture of bored loneliness and infrequent dances, his attack on the kind of education given to women, even his quotations from *The Bride of Lammermoor* can all be seen as offering Flaubert possibilities of adaptation and experimentation. This is not to argue any direct influence, but rather to suggest that to read *Madame Bovary* as part of this tradition is to respond to it in a particularly fruitful way.

Balzac's witty, cynical and epigrammatic *Physiologie du mariage*, first published in 1829, is of course a deliberately provocative attempt to ensure a *succès de scandale* and it borrows both openly and covertly from Stendhal. Nevertheless, it contains much that seems to cast light on *Madame Bovary*, even if, like Flaubert's own *Dictionnaire des idées reçues*, it is in many ways a cleverly orchestrated collection of contemporary clichés. Balzac's attack on the education given to girls, particularly in boarding schools, his image of the power of novels to present a vision of love other than that which a husband can provide, and particularly his description of women turning to religious fervour in an attempt to avoid sexual temptation, all help to place Emma's responses in a broader context. Balzac's comic attack on allowing women to read is particularly close to the debate between Charles's mother and Homais on whether or not to prevent Emma reading, a debate Flaubert eventually removed from the published version of his novel:[18]

> Laisser une femme libre de lire les livres que la nature de son esprit la porte à choisir! . . . Mais c'est introduire l'étincelle dans une sainte-barbe; c'est pis que cela, c'est apprendre à votre femme à se passer de vous, à vivre dans un monde imaginaire, dans un paradis.(original ellipsis)[19]

Flaubert's own habits of voracious reading, therefore, have enabled him to absorb so much contemporary literature that in *Madame Bovary* he constantly responds, often in parodic or ironic mode, to the technical and thematic preoccupations of other writers, not merely in their approaches to love but also, more broadly, in their vision of the values of existence.

THE BELIEF IN PROGRESS

However much Flaubert may delight in his parodies and mockery of Romanticism, however sharply he depicts the self-seeking cynicism of the sceptics and roués, he keeps his bitterest tone for the bourgeois. The 'école du bon sens', with its poeticization of the bourgeoisie and its depiction of a dual and hypocritical morality, and Louis Reybaud's *Jérôme Paturot*, with its famous assertion that he who aspires to perfection is a poet, for the best in earthly existence is the unknown, the ideal, as in poetry,[20] as well as Baudelaire's diatribe against this literary movement, which elevated the philistinism of the middle-classes and poured scorn on poets and artists, provides the kind of background against which this aspect of *Madame Bovary* is best seen.[21] Homais, the bustling, self-opinionated cliché-monger, acts as a perfect foil for both Emma and Rodolphe, but only because, with characteristic subtlety, Flaubert reveals in him moments of kindness, a desire for the improvement of society, even ideals, of a sort, which prevent us from categorizing him as uniquely villainous. The really ruthless exponent of progress, the uniquely self-seeking manipulator of others, is represented by Lheureux, into whose mind, significantly, we rarely see. Equally typical of Flaubert is his refusal to raise Lheureux to epic or mythical status, as Hugo does with Javert in *Les Misérables*, for instance, or to give him the personal magnetism of Balzac's symbol of evil, Vautrin. Similarly, however much Homais's profession may parodically recall the evil scientist of German Romanticism, particularly of Hoffmann's tales, Flaubert constantly subverts such echoes as soon as he has set them up.

In terms of social hierarchy, pharmacists, under the July Monarchy, could become highly prosperous, but, a contemporary guide to careers asserts, 'vain pride' kept many young men from entering the profession.[22] No inkling of social leprosy seems to cross Homais's mind. From the moment he first enters the text in his velvet bonnet his face expresses nothing but self-satisfaction (76), and he brackets his profession with that of 'un jurisconsulte, un médecin' and 'un négociant qui a des relations considérables' (78).[23] His attack on the priest's refusal to take a glass of wine in the scene where Homais and Mme Lefrançois await the arrival of the Bovarys – an attack made after the priest has left – and his pompous affirmation of his personal religion, may present him from the outset as self-satisfied and self-opinionated, as indeed the rest of the novel reveals him to be. But Homais, that walking dictionary of clichés, cannot lightly be dismissed as the mere butt of Flaubert's sarcasm. In one of his scenarios Flaubert wrote: 'Homais vient de *Homo* = l'homme.'[24]

If one can argue that an analysis of Emma's imagination reveals the central motifs of Romanticism, it is certainly true that Homais's possessions, convictions and use of language catalogue the Bourgeois and suggest the fragility of man in general. The 'bonnet grec' his daughter makes for him (which gives the face an air of majesty, as the *Dictionnaire des idées reçues* informs us), his

unshakeable belief in progress, his conviction of his own ability
to comment on everything ('problème social, moralisation des
classes pauvres, pisciculture, caoutchouc, chemins de fer, etc.'
(351)[25]), even the interest he takes in his children[26] and his
eventual shame at his own middle-class position (351) all mark
him as bourgeois to his finger tips.

Equally typical of his class is his belief in the power of the
written word both to inform – like Bouvard and Pécuchet, he
gleans his pharmaceutical knowledge less from experiments than
from reading brochures and 'papiers publics' (138), a reminder
of the growing importance of science and the proliferation of
vulgarizations of scientific discoveries and theories – and to
persuade, hence his desire to change the world through his
journalism. For him, language and the manipulation of language
are a sign of standing: if he calls Charles 'docteur' it is in part
because of his conviction that the very use of such a term
reflects glory on the person using it (171). Not that his belief
in his own worth seems in much need of bolstering up, since he
so frequently quotes, in support of generalizations, stories about
himself that seek to present him as sharing the characteristics
of great men: the absent-mindedness of those absorbed in
great thoughts, for instance, is illustrated by Homais with the
following ridiculous parallel: 'Moi, par exemple, combien de
fois m'est-il arrivé de chercher ma plume sur mon bureau pour
écrire une étiquette, et de trouver, en définitive, que je l'avais
placée à mon oreille!' (78).[27]

His anticlericalism is also typical of the age, but whereas for
many the doubts about the Church stemmed from its role
in politics, particularly in the years leading up to the 1830
revolution when it sought to regain some of the power lost
in the Revolution of 1789, Homais's reasons are concerned
more with his own fear of death, and the fact that the church
constantly reminds him of his own mortality. The triviality of
his arguments against the priest Bournisien – the fact that the
Bible contains salacious passages, the accusation that priests
dress as 'bourgeois pour aller voir gigoter des danseuses' (224)[28]
– does not of course prevent him from congratulating himself
subsequently on soundly defeating his opponent: Homais shares
with the Romantics the ability to see the past as perfect, when
he wishes to. Even over Emma's corpse Homais and Bournisien

continue to argue, except for moments when they fall asleep, finding equality in this simulacrum of death – 'ils étaient en face l'un de l'autre, le ventre en avant, la figure bouffie, l'air renfrongé, après tant de désaccord se rencontrant enfin dans la même faiblesse humaine' (339).[29] And finally, they break their fast together, eating and drinking in a scene of particular, and characteristically Flaubertian, grotesqueness. Bournisien's black joke – 'nous finirons bien par nous entendre' (341)[30] – arouses no denial from Homais: no amount of belief in progress can prevent the coming of the end.

Even those acts and convictions of Homais that suggest he may for once be motivated by kindness are not free from a degree of self-seeking: the friendliness he shows the Bovarys when they move to Yonville stems from his fear of being betrayed to the authorities for breaking the law forbidding pharmacists to practice medicine, and the desire to abolish superstitious cures for illnesses reveals not so much enlightenment as a determination that those who are ill should pay him rather than priest or wise woman for advice. Nevertheless, his final apotheosis is double: honoured by the state, he is also a source of stunned amazement to his wife:

> Il s'éprit d'enthousiasme pour les chaînes hydro-électriques Pulvermacher; il en portait une lui-même; et, le soir, quand il retirait son gilet de flanelle, madame Homais restait tout éblouie devant la spirale d'or sous laquelle il disparaissait, et sentait redoubler ses ardeurs pour cet homme plus garotté qu'un Scythe et splendide comme un mage (351).[31]

The marvellous blend here of flannel and gold, together with the exotic and mythical points of comparison, are what give this splendid passage its punch and transpose Homais at last from individual to symbol, the bourgeois garotted by gold, but commanding the respect due to the sorcerer.

CLASS AND TRADE

From the opening pages, with their depiction of the way in which both children and teachers impose on individuals patterns of behaviour they are obliged to copy slavishly,[32] to the concluding lines, which record Homais's reward for conforming to the image of the successful man, *Madame Bovary* reveals the mechanisms of middle-class society, the way in which it creates a form of fatality every bit as inescapable as that inflicted by the gods of antiquity.

The power of the middle classes is revealed partly through the evocation of the two other classes, the aristocrats and the peasants. The former, briefly invading the monotony of life at Tostes, may paint before Emma's eyes a picture of variety, exoticism, attained desires, but the narrative voice forces on us an image of physical decay: although for Emma the old duke, decrepit and senile, represents 'quelque chose d'extraordinaire et d'auguste', he is for the narrator 'ce vieil homme à lèvres pendantes'(50).[33] It is also an image of deception, metonymically conveyed by the decorous society woman whose dropping of a fan is a means of conveying a note, presumably an assignation. The aristocracy offers, in addition, an image of empty conversations revolving around voyages to Italy from which are extracted the kinds of cliché that could equally well have been produced by staying at home, the massive size of the pillars at Saint Peter's, the roses at Genoa, the moonlit Colosseum.

The peasants, too, briefly sighted looking in at the Vaubyessard ball, have none of the unspoilt natural nobility they are granted in George Sand's rustic novels or Pierre Leroux's socialist tracts. Tuvache's elliptical summing up of Catherine Leroux's long years of service and the inadequacy of the reward she receives are of course a searing condemnation of bourgeois values, but there is nothing in the description of the woman herself to suggest that she offers any kind of model to Emma.[34] What marks the peasants above all is their incomprehension of the world: they are presented as speechless (29), filled with 'ébahissement' (210), 'effarouché[s]' (155), mute and placid as animals (155), 'effrayé[s]' (314). Indeed the only time they are allowed to communicate at the same level as the aristocracy is in the sanctified world of the opera: 'des paysans et des seigneurs, le plaid sur l'épaule, chantaient tous ensemble une chanson de chasse' (228),[35] the 'tous ensemble' of course signalling the vast and ironic gap between Emma's world and that of romantic opera.

Paradigmatic of the society in which Emma finds herself at Yonville, the scene at the beginning of the second section of

the novel presents, in person or by allusion, the central figures
of the text's bourgeoisie, at once individuals and representatives
of social types. A scene brought intensely alive by focusing
attention on tiny details – Homais's green slippers, Binet's
boots bulging over his toes, the curé's ruddy face, the mud
plastering the coach – it is also full of the noises of the inn: Mme
Lefrançois complaining about all she has to do, the laughter from
the billiard room, the crackling of the fire, and the comic and
sinister sounds from the poultry yard as the servant dashes about
trying to kill the fowls. And while much of the conversation
seems little more than dull gossip about the fussiness of the
tax-collector or the priest's refusal to accept the offer of a glass
of wine, the social positions of principal figures, as well as their
aspirations, are being suggested and many of the novel's central
themes are expanded.

   In terms of material well-being, Guillaumin, the local notary,
not present in person in this scene but metonymically
represented by his house, is the wealthiest of the bourgeoisie. Traditionally regarded as well-off respectable men,
who, according to a contemporary account, could 'prevent
divisions between relatives, . . . diminish the demands of a
greedy or discontented creditor, save an unfortunate debtor
from complete ruin; protect minors, women and absentees in
the inventory, accounting and division of bequests',[36] notaries
do not have a good press in *Madame Bovary*. One of them,
far from protecting the financial concerns of women, runs
off with most of the savings belonging to Charles's first wife,
others are described as having 'si mauvaise réputation'(261),
while Guillaumin himself promises to obtain shares for the
ambitious salesman Lheureux (217), with whom, moreover,
he is closely connected through various financial deals (308)
and, of course, as the presence of the statue of Love outside
his expensive house may well indicate, offers to lend Emma
the money she needs in exchange for sexual favours. Only in
this final scene with Emma does Guillaumin speak. Elsewhere
he is silent, but he is frequently mentioned as present, listening
to the interminable chatter of Homais. He alone is in a position
to offer Emma legal advice in her predicament, yet he remains
the most passive of all the main characters in Yonville society:
it is hardly surprising, then, that the *Dictionnaire des idées reçues*

should contain the following item under 'notaires': 'maintenant, ne pas s'y fier'.[37]

The initial description of Yonville also explores the local church and cemetery, preparing the scene at the end of the novel, where the adolescent Justin is found weeping over Emma's tomb, by linking the graveyard and the beadle's vegetable plot. Adumbrated here is the church's constant failure to interpret desire in other than purely materialistic terms – Emma, seeking help from the priest, finds herself lumped together with cows suffering from 'l'enfle', mothers without bread, and those with poor digestion, while Justin, weeping over Emma's tomb, is accused of having designs on Lestiboudois's potatoes. This failure is anticipated not only in the portrayal of the Virgin as pagan goddess but also in the way in which the dead are seen as a means of fertilizing the vegetables. The black jokes are particularly in evidence here: Lestiboudois, being both grave-digger and beadle, is described as 'tirant ainsi des cadavres de la paroisse un double bénéfice' (74), and the connection is reinforced by the priest's assertion: 'Vous vous nourissez des morts' (75).[38] The priest's arrival at the inn is presented in terms parodic of the gothic novel, for the narrative eye, as if briefly incapable of interpreting the social significance of Bournisien's garb, records at first merely a man clad in black, whose sudden appearance makes the inn-keeper shudder (78). But whatever the suggestions conjured up of Death come to summon his own, they are mockingly swept away by his rosy face, his athletic figure and the absent-mindedness that has caused him to forget his umbrella. Bournisien's role throughout the novel is indicative of the church's failure to respond to contemporary changes in the expectations and desires of its parishioners. Curiously, the confessional plays no important role in the novel: it is left for the Spanish variation on the *Madame Bovary* theme, *La Regenta*, to explore the complex relationship of trust and deception, of a personal and spiritual struggle for power, and to take further the sensuality of the confessional, with its shadowy enclosure and its whispered communications, that is touched on briefly in the evocation of Emma's convent years.

Also present in the inn is the tax-collector Binet, known for his punctuality and his fussiness, despised by Homais for his lack of social graces and envied by him for his money, as

his sharp repetition of Mme Lefrançois's claim that Binet
has 'means' suggests. The reference to Binet's twin passions
prepares later scenes in the novel: the indication of his love
of hunting points forward to the morning he discovers Emma
returning from Rodolphe's house, when he himself is out
illegally duck-shooting; the allusion to his compulsive creation
of wooden napkin-rings anticipates not only the scene where
Emma, stunned by Rodolphe's letter breaking off the affair,
is tormented by the continuous hum of the lathe, and that in
which she begs him for money, but also the moment when,
in a carefully contrived parallel to Emma's interview with
Bournisien, he urges Léon to solve his woes by buying himself
a lathe.

Equally important, both for its preparation of the novel's
future development and its sketching in of the town's social
structure, is the appearance of Lheureux, who arrives on the
coach with the Bovarys. Deliberately playing down the black
shadow Lheureux is to cast over Emma's existence (in terms of
the gothic he is indeed the figure of death the reader is mocked
for having seen in Bournisien)[39] the narrative voice merely
reproduces the salesman's attempted consolation of Emma for
the loss of her dog, spinning her increasingly unlikely tales of
pets returning to their owners, as later he is to offer her the
dangerous consolation of apparently endless credit. Travelling
salesmen, depicted in Balzac's novels as shabby down-at-heels
starvelings, or as garrulous profiteers like Gaudissart, and
portrayed in the world of the pantomime as the sinister,
wheeler-dealing 'marchands d'habits',[40] are typical of the rising importance of commerce over the traditional professions.
Significantly, Lheureux not only travels with his goods but
also has a shop in Yonville. His combination of 'faconde
méridionale' and 'cautèle cauchoise' (105),[41] the sharpness of
mind that enables him to perform mental calculations that
astonish even the tax collector and the suppleness of attitude
that hides overwheening ambition behind an obsequiousness
that keeps his back bent 'dans la position de quelqu'un qui
salue ou qui invite' (106)[42] make him the sinister representative of true bourgeois materialism, the force that realizes,
before the publication in French of Darwin's theories, that
survival depends on destroying others. Significantly, Homais,

after Charles's death, takes a leaf from Lheureux's book when, supported by public opinion and tolerated by the authorities, he victoriously wages war on doctors attempting to settle in the town.

Although the individual may conceive of herself as unique, society perceives the individual as part of a class, of a group of workers or professionals in a particular field, as belonging to a certain income bracket. One of the ways in which *Madame Bovary* suggests the social forces at work is by referring to individuals through a series of periphrases which, since it subverts the sense of uniqueness conveyed by the choice of their given name, depicts them instead as part of a series. The ironic consequences of forcing on the reader's attention the social position of the character concerned can be considerable, and the technique is certainly one of those in which the text's corrosive mockery operates most potently.

Charles, seen by Homais as potential nark, is denoted by his profession when the pharmacist, terrified of being caught a second time breaking the law forbidding those not medically qualified from practising, sets out to curry favour with him, in the days before he has time to discover Charles's character: 'tous les matins, Homais lui apportait *le journal*, et souvent, dans l'après-midi, quittait un instant la pharmacie pour aller chez l'officier de santé faire la conversation' (89: original emphasis).[43] In the midst of the débâcle of the *pied-bot* operation, when Charles's inability to carry out such a complicated operation is so cruelly exposed, the surgeon Canivet sums up the medical fraternity's scorn for the *officiers de santé* when he describes his own calling as 'un sacerdoce, quoique les officiers de santé le déshonorassent' (188).[44] But perhaps the most telling use of this periphrasis occurs when Charles first comes to Les Bertaux, summoned because père Rouault has broken his leg: the child waiting to guide him may ask if he is the doctor and Charles may reply that he is, but the narrative voice implacably rejects such a claim by referring to him immediately as 'l'officier de santé' (14).

Although, of course, periphrasis is not always used for ironic purposes,[45] the moments when it does appear are frequently those when the reader's sympathies are alienated from the character by techniques such as juxtaposition or narrative intervention. Homais, at his most eager for an event that will bring Yonville to the notice of the world as a centre of progressive thinkers, has the philanthropic pedestal on which he stands jerked from under him as he attempts to persuade Hippolyte to undergo the operation: 'Du reste, reprenait le pharmacien, ça ne me regarde pas! c'est pour toi! par humanité pure!' (179).[46] Léon at his most Romantic is unceremoniously stripped of the individualism central to the Romantic concept at the moment when he is waxing most lyrical about literature: 'En effet, observa le clerc, ces ouvrages ne touchant pas le cœur, s'écartent, il me semble, du vrai but de l'Art.' (86)[47]

The alienating possibilities of this technique are particularly evident at certain points when the narrative, instead of referring to Emma by her first name, gives her her married title: at the Vaubyessard ball, for instance, her delight on seeing so many exotic foods is conveyed through a passage of *style indirect libre* introduced by direct reference to her as Emma, but her lack of social experience and her provincialism are highlighted in the following sentence, which alienates us from her: 'Madame Bovary remarqua que plusieurs dames n'avaient pas mis leurs gants dans leur verre' (50).[48] Most forceful, perhaps, is the use of the title at moments when Emma is least mindful of her married state: thus, when Léon visits her in her hotel at Rouen and claims to have returned time and again to a depiction of the Muse because it reminds him of Emma, the external narrative voice comments: 'Madame Bovary détourna la tête, pour qu'il ne vît pas sur ses lèvres l'irrésistible sourire qu'elle y sentait monter' (238–9).[49] The refusal to use *style indirect libre* intensifies the mockery here, when we might like to feel she is tempted to laugh at the cliché of love-lorn young man gazing at an equally hackneyed muse, forget-me-nots entwined in her tumbling hair, but the smile, as a later sigh suggests, is more likely to be one of self-satisfaction.

WOMEN

The social structures represented in *Madame Bovary* are, of course, the creation and the province of men. As L. Czyba points out, 'liées par le mariage indissoluble, privées d'autonomie, condamnées à répéter des comportements séculaires, les femmes apparaissent invariablement comme des victimes'.[50] And she indicates as a 'corollaire du mariage bourgeois, fondé sur l'intérêt, et du statut des femmes mariées réduites au rôle de reproductrices, la nécessité des amours adultères, seuls synonymes de plaisir et de volupté'.[51] Divorce, permissible under certain circumstances during the Napoleonic empire, was abolished in 1816 and not allowed again until 1884, and although men could legally indulge with impunity in adultery, women were liable to imprisonment for from three months to two years, although Tanner suggests that this law was not actually put into practice.[52] Certainly, as George Sand reveals in *Indiana*, women were regarded in the eyes of the law as minors.

In *Madame Bovary*, the significance of whose title in defining ✓
Emma only as married woman, not as individual, has frequently been pointed out, the women presented to us are almost all defined by their relationship to men. Only one is depicted as happily married: Mme Homais, and she has so little of the feminine that neither Léon nor Justin, although they board with the pharmacist, perceive her as anything other than a producer of children. (The narrative voice, however, hints at undetected passion in the expression: 'sentit redoubler ses ardeurs', quoted above, and a recent novel chooses her as heroine and reveals a sexual appetite we might not necessarily have suspected.)[53] The unhappiness of marriage is far more in evidence, not merely through Emma, but in the evocation of Charles's first marriage, with his wife begging for some syrup for her health and a little more love (13), and, too, in his parents' relationship. The concision with which the text conveys the existence of Mme Bovary mère, after her husband has devoured her small fortune, makes it all the more bleak an indication of what women could be subjected to:

> [elle] avait été folle de lui autrefois; elle l'avait aimé avec mille servilités qui l'avaient détaché d'elle encore davantage. Enjouée jadis, expansive et tout aimante, elle était, en vieillissant, devenue . . . d'humeur difficile, piaillarde, nerveuse. Elle avait tant souffert, sans se plaindre, d'abord, quand elle le voyait courir après toutes les gotons de village . . .. Puis l'orgueil s'était révolté.

Impotent

Alors, elle s'était tue, avalant sa rage dans un stoïcisme muet, qu'elle garda jusqu'à sa mort (7).[54]

Apart from the servants, only two women are depicted as working: Mme Lefrançois, who carries on as innkeeper after her husband's death, and the wet-nurse, who supplements in that way the earnings of her husband (96). Emma's social position, of course, precludes any possibility of her working and finding in that way an outlet for her energies.

No one in the novel is more sharply aware of the limitations imposed on women than Emma herself is. If, like Charles's mother, she could produce a son, she believes, however, that she would be able to live out some of her fantasies through him, as Mme Bovary mère does through Charles:

cette idée d'avoir pour enfant un mâle était comme la revanche en espoir de toutes ses impuissances passées. Un homme, au moins, est libre; il peut parcourir les passions et les pays, traverser les obstacles, mordre aux bonheurs les plus lointains. Mais une femme est empêchée continuellement. Inerte et flexible à la fois, elle a contre elle les mollesses de la chair avec les dépendances de la loi (91).[55]

Yet even here Emma's thinking reflects her reading: numerous intertexts suggest themselves, but none more strongly than Borel's *Madame Putiphar* (inscribed in the text through the painting in Guillaumin's dining-room) whose heroine names her son Vengeance, with the specific aim of bringing him up to exact on society the revenge her gender prevents her from carrying out herself. Indeed, however much sympathy Flaubert reveals for women, it would be false to suggest that he treats them with any less irony than the men in the novel. In a letter to Louise Colet he comments at some length about what he sees as the typical errors of the sex : 'ce que je leur reproche surtout, c'est leur besoin de poétisation, . . . si une femme aime un goujat, c'est un génie méconnu, une âme d'élite etc., si bien que, par cette disposition naturelle à loucher, elles ne voient pas le vrai quand il se rencontre, ni la beauté là où elle se trouve.'[56]

Although childhood is not a dominant theme in the literature of the age, *Madame Bovary* contains various indications of the

role children played in society. The habit of sending children
to wet-nurses rather than the mother breast-feeding them was
widespread, despite the polemics of Rousseau in *Emile*, first
published in 1762.[57] Homais, always better at theory than at
practice, supports Rousseau's theories concerning children:
'Moi, je trouve que les mères doivent instruire elles-mêmes
leurs enfants. C'est une idée de Rousseau, peut-être un peu
neuve encore,[58] mais qui finira par triompher, j'en suis sûr,
comme l'allaitement maternel et la vaccination.' (266)[59] This
laudable conviction does not prevent the Homais children
from being constantly grubby and very badly behaved ('toujours
barbouillés [et] fort mal élevés') (88), while the implicit trust
in maternal abilities is put rather sharply to the test by Mme
Homais's mania of making the children wear, at least until they
are four years old, 'des bourrelets matelassés' (119).[60]

Both the subtlety and the complexity of *Madame Bovary* derive
at least in part from the way in which the novel reveals, against
the intellectual background of the age, the play of social forces,
through the careful counterpointing of Emma and Homais,
the fine shading in the portrayals of Léon, Rodolphe and
Charles, and the wider range suggested in the minor characters,
particularly Lheureux, Félicité and Justin. Nevertheless, the
creation of a social background and the balances and tensions set
up between the characters are only some of the novel's structural
features: my next chapter, therefore, will deal more explicitly
with the major question of the devices on which Flaubert drew
to construct *Madame Bovary*.

NOTES: CHAPTER 3

1 Du Bos, *Approximations*, p.166: 'if Flaubert pursued, with such tenacious
  hatred, stupidity as it appears in certain modes of speech, it is because,
  to a considerable degree, he had to combat them in his own means of
  expression'. Compare Sartre's assertion that 'Gustave nous parlera plus tard
  des idées reçues avec un humour d'autant plus âcre qu'il a reçu toutes les
  siennes' (*L'Idiot de la famille*, p. 165): 'Gustave will later speak of received
  wisdom with all the more bitterness in that he received all his own.'
2 *De L'Allemagne* (Paris: Charpentier, 1852), p.365: 'the mass of romantic
  novels published in Germany has made people consider as a bit of a joke
  the descriptions of moonlight, harps playing at night in valleys, in a word all
  the well-known means of gently cradling the soul. But, nevertheless, there is
  in all of us a natural tendency to take pleasure in these facile novels; it's up
  to the genius to seize that tendency that people are still trying to crush'.

3 ibid, p. 366: 'the human spirit is far less eager, these days, for events, even the best combinations of events, than it is for observations on what takes place in the heart'.

4 ibid, pp. 526–7: 'Werther had made exalted sentiments so fashionable, that almost no one would have dared appear dry and cold, even if that were their natural character. That is what gave rise to the *obligatory enthusiasm* for the moon, the forests, the countryside and solitude; that is what produced those nervous illnesses, those pretentious voices, those glances which sought to be seen, in a word the whole rigmarole of sensitivity.'

5 ibid, p. 620: 'what magic the language of love borrows from poetry and the arts! how beautiful it is to love with the heart and the mind! thus to vary in a thousand different ways a feeling that a single word can express, but for which all the words in the world still fall far short! to steep oneself in masterpieces of the imagination all of which spring from love, and to find, in the wonders of nature and human genius, a few more expressions to reveal one's own heart!'

6 ibid, p. 72: 'in France, there is, on every subject, so many fixed expressions, that a fool, with their help, sometimes speaks quite well, and even, momentarily, resembles a man of wit'.

7 Corr, II, p. 362.

8 Marie d'Agoult [Daniel Stern], *Nélida* (Paris: Calmann-Lévy, 1987), pp. 8–9, 'the solemn charm which attracts and seduces lively imaginations'; 'the poetry of the cloisters'.

9 'a poet's heart in an angel's form, a lyre with strings of bronze'.

10 'do you not know that there are souls who suffer unceasing torments . . . They stand in constant need now of dream, now of action, now of the purest of passions, now of the most unrestrained of pleasures'.

11 'these irresistible attractions draw their cause from some former existence'.

12 Gautier, *Emaux et camées* (Genève: Droz, 1947), p. 5: 'Thus arise those sympathies, imperiously sweet, through which attentive souls everywhere recognize each other as sisters.'

13 'two crossed swords, below a skull and a guitar'.

14 'the exaltation of her soul and the lace of her skirt'.

15 'it causes them so little ill and us so much pleasure'; 'love was treated like glory and religion, as an old illusion'.

16 P. Moreau, *Amours romantiques* (Paris: Hachette, 1963), p. 34: 'romanticism never wearied of drawing up a Map of Love or of Pleasure'. See his chapters I and II for other studies of love.

17 Stendhal, *De l'amour* (Paris: Garnier-Flammarion, 1965), p. 32: 'novelistic ideas seize you by the throat and you believe you're in a state of melancholy and love'.

18 See Chapter 5, p. 90.

19 Balzac, *Physiologie du mariage* (Paris: Garnier-Flammarion, 1968), p. 142: 'Leave a wife free to read those books her natural inclinations lead her to choose! Why, that's like throwing a spark into a powder keg; worse than that, it's teaching your wife to do without you, to live in an imaginary world, in a paradise.'

20 L. Reybaud, *Jérôme Paturot à la recherche d'une position sociale* (Paris: Paulin, 1845), p. 334: on this see my *Baudelaire's Literary Criticism* (Cambridge: Cambridge University Press, 1981), pp. 32–7.

21 Baudelaire, *Œuvres complètes* II, pp. 38–43.

22 Quoted in T. Zeldin, *France*, p. 90.

23 'a jurisconsult, a doctor, a businessman with considerable connections'.

24 'Homais comes from *Homo* = man.'
Various critics have pointed out suggestions embedded in the characters' names. Emma has been seen as Femina (N. Schor), or Embla, mentioned by Grimm as the name of the first woman (M. Lowe), Charles as Karl or Kerl and therefore 'male' (M. Lowe).

25 'the social problem, moralization of the poor, pisciculture, rubber, railways, etc.'.

26 It was oly relatively recently that men had, in general, begun to interest themselves directly in the education and well-being of their children: see P. Ariès, *L'Enfant et la vie familiale sous l'Ancien Régime* (Paris: Plon, 1973), L. de Mause (ed.), *The History of Childhood* (London: Souvenir Press, 1976) and L. Pollock, *Forgotten Children* (Cambridge: Cambridge University Press, 1983). The *Dictionnaire des idées reçues* notes under 'enfants': 'affecter pour eux une tendresse lyrique, quand il y a du monde'.

27 'How many times, for example, have I myself searched for my pen on my desk in order to write a label and eventually found I'd put it behind my ear?'

28 'in civilian clothes to go and watch dancing girls wriggling about'.

29 'they were opposite each other, their stomachs bulging, their faces puffed up, with a bad-tempered air, united at last, after so much discord, by the same human weakness'.

30 'we'll surely find agreement in the end'.

31 'he was an enthusiastic supporter of Pulvermacher's hydro–electric chains; he wore one of them himself, and, in the evening, when he took off his flannel vest, Mme Homais was quite bedazzled by the gold spiral which hid him, and felt her ardour redouble for this man who, while more tightly garotted than a Scythian, appeared as splendid as a sorcerer'.

32 Compare the catechism scene and Rousseau's statement in *Emile*: 'si j'avais à peindre la stupidité fâcheuse, je peindrais un pédant enseignant le catéchisme à des enfants' (*Emile* (Paris: Garnier-Flammarion, 1966), p. 335: 'if I wanted to depict annoying stupidity, I'd depict a pedant teaching children their catechism'). *Emile* is one of the books Flaubert says he has read while at work on *Madame Bovary*.

33 'something extraordinary and august'; 'this old man with drooping lips'.

34 It is equally difficult to agree with H. Levin, *The Gates of Horn*, p. 266, for whom the introduction of Catherine Leroux is 'a standing rebuke to Emma's course of conduct' as it is with M. Lowe, who insists that she is 'another representative of an eternal characteristic' and therefore another version of Emma (*Towards the Real Flaubert*, p. 49).

35 'peasants and lords, with tartan shawls over their shoulders, sang a hunting song all together'.

36 E. Clerc, *Théorie du notariat pour servir aux examens de capacité*, quoted in T. Zeldin, *France 1848–1945*, p. 43.

37 'these days, one should have no faith in them'.

38 'thus drawing a double benefit from the corpses of the parish'; 'You feed on the dead'.

39 M. Lowe suggests his name is a translation of the Eumenides, the Happy Ones, as the Erinnyes (the Bad Ones) were euphemistically termed (M. Lowe, op. cit., p. 89) but the irony of his name is surely sufficient without such an ingenious explanation.

40 See J. Storey, *Pierrots on the Stage of Desire*.

41 'southern volubility and the cunning of the Cauchois region'.

42 'in the position of a person bowing or inviting someone'.

43 'every morning, Homais would bring him *the paper* and often, in the afternoon, he would leave the pharmacy for an instant to visit the health officer and make conversation'.

44 'A priesthood, although the health officers dishonour it' See T. Zeldin, op. cit., p. 34, for the attacks launched on the *officiers de santé* by the medical profession.

45 French avoidance of repetition of proper names is far more meticulous than that of English, resulting for instance in Carlyle being referred to as 'le prophète de Craigenputtock'. James Joyce brilliantly parodies this stylistic tic with his phrase: 'the one-armed hero of Trafalgar'.

46 ' "Besides", the apothecary went on, "it's no business of mine! It's for you! It's out of pure humanity!" '

47 ' "Indeed", the clerk observed, "since these works do not touch the heart, they turn aside, so it seems to me, from the true aim of art." '

48 'Mme Bovary noticed that several ladies had not placed their gloves in their goblets'.

49 'Mme Bovary turned her head away, so that he would not see on her lips the irresistible smile she felt appearing'.

50 *Les Femmes dans les romans de Flaubert* (Lyon: Presses universitaires de Lyon, 1983), p. 51: 'tied by indissoluble marriage, deprived of autonomy, condemned to repeat centuries-old behaviour, women invariably appear as victims'.

51 ibid, p. 39: 'corollary of middle-class marriage, which was based on financial interests, and on the status of married women reduced to their reproductive role, the necessity for adulterous love afffairs, the sole synonyms of pleasure and sexual satisfaction'.

52 See T. Zeldin, p. 343, and Tanner, p. 14.

53 S. Monod, *Madame Homais* (Paris; Belfond, 1987).

54 'In the past she had been mad about him; she had loved him with a thousand servilities which had alienated him from her even more. Once playful, expansive and utterly loving, she had become, as she grew old, difficult, complaining, nervous. She had suffered so much, without complaining, at first, when she saw him running after all the skirts in the village ... Then her pride had revolted. She had held her tongue, swallowing her rage in a silent stoicism, which she maintained until her death'.

55 'this idea of having a male child was like an expected revenge for all her past powerlessness. A man, at least, is free; he can explore passions and lands, cross obstacles, taste the most distant joys. But a woman is constantly prevented from doing so. Inert yet at the same time flexible, she has against her the weaknesses of the flesh and the dependence created by the law.'
   For Sartre, curiously, this is yet another indication that Flaubert as a child felt that his mother wanted a girl (*L'Idiot de la famille*, p. 722).

56 Corr, II, p. 80: 'what I criticize them for above all, is their need to poeticize ... If a woman loves a churl, he's a misjudged genius, a superior soul, etc., with the result that, given this natural inclination to squint, they don't see truth when they meet it, or beauty where it is to be found.'

57 See T. Zeldin, *France 1848–1945*, p. 317, and E. Badinter, *L'Amour en plus*. L. Bopp's remark on noting that both Charles and Berthe are sent away as infants – 'ah! familles!' (*Commentaire sur 'Madame Bovary'* (Neuchâtel: A la Baconnière, 1951), p. 16) – misleads by imposing twentieth-century views on a nineteenth-century society.

58 Some eighty years after the publication of Rousseau's work.

59 'I myself consider that women should teach their children themselves. It's an idea of Rousseau's which may still be a bit new, but which I'm sure will eventually triumph, like breast-feeding and vaccination.'
60 'padded rolls'.

CHAPTER 4

Structures

Although Flaubert announced in a letter to Louise Colet that he had begun his novel on 19 September 1851, there can be no doubt that he had been pondering it for some considerable time beforehand, and that when he started the task of writing it, he had already drawn up a detailed and complex plan to which he was to adhere remarkably closely, whatever additions may subsequently have been included. The detailed plans, scenarios and drafts left after the novelist's death have been carefully documented, notably by the Rouen librarian Gabrielle Leleu, who has published not only a two-volume edition of the sketches and fragments, but also, in conjunction with the critic Jean Pommier, a 'new version' of the novel incorporating much of the material Flaubert finally rejected. The development of the scene describing the agricultural fair has also been reproduced in a work providing the numerous drafts and rewritings of this remarkable episode. These draft versions, together with Flaubert's frequent analysis of his aims and techniques in letters to Louise Colet or Louis Bouilhet, are a richly rewarding source of information about the novel's composition.

The meticulous planning of *Madame Bovary* reflects Flaubert's frequently reiterated conviction that difficulties encountered in writing arise above all from a lack of order. Persuaded that if writers had a clear picture of the image or emotion they wished to represent the perfect expression would inevitably result, Flaubert often returned to his early plans, refining and clarifying them. In contemplating his scenarios, a central concern, constantly expressed in his letters and reflecting the complexity of his endeavour, is the need for conviction in the sequence of analysis and events, the ideas and the emotions. 'Ce qui est atroce de difficulté', he complains to Louise Colet, 'c'est l'enchaînement des idées et qu'elles dérivent bien naturellement les unes des autres.'[1] One of the major reasons behind this preoccupation is the fear that his novel, being concerned more with ideas than with facts, may fail to seize the reader's attention, and the belief that success, therefore, depends on the reader's being carried along by a tightly controlled structure. This conviction has various important consequences, in terms of both the balance of the novel and the determination to find physical analogies for states of mind. As he puts it to Louise Colet in November 1852:

> l'enchaînement des sentiments me donne un mal de chien, et tout dépend de là dans ce roman; car je maintiens qu'on peut tout aussi bien amuser avec des idées qu'avec des faits, mais il faut pour ça qu'elles découlent l'une de l'autre comme de cascade en cascade, et qu'elles entraînent ainsi le lecteur au milieu du frémissement des phrases et du bouillonnement des métaphores.[2]

In this elliptical expression he ties together three central concerns: the psychological exploration of his characters and their society; the physiological response to the sounds and rhythms of the sentences; and the power of metaphor to give concrete form to abstract concepts. And even in a letter dashed off in the weariness and tension that followed a day struggling with the difficulties of writing, the language he uses indicates the intensity of his vision: the image of the waterfall, the force of the two words 'frémissement' and 'bouillonnement', the determination to pull the reader along with him, all suggest not only the nature of the challenge he set himself, but also the intellectual stimulation he derived from it, however much he may pretend to bemoan the 'mal de chien' it causes him.

What he sought above all in his plan was unity, to prevent individual details from dominating the overall harmony. There are frequent laments in the correspondence that the novel lacks proportion, that too much has to be devoted to the psychological preparation in comparison with the dramatic section. Although he found reassurance in the fact that the novel was above all a biography rather than an adventure tale, he still suspected that *Madame Bovary* might seem to offer a great defect in that the exposition and the conclusion greatly outweighed, in material terms, the action itself, like a sandwich with too much bread and too little filling. And yet, as he points out, in this it reflects life itself: 'un coup dure une minute et a été souhaité pendant des mois! Nos passions sont comme des volcans: elles grondent toujours, mais l'éruption n'est qu'intermittente.'[3] A specific example of this preoccupation with balance and harmony is provided by the scene of the agricultural fair, where Flaubert has to walk a knife-edge between making the episode disproportionately long, and failing to keep it sufficiently well-rounded. The different aspects of the challenge he faced are sharply etched in a letter of 1853, again to Louise Colet: 'c'est un dur endroit. J'y ai *tous* les personnages de mon livre en action et en dialogue, les uns mêlés aux autres, et par là-dessus un grand paysage qui les enveloppe. Mais, si je réussis, ce sera bien symphonique' (original emphasis).[4] Given the importance Flaubert attached to structure, therefore, no reading of *Madame Bovary* can be complete if it fails to respond to the ways in which the novel is articulated.

THE EVOLUTION OF THE TEXT

The theoretical position explored and developed in Flaubert's letters is of course elaborated in the scenarios and drafts prepared for *Madame Bovary*. The first of these, which covers a mere two pages, already contains a clear depiction of the main outlines and the two central characters, tracing Emma's development from her marriage to her suicide, with brief references to a 'besoin poétique de luxe', the reading of novels, and the 'mémoires de fournisseur'.[5] Charles is summed up succinctly as an 'esprit doux sensible, droit juste obtus, sans imagination', while Emma, typified here by a reference to a 'longue attente d'une passion et d'un événement qui n'arrivent pas',[6] is further characterized in a subsequent scenario: 'sans goût artistique, elle est peu artiste mais poétique'.[7] This second scenario, moreover, insists on the importance, for the subsequent development of their relationship, of the scene in which Rodolphe seduces Emma: 'il faut que le 1er coup comme couleur domine tout le reste de la passion – qu'il y en ait toujours dessus le reflet'.[8] Léon and Rodolphe, at first indicated merely in vague terms, are more precisely depicted in a third scenario, which is far more detailed in its suggestion of the various developments. Léon is described as being similar in nature to Charles, but with more intelligence and less kindliness, while Rodolphe, a man of experience, seizes Emma 'en blaguant et lui remue vigoureusement le tempérament'.[9] The expression here serves to remind us of the sharp contrast between what Flaubert could say in drafts and letters meant for personal and private consumption, and the more sober language demanded in the published version, where so much had to be implied or hinted at through subtle phraseology or a particular choice of image.[10]

However precise the first scenario may be, and however little Flaubert deviates from the main lines he has set down for himself, there are aspects which are introduced at a later stage.

First, the initial scenario does not foresee the platonic nature of Emma's initial relationship with Léon, which Flaubert explains in one of his detailed drafts through a note emphasizing his fascination with the psychological development of his characters: 'pourquoi n'est-elle pas empoignée par l'amour de Léon. – est trop jeune, ne s'explique pas, les passions vraies ne se font pas remarquer, comme les *organes* qui ont une membrane protectrice'(original emphasis).[11] Such a comment draws our attention to the fact that, in the drafts and in letters written at the time, Flaubert reveals an undeviating interest in the psychological development of his characters, in the reasons underlying responses and emotions: this interest gives the lie to critics who uphold him as an exponent of the purely self-reflexive nature of language.

The character of Homais, too, is not mentioned in the early drafts, appearing only in the section Pommier and Leleu have labelled as IX, where he springs into being as a stout, serious little man, a joker, an intellectual with smallpox scars, already described as a correspondent for the Rouen newspaper.[12] It is at this point that the novel takes on its unique character, with the personal story of Emma finding its balance in the depiction of Homais, whose convictions, ambitions, successes and failures are henceforth worked into the text as a constant counterpoint to her own.

Although he returned at various points to his sketches and drafts, Flaubert, once embarked on the writing of his novel, pursued a chronological path that can be charted through his correspondence. In April 1852, for example, he was at work on the ball scene, and spent a day peering through coloured glass to prepare for a description of a kiosk in the gardens of the Vaubyessard chateau, an episode subsequently suppressed. By September he was launching himself into the second part of the novel, with the visit to the wet-nurse occupying his attention in December, and the scene where Rodolphe's manservant is bled mentioned in the following July. From then to December 1853 he struggled with the complex symphony of the agricultural fair. In various letters he refers to the difficulty he experienced in orchestrating what was to become one of his most famous scenes. A letter to Louise Colet written in October 1853 is typical: 'le fond de mes *comices* est à refaire, c'est-à-dire tout mon dialogue d'amour dont je ne suis qu'à la moitié. Les idées me manquent. J'ai beau me creuser la tête, le cœur et les sens, il n'en jaillit rien.' (original emphasis)[13] The realization that this scene offered such possibilities for the exploration of character, the analysis of society and the experimentation with language that are central preoccupations in the novel as a whole, and the great development subsequently accorded it can be seen as one of the seminal moments in the history of the novel form, even if the effort Flaubert put into it can be detected in its moments of exaggeration and over-emphasis.

By mid-December he had embarked on the scene in which Rodolphe seduces Emma, remarking on Christmas day, rather inappropriately, perhaps, given the date, that 'Ma Bovary est sur le point immédiat d'être baisée.'[14] This scene seems to have convinced him again of the joy of writing: 'c'est une délicieuse chose que d'écrire! que de ne plus être *soi*, mais de circuler dans toute la création dont on parle. Aujourd'hui, par exemple, homme et femme tout ensemble, amant et maîtresse à la fois, je me suis promené à cheval dans une forêt.'[15] By April he was preparing the disastrous operation on Hippolyte's club-foot, announcing to Louise Colet that he had spent an entire evening abandoning himself to furious surgery.[16]

After the break-up of the relationship with Louise Colet and the resultant cessation of their correspondence, the progress of the novel becomes more difficult to chart, but letters to Louis Bouilhet provide some clues. In May 1855 Flaubert mentions the love affair between Emma and Léon,[17] and later that month he reports a desire to introduce into the novel an episode describing the '*cheminots*' which he evokes as alimentary turbans ('turbans alimentaires').[18] By September he was struggling with the difficulties of exploring Emma's financial problems in suitable narrative terms, despairingly depicting the explanations as posing insurmountable problems.

Whatever problems individual items may have posed him, it is clear that, from an early stage, Flaubert had a sharp image of the overall structure of *Madame Bovary* and that changes to the development envisaged in the first drafts arise from an increased sense of the psychological complexities of his characters. The tripartite movement suggests an inexorable unfolding of personal destinies, where character and social circumstance combine to create a sense of inevitability. The depiction of Charles and Emma in childhood and in the early days of their marriage prepares for the sense of dissatisfaction the young woman feels, as well as justifying the calm contentment of Charles himself. The first chapters of the second part, charting the growing closeness of her relationship with Léon, reflect a sudden burst of additional insight on Flaubert's part, as he realizes how much more forceful the study of her personality and how much more convincing the intensity of her response to Rodolphe will be, if inexperience and shyness prevent Emma and Léon from admitting their desire for each other. The longing for a permanent intensity, prepared by the scenes in the convent, confronted with the cynicism of Rodolphe's character, leads inescapably to the sudden disillusionment with love caused by Rodolphe's departure and this, in turn, causes the frenetic, turbulent and disquieting nature of the relationship with Léon. Just as it was inevitable that Rodolphe's experience had led him to demand of sexual love something sharply at odds with Emma's search for permanence, so it is obvious that Léon's spineless and passive nature will quickly tire of a relationship predicated on intensity. These experiences of disappointed emotion, with the failure of either maternal love or religious ardour to give Emma a sense of fulfilment, combine with the more easily definable despair caused by her financial predicament, and culminate, again with a sense of inexorability, in her suicide as the only possible response left to her, given her own nature, that of the men she has met, and that of society more generally. The novel's overall structure, therefore, is firmly moulded to convey a triple destiny – that of Emma, Charles, and Homais – which is the product of carefully analysed psychological tendencies and social pressures.

The gradual unfolding of the narrative reflected in Flaubert's letters shows the extent to which he continued along the general plan outlined from the beginning and the way in which he expanded it to include scenes and characters not initially mentioned. Indeed, many of his most powerful structural devices seem to have occurred to him in the act of writing the text, or arise more straightforwardly from the need to provide transitions from one section to another or to convey psychological or social suggestions indirectly. No one, for example, can overlook the fact that neither the opening nor the conclusion of *Madame Bovary* focuses on Emma herself. The refusal to allow her the privileged status she longs for is not merely, therefore, a factor depending on herself as individual or the society in which she finds herself: it is inscribed in the very structure of the novel. Five aspects of the structure demand further attention: the transitions between chapters, the nested stories, the technique of juxtaposition, the role of repetition and the networks of metaphors.

TRANSITIONS

The art of transition, both between chapters or books within the novel and between scenes in a chapter, was one Flaubert, with the meticulous attention he paid to the total effect of a work of art, considered of great importance. A letter to Louise Colet in 1854, at the time he was working on the beginnings of the affair between Emma and Rodolphe, reveals just how much of his energies went into such links: 'avant le dit passage, j'en ai une transition qui contient 8 lignes, qui m'a demandé 3 jours, où il n'y a pas un mot de trop, et qu'il faut, pourtant, refaire! encore! parce que c'est trop lent'. [19]

This care is reflected, too, in a desire to summarize certain aspects or events which are also described in detail. Homais's newspaper article about the fair serves at least a triple purpose, indicating much about the nature of the man and the role of the press, but also, as Flaubert explains in a letter to Louis Bouilhet, 'il rehausse les comices, et les fait paraître plus courts, parce qu'il les résume'.[20] A further example of this technique, imbued with special irony in that it precedes rather than follows the main events, is Rodolphe's depiction, after his first encounter with Emma, of a possible relationship between them: 'avec trois mots de galanterie, cela vous adorerait, j'en suis sûr! ce serait tendre! charmant! . . . Oui, mais comment s'en débarrasser ensuite?' (134).[21] This kind of summary is also used as a transition between chapters. In part I of the novel, the third chapter concludes with a passage offering a brief résumé of the wedding, while the following chapter then describes that wedding in detail. The device is given a slightly different twist in the second part, where chapter 4 ends with a general statement about love coming, not, as Emma thinks, in a sudden overwhelming flash, but as the result of a slow accumulation of meetings and emotions, while chapter 5 proceeds to illustrate this maxim with regard to Emma's feelings about Léon.

Frequently Flaubert uses as a linking technique a brief reference at the end of a chapter leading to a detailed description in the following chapter: an invitation to Emma to inspect her new home leads to a full description of the house at Tostes, for instance, Rodolphe's decision to use the fair as an excuse to see Emma again and embark on his seduction of her leads into the detailed description of the fair itself and, towards the end of part II, a reference to Charles's financial worries acts as a hinge between the description of Emma's illness and an exploration of the couple's financial situation. Occasionally the transitions between chapters introduce a temporal switch. Emma's ponderings on her marriage lead into a flashback recalling her education in the convent against which background her disappointment is more easily understood. Similarly, in part III, chapter 9 ends with the arrival of Emma's father, introducing at the beginning of chapter 10 a flashback to the moment when the letter informing him of his daughter's suicide arrived and his subsequent reactions.

These transitions can, of course, be particularly ironic. Part II, chapter 2, for instance, concludes with Emma's naïve belief that because her life so far has been dull, the remainder will be better, while the opening passage of chapter 3 shows her looking out from her window and catching sight of Léon, who is, of course, to present yet more cause for disappointment. Ironically, too, the débâcle of the club-foot operation, which concludes Part II, chapter 11, leads into an affirmation of a renewal of desire between Emma and Rodolphe. However varied Flaubert's use of these transitions may be, the importance he places on them and the care with which they are created are an essential part of the means by which the novel produces for the reader a conviction of inevitability, of an unfolding of events that could not have been otherwise. This is rather different, I would contend, from Culler's affirmation that Emma is 'fated to be destroyed by the irony of Flaubert's prose':[22] both the irony and the fatality derive not merely from the language but also, among other things, from the novel's particular architecture.

NESTING

Many critics have commented on the way in which Emma's story is nested in that of Charles, and on the frequency with which other stories are nested within hers.[23] Of course *Madame Bovary* is not unique in delaying the introduction of the central character: *Corinne, La Chartreuse de Parme, Illusions perdues, Lucia de Lammermoor, Ulysses,* not to mention *Tristram Shandy* would all be cases in point. Flaubert may be parodying or simply following convention here. What is certainly parodic is the first-person assertion: 'il serait maintenant impossible à aucun de nous de se rien rappeler de lui' (9),[24] which is both preceded and followed by a detailed evocation of him in social, physical and psychological terms. But it is not merely the way in which the novel both opens and closes with a focus other than Emma herself, but also the beginnings and endings of the individual sections which allow *Madame Bovary* to deny Emma the primacy for which she longs. The first section closes with the news that she is pregnant, thus introducing a story whose protagonist is someone other than Emma; the second part opens with a description of Yonville, during which the narrative voice asserts that nothing has changed in the town since the events related, thereby offering an ironic gloss on Lamartine's 'Le Lac', and it closes on another story, that of Lucia de Lammermoor, while also pointing forward to the affair with Léon; and the third section opens with a recapitulation of Léon's life since he left Yonville. Even Charles's insistence that Emma be buried in three coffins can be seen as offering a *mise en abyme* of the novel's nested structure.

The multiplicity of stories included in the general framework is drawn from three main areas, the world of the novel, the domain of fiction, and the linking corridor of the characters' imaginations. To the stories recounting the childhood of the central characters are added succinct summaries of other lives: that of the old spinster who mends the linen in the convent, that of la Guérine, and that of the singer Lagardy's rags-to-riches career. Some form an obvious structural function, such as the bankruptcy of the Café français, brought about by Lheureux, which points forward to Emma's own financial ruin, while others offer a cogent summing up, refracted by a more perceptive mind, of events whose full force have not yet been entirely revealed, or which have been blunted by being presented through the mind of a less clear-sighted character, and deliberately diluted by being portrayed according to a larger time-scale. Such a moment occurs when Emma tells Guillaumin of her debts, and her story encounters in the notary's mind his own succinct résumé of events:

> il savait (et mieux qu'elle) la longue histoire de ces billets, minimes d'abord, portant comme endosseurs des noms divers, espacés à de longues échéances et renouvelés continuellement, jusqu'au jour où, ramassant tous les protêts, le marchand avait chargé son ami Vinçart de faire en son nom propre les poursuites qu'il fallait (308).[25]

Suddenly the reader is made acutely aware of the web spun for Emma, a web whose threads we have hitherto only occasionally and imperfectly glimpsed.

No story is more succinct in its outline nor more telling in its unspoken implications than Tuvache's account of Catherine Leroux's life: – 'Cinquante-quatre ans de service! Une médaille d'argent! Vingt-cinq francs! C'est pour vous' (155).[26] This elliptical treatment of Bergsonian *durée* as opposed to chronologically measured time is yet another form of the Flaubertian silence,[27]

or the blanks on which Proust and Thibaudet comment so
suggestively, where the reader is invited to round out the
tale so tersely presented to us.[28] If, as her name suggests
and in accordance with Flaubert's claim that his novel would
'chatouille[r] doucement mainte plaie féminine',[29] Emma is to be
perceived as typical at least of a certain sort of woman, then the
nested stories concerning other women – Madame Bovary mère,
Catherine Leroux, la Guérine, Lucia de Lammermoor, even,
obliquely, the woman who rescued Lagardy from poverty and
was then abandoned by him – are all comments both on possible
aspects of Emma and on the structures of society. The nested
story is, therefore, not merely a means of manipulating narrative
focus but also a device allowing for impersonal commentaries
and judgements, and for creating further resonances.[30]

The characters in *Madame Bovary* are all persistent tellers of
stories: from Charles's mother telling tales to the child (8),
through Père Rouault recounting his wedding and the early days
of his widowerhood (22), to Homais, retelling stories read in the
newspapers or creating them to feed back into the newspapers
(the accident he claims the blind beggar provoked, for instance),
Léon inventing for Emma's benefit a story of his student life
in which she is the constantly remembered guiding light, and
Emma herself, wrapping her love-life in lies (276) as her own
story is wrapped in that of others, all are involved in patterns of
interpretation and manipulation of the inchoate world in which
they find themselves. The longing to impose pattern on disorder
is symbolized by Binet's obsessive production of the perfectly
proportioned napkin rings, but the clearest symbol of the
wish-fulfilling nature of story-telling, which Freud was to see as
posing the fundamental problem for aesthetic creation,[31] occurs
right at the end of the novel, when Homais, frustrated in his
desire to be honoured by his country for services rendered, 'fit
dessiner dans son jardin un gazon figurant l'étoile de l'honneur,
avec deux tordillons d'herbe qui partaient du sommet pour
imiter le ruban' (354).[32] The world as garden, metonymical space
standing for a creation entirely controlled by the bourgeoisie, is
reduced here to a representation of what in itself is a symbol,
the star and its ribbons, but a representation deprived of all
authority since Homais has no power to confer the honour he
so craves. From *locus amœnus* the garden is transformed into

the bourgeois space *par excellence*, stripped of all its romantic associations, uniquely and specifically functional, even if its function is a lie. One of Flaubert's best jokes about Homais, it is also a wry comment on the representational claims of the wish-fulfilling narrative.

In narratological terms, the nesting technique is one means of creating those shifts of focus that make *Madame Bovary* so challenging, one of the devices by which Flaubert forces his reader constantly to question the identity of the voice presenting the information given, and therefore to question the nature of that information. But it also has a function that is far more closely associated with social criticism. First, the technique shifts the centre of authority away from a clearly delineated authorial persona, offering as a result an image of a world devoid both of the authority of an omniscient and omnipotent God, and of a monarchical figure of government. The bourgeois world the novel depicts has a power structure far more complex and far less easily locatable than that of pre-revolutionary monarchy, and where Balzac uses direct intervention in his texts to specify that source of power as money, Flaubert largely retains his impersonality but suggests through the very structures of his narrative the dispersal of power. Secondly, by refracting our vision of Emma, he indicates the way in which the individual, and particularly the female individual, is removed from the centres of authority. Since she feels herself to be exiled from Paris and alienated socially from positions of local authority by gender, Emma's social powerlessness is a symbol of her inability to alter the conditions of her existence. The nesting technique combines with the fact that, unlike the heroines of eighteenth-century novels, or even the novels of Balzac, Emma has no peer in whom she can confide, to reveal her sense of being an outsider in a masculine world. The *fatalité* that destroys her is above all that of gender: the misogyny of nineteenth-century French society, whose laws kept women to the status of minors and whose customs rejected all of their skills apart from those specifically concerned with house and family, created a phallocratic authority in which Emma has, quite literally, no identity to assume unless she manages to produce a son through whom she can live out her fantasies of freedom and power.

JUXTAPOSITION

However revealing the nesting technique may be, in both
social and metaphysical terms, it is only one of the structural
devices Flaubert employs with such wily power. The skill with
which he places events or metaphors side by side is equally
effective. Indeed, H. Levin insists that 'meaningful juxtaposition is Flaubert's signature, where Balzac's was miscellaneous
accretion'.[33] Sartre's belligerent assertion that, despite the value
he placed on an initial plan, 'Gustave, Dieu soit loué, n'a jamais
su "faire un plan": grâce à quoi la "composition" de cet ouvrage
est une surprenante merveille',[34] reveals, of course, that, as so
often, he is exploring here less Gustave Flaubert than Jean-Paul
Sartre, for *Madame Bovary* is particularly rich in the suggestions
and implications that can be conveyed by juxtaposing ideas or
images. That Flaubert was fully conscious of such suggestions is
clearly and frequently indicated in his letters. Such juxtaposition
represents a further area in which authorial presence can be
detected while authorial voice remains silent. An exploration
of certain examples of the technique reveals much about the
way the reader is being both manipulated and stimulated into
an interpretative response.

During Charles's first visit to the Rouault farm, he accidently
collides with Emma when both bend down to pick up his
whip. The text provides us with an external description of
their embarrassment, then cuts immediately to the statement
that instead of returning to the farm three days later, as he
had promised, it was the very next day that he paid his
next visit (18), leaving to us the not too arduous task of
drawing the obvious conclusions. While the purpose of this
juxtaposition is primarily psychological, the technique may
carry considerable moral weight. For instance, after depicting
Emma's boredom as such that she wants both to die and to live
in Paris, the narrative voice provides the uncommented image
of Charles riding through the rain and snow (62). A similar kind
of unmediated juxtaposition, but one which is far more sinister,
occurs in the course of Emma's affair with Léon. Leaving Rouen,
Emma indulges in a fit of despair that might make us forget that
she sees him every Thursday: 'elle sanglotait, appelait Léon, et
lui envoyait des paroles tendres et des baisers qui se perdaient au

vent' (272).[35] Immediately the angle of vision swivels, bringing
in the character of the blind beggar: 'un amas de guenilles lui
recouvrait les épaules, et un vieux castor défoncé, s'arrondissant
en cuvette, lui cachait la figure; mais, quand il le retirait, il
découvrait, à la place des paupières, deux orbites béantes
tout ensanglantées.'(272)[36] The semi-echoes set up between
'sanglotait' and 'ensanglantées', and the parallelism between
Emma's 'paroles tendres' and the beggar's song, with its trite
images of love – sun, birds, leaves[37] – are enough to convey
the moral point, with no need for authorial intervention. The
deflating power of juxtaposition is perhaps most clearly revealed
when Emma's sense that she is worth more than her destiny
is qualified by the depiction of the wig-maker at Tostes: 'lui
aussi, le perruquier, il se lamentait de sa vocation arrêtée, de
son avenir perdu, et, rêvant quelque boutique dans une grande
ville, comme à Rouen, par exemple, sur le port, près du théâtre,
il restait toute la journée à se promener en long' (66).[38] There
is no need here for an intrusive narrative voice telling us that
his time would have been better spent actively promoting his
ambitions, or that Emma's longings are in no way qualitatively
superior to the more materialistic aspirations of the wigmaker.

At times, juxtaposition may offer a means both of further
exploring the psychology of the characters and of preparing
dramatic ironies. The interlocking of Emma's various desires
– both sexual and material – and the way in which desire itself
is for her a longing to appropriate the other, is conveyed, for
instance, in a passage which also points forward to Emma's
ultimate bankruptcy. When Emma first realizes that Léon desires
her, we are told that she falls asleep with her mind filled with a
new enchantment (105). The next sentence, however, introduces
Emma's Nemesis in the form of the draper, Lheureux, the
'marchand de nouveautés' (105), who is to introduce her to
another enchantment, the magic wand of credit, which allows,
for a limited period, instant appropriation of whatever material
wares her heart desires.

The technique of juxtaposition can also enact a failure to
communicate: on numerous occasions – after the wedding, or
when the young couple know they are expecting a baby, or
when Emma dreams of eloping with Rodolphe while Charles
envisages a tranquil domestic future – Charles's response to an

event is simply followed by that of Emma, with no transition that might indicate a sense of shared or even communicated experience between the two, and no intervention of direct authorial comment.

REPETITION

While juxtaposition creates a feeling of discontinuity, other techniques promote a sense of the inexorable forward movement of time or intensify our awareness of the repetitive nature of existence. The theme of repetition is one that critics have frequently – indeed repeatedly – commented on,[39] T. Tanner even coming to the conclusion that 'what emerges in the book is that the whole society itself is permeated with this kind of *compulsion to copy* that Charles learns at school as an exercise' (original emphasis).[40] This series of circles and repetitions has as its prime function the rejection of any claim an individual might have to uniqueness. From the opening sentences of the novel, Charles is presented as just one in a constantly recurring series, a 'nouveau' who will rapidly be supplanted by yet another 'nouveau'. Emma, whose reading of novels is based on the desire to substitute herself for the central characters, fails to see that far from being the heroine of a unique adventure she is merely one in a chain: a chain of adulterous women, Charles's second wife, one mistress among many for Rodolphe, the constantly recurring 'elle' of the works Léon reads. The waltz scene in the section describing the Vaubyessard ball is an evident *mise en abyme* of this theme of repetition, with Emma whirled around completely in the control of her partner, then left leaning against the wall with her hands over her eyes and realizing when she comes to herself that her partner is already one of a group of three requesting the right to dance with another woman. Moreover, it is quite possible that there is a further element of repetition here, in that the topos of the waltz scene is yet another cliché of the sentimental novel. Marie d'Agoult, for instance, uses it with particular melodrama in her confessional novel, *Nélida*, which was published some ten years before *Madame Bovary*:

> Et Timoléon attachait ses yeux enivrés sur les yeux de la
> jeune fille inquiète; il osait presser doucement sa taille

flexible; et sa main, sans serrer la sienne, la retenait et l'enchaînait par un magnétisme inexplicable. A mesure qu'ils rasaient le sol, d'une vitesse toujours redoublée, au son d'une musique dont le rhythme impérieux arrachait Nélida à elle-même, l'étourdissait, lui donnait le vertige, la jeune fille émue, palpitante, poussée par une impulsion irrésistible dans un tourbillon de lumière et de bruit, sentait monter à son cerveau les perfides exhalaisons du jasmin.[41]

It is not just Emma and Charles who are presented in this way, as part of a series rather than as individuals: Léon and Rodolphe, of course, are also part of the series of Emma's lovers; Emma in need of money turns to a series of possible creditors – the notary, Binet, Rodolphe; even the senile and dribbling marquis at the Vaubyessard chateau is famous for having been one in a series of Queen Marie-Antoinette's lovers, between MM. de Coigny and de Lauzun (50). This image of endless repetitions of the same is also present in a passage Flaubert decided to omit from the final version of *Madame Bovary*, in which Homais, surely the character with the strongest sense of his own *unicité*, perceives himself reflected in the glass jars of his pharmacy and in his delirium begins to doubt his very existence: 'ne suis-je qu'un personnage de roman, le fruit d'une imagination en délire, l'invention d'un petit paltaquot que j'ai vu naître et qui m'a inventé pour faire croire que je n'existe pas.'[42] Flaubert's decision to remove this wonderfully comic surrealistic shift shows his determination to remain within the conventions of the traditional novel as part of the wager he had set himself in writing *Madame Bovary*. The 'imagination en délire' may well be Flaubert's, but the challenge he rises to in this novel is to prove his ability to control that imagination and use it for other purposes.

The idea of repetition is also embedded in the study of relationships. Emma's longings to find the ideal man suggested by her reading make her turn from Charles to Léon to Rodolphe, then to Léon again, while her inability to distinguish between secular and religious love make her conceive of God as yet another potential lover (see 330–1).[43] The seduction scenes themselves are sufficiently similar to confirm the novel's explicit assertion of the eternal monotony of passion (196). If Rodolphe finds her open to his suggestions during the *comices agricoles* it is in part because he is continuing a process already begun by another at the Vaubyessard ball and continued, however ineffectually, by Léon: 'il lui sembla qu'elle tournait encore dans la valse, sous le feu des lustres, au bras du vicomte, et que Léon n'était pas loin, qui allait venir . . . et cependant elle sentait toujours la tête de Rodolphe à côté d'elle' (151).[44]

An equally important function of repetition is to suggest the failure of any of these characters to learn, making the novel, for all its beginnings in the classroom, a parody of the *Bildungsroman*. Even Homais, who in many ways seems to develop his position as the novel progresses, merely repeats his failure, when, despite the experience he might have gained in the club foot operation, he still believes himself capable of curing the blind beggar. Nevertheless, it is due to the complexity of Flaubert's vision that he can suggest the way in which repetition, far from being an inevitable source of monotony, may also bring pleasure, as for instance in the depiction of Charles's satisfaction each time he opens the door into the room where he plays dominoes, or the way in which he indicates the delight Emma and Léon feel at repeating the same gestures each Thursday.

To such temporal juxtapositions are added accumulations and contrasts of different linguistic registers, as when Rodolphe's honeyed words against the backdrop of the prize ceremony at the agricultural fair threaten Emma's vision of love as something ethereal, since the animality of desire is always at the forefront here, punctuating the words of love like a Greek chorus constantly revealing what lies beneath the veneer of language:

—Cent fois même j'ai voulu partir, et je vous ai suivie, je suis resté.
'Fumiers.'
—Comme je resterais ce soir, demain, les autres jours, toute ma vie!
'A M. Caron, d'Argueil, une médaille d'or!'
—Car jamais je n'ai trouvé dans la société de personne un charme aussi complet.
'A M. Bain, de Givry-Saint-Martin!'
—Aussi, moi, j'emporterai votre souvenir.
'Pour un bélier mérinos...'

—Mais vous m'oublierez, j'aurai passé comme une ombre.
'A M. Belot, de Notre-Dame. . . '
—Oh! non, n'est-ce pas, je serai quelque chose dans votre
pensée, dans votre vie?
'Race porcine, prix *ex æquo*'(153).[45]

Whether we decide to substitute Rodolphe for the merino ram
here or conclude that the equal first prize for pigs should be
awarded to him and Emma, rather than to Lehérissé and
Cullembourg with their splendidly Rabelaisian names, what
emerges, of course, is that Rodolphe's romantic language
unravels to reveal sheer animality. The same code operates,
moreover, in the scene where Emma and he first make love, for
it is Rodolphe's claim of courtly adoration – 'vous êtes dans mon
âme comme une madone sur un piédestal, à une place haute,
solide et immaculée. . . . Soyez mon amie, ma sœur, mon ange!'
(165)[46] – that precipitates the act of physical love. Even here,
the sense of *déjà vu* is overwhelming, for a comparison with the
waltz scene at the ball reveals parallels already adumbrated by the
image of the circle (54). There, too, Emma's dress catches against
the clothes of the man, as her riding-habit clings to Rodolphe's
jacket, her head falls against the vicomte's chest as it does against
Rodolphe's shoulder, and in both cases she escapes from reality
by covering her eyes with her hand.

The waltz continues, moreover, with Léon, whose seduction
of her in the cathedral also takes place against the backdrop of
a conversation, this time that of the guide pointing out the
beauties of the cathedral. The religious terminology Rodolphe
had used – 'madonna', 'immaculate', 'angel' – is echoed here as
one of the repetitions, but there are also premonitory rumblings
of the great theme of death when the guide, who, for his part,
is of course simply repeating the patter he gives all visitors,
comments on one of the tombs by asserting, in what one is
tempted to see as a *mise en abyme* of the entire novel: 'il
n'est point possible, n'est-ce pas, de voir une plus parfaite
représentation du néant?' (247).[47] Moreover, in the same way
that the agricultural show offered a physical representation of
the animality of desire, so too the cathedral is presented as
giving concrete form to erotic longing. Seen through Léon's
eyes, the church is a gigantic boudoir: 'les voûtes s'inclinaient

pour recueillir dans l'ombre la confession de son amour;
les vitraux resplendissaient pour illuminer son visage, et les
encensoirs allaient brûler pour qu'elle apparût comme un ange,
dans la fumée des parfums' (245).[48] The sensual intensity of this
passage, with its appeal to the senses of sight, hearing and smell,
serves to heighten the constant slippage operating between the
spiritual and the physical, and to recall Emma's adolescence
in the convent, with its same heady blend of sensuality and
mysticism. An even more obvious substitution is provided
when the guide urges the couple to view the cathedral spire:

> Léon fuyait; car il lui semblait que son amour, qui, depuis
> deux heures bientôt, s'était immobilisé dans l'église comme
> les pierres, allait maintenant s'évaporer, telle qu'une fumée,
> par cette espèce de tuyau tronqué, de cage oblongue, de
> cheminée à jour, qui se hasarde si grotesquement sur la
> cathédrale comme la tentative extravagante de quelque
> chaudronnier fantaisiste (248).[49]

The endless potential for substitution is intimated here as the
text moves towards finding a simile for the steeple, continually
suggesting that what is at issue is yet another kind of erection.
And the repetitions continue as Emma, unable to flee with
Rodolphe in the coaches of her dreams, accepts instead a
debasement of the dream when she makes love with Léon
in a cab, that 'lourde machine' (249). As Sartre argues, 'en se
donnant au jeune clerc, Emma se parodie; c'est une charge, cette
coucherie, l'imitation hystérique de l'instant unique, à jamais
perdu'.[50]

Hysterical imitation runs through the whole of the novel.
Rodolphe's soft leather boots and velvet coat instantly put
him in the category of the ideal man Emma dreams of in
the early days of her marriage (42), but the fact that he
carries a knife in his pocket, revealed when he repairs the
bridle after seducing Emma, also turns him into a substitute
Charles (104). And when Léon visits Yonville to see Emma,
the meetings take place in the alcove, where she met his
predecessor (264), as the narrative voice points out, although
we are left to discover for ourselves the additional substitution:
they chat under an umbrella, lit by flashes of lightning (264) in
unconscious imitation of the early days of her courtship with

Charles (19). Even Charles's preparations for Emma's funeral, in which he assumes her romantic nature, reproduce the black velvet of the ideal husband's jacket in the form of a funeral cloth (334), transforming death into the ultimate lover. The emblem of imitation inscribed in the text is of course Binet, whose very name, as T. Tanner points out, suggests duplication,[51] and whose task is to reproduce, in the lesser medium of wood, 'une de ces ivoireries indescriptibles . . . ne servant à rien' (311–12).[52] But Binet, whose task is coming to an end at the same time as the novel approaches its conclusion, is also there as Flaubert's most caustic and self-critical reflection of the author, copying an imitation of empty complexity, which has its echo in the 'aboli bibelot d'inanité sonore' of Mallarmé's poem, 'Ses purs ongles'.

POETIC SYMBOLISM

The principle of repetition, therefore, is one of the central structuring devices in *Madame Bovary* and recurs in a slightly different form in what A. Fairlie has called the patterns of poetic symbolism.[53] Well-known examples are the floating butterfly shapes created when Emma burns her wedding bouquet and when she throws from the cab window the shreds of the letter she had written for Léon; the cry she hears after making love to Rodolphe for the first time and that she herself emits at the opera; the moments when her clothes become caught on vegetation, the first time as she walks to her wedding, the second when she goes out riding with Rodolphe. Threaded through the narration, these patterns not only tauten the novel's structure but also cast an ironic light over events by suggesting that what seems special and unique is merely yet another version of the same, life's sardonic joke in which individuality is only a mock for monotony.

The sense of repetition is further increased by the recurrent use of certain metaphors. Indeed, any reader of the published version of *Madame Bovary* is likely to be struck by the way in which Flaubert's images cluster around certain motifs, such as food and drink, animals, architecture, the countryside. Rather than see this as representing a somewhat impoverished imagination, as certain critics have done, it is no doubt more

accurate to historicize it and perceive it as reflecting further
hackneyed patterns of thought and speech recorded by Flaubert
in his observations of his contemporaries.[54] Throughout the
novel there is an unmistakable sense of joy in picking out what
is representative of the time.

Eating and drinking are central pastimes in the novel, as of
course they were in the society of the time. Indicative of the
characters' desire to appropriate the world, they are also symbols
of the way in which the weaker are at risk of being devoured by
the stronger. Images of wine set up a sequence of echoes, from
the early description of Charles's mother gradually becoming
bitter, as wine turns to vinegar when the air gets to it (7),
through the depiction of Emma allowing herself to be debased
by her passion for Rodolphe to such an extent that 'son âme
s'enfonçait en cette ivresse et s'y noyait, ratatinée, comme le
duc de Clarence dans son tonneau de malvoisie' (196–7),[55] to
a glimpse of Charles after Emma's death, finding in Berthe's
company a delight mingled with sad memories, a pleasure, we
are told, that is mixed with bitterness, like those poorly-made
wines that smack of resin (350). Homais, of course, representing
the rise of the bourgeoisie, is associated with no such images,
knowing on the contrary how to care for ailing wines (100).
Emma is reduced to a comestible object by the depiction of
Charles's happiness in the early days of their marriage – 'il s'en
allait ruminant son bonheur, comme ceux qui mâchent encore,
après dîner, le goût des truffes qu'ils digèrent' (35)[56] – as well as
by the more cynical Rodolphe, whose vision of her as fruit ripe
for the plucking is suggested by the peaches they hear falling
on their final evening together and symbolized in the basket of
apricots in which he hides his letter. This symbol, furthermore,
is also taken up by Léon, who, during his time in Paris, thought
of Emma as a vague promise hanging in the future, like a golden
fruit hanging in fantastic foliage (236).

The rural landscape in which Flaubert places his characters
provides numerous clustered images, whose function is to
underline the physical nature of emotions and longings that
Emma tends to perceive as more ethereal. Charles is forever
summed up in the early comparison between him and a 'cheval
de manège, qui tourne en place les yeux bandés, ignorant de
la besogne qu'il broie' (10).[57] The memory of this comparison

highlights the yawning gap between the couple when Emma is described as having abandoned ideas of a religious vocation as horses pulled by the bridle stop dead and drop the bit from between their teeth (41). The exploitation of Charles is underpinned by the way in which horses become agents in his cuckolding, not merely the horses that carry Rodolphe and Emma to the forest-clearing where they first make love, and those that pull the *Hirondelle* to Rouen and the reunions with Léon, but also those that are an integral part of Emma's reveries: the black horse with its white-plumed knight of her convent musings (38), the horses galloping to the promised land where the lemon trees bloom. The irony, therefore, is all the more mordant when Charles's final meeting with Rodolphe comes about because Charles, now bankrupt, is forced to sell his horse at the Argueil market.[58] The rural motifs that dominate the backdrop to the conversations between Emma and Léon on the visit to the wet-nurse and between Rodolphe and Emma at the agricultural fair, picked up again when Rodolphe meets Charles at Argueil in a parodic travesty of the *comices* scene – it is Rodolphe this time who chats on about farming, animals, fertilizers (355) – are also vital to the description of Emma's beauty at the height of her affair with Rodolphe: 'ses convoitises, ses chagrins, l'expérience du plaisir et ses illusions toujours jeunes, comme font aux fleurs le fumier, la pluie, les vents et le soleil, l'avaient par gradations développée' (199).[59] The concision with which the manure is acknowledged while the presence of the flowers is emphasized gives particular weight to a psychological point Flaubert frequently raises in his letters: the way in which, under certain circumstances, the whole personality of an individual suddenly comes intensely alive.

The countryside inhabited by the characters thus supplies many of the images, creating a landscape that acts as a commentary on their aspirations and vices, without becoming the emotionalized nature of Romanticism. In a similar way, the buildings they frequent and live in, as well as those in their reveries, offer a source of structuring imagery. Emma's father, after the wedding, feels as sad as one does in an empty house (32); Emma's life at Tostes strikes her as being as cold as a loft whose skylight faces north (46); on Léon's departure, sorrow enters her soul like winter wind howling in abandoned castles (126).

Against this series of solid comparisons, Emma's longing to escape is given physical form by a series of metaphors predicated on birds and flight. Before her marriage, for instance, love had appeared to her like 'un grand oiseau au plumage rose planant dans la splendeur des ciels poétiques' (41);[60] in the first days of her marriage, the flowers she drops from her window as she bids farewell to Charles circle like birds as they fall, only to land on the ill-groomed mane of Charles's old white mare (35); her longing for Léon in her early days at Yonville is conveyed in an image that exchanges the exotic pink-feathered bird for a far more familiar species, when we are told that her thoughts fly to Homais's house, where Léon boards, 'comme les pigeons du *Lion d'or* qui venaient tremper là, dans les gouttières, leurs pattes roses et leurs ailes blanches' (110);[61] at the *comices*, when Rodolphe puts his hand on hers, he imagines its as a 'tourterelle captive qui veut reprendre sa volée' (153),[62] while the first love scene with Rodolphe includes a reference to hummingbirds; and faced with Charles's failure to treat Hippolyte's club foot, Emma finds her dreams 'tombant dans la boue comme des hirondelles blessées' (189).[63] Both pigeons and swallows combine here with the *métaphore filée* of water and mud, suggesting an element to which they are alien, as Emma perceives herself to be lost in an alien world. Significantly, perhaps, while Emma is associated with images of wild birds, Homais is first seen standing under a caged bird. Again, while this patterning may not be conscious, its subtle effect on the reader is none the less part of the novel's force.

An equally important element of that force is the movement between narrative voices, the ability to change the focus of perception from character to character, or from a character to an external narrator through an almost seamless shift whose features my next chapter will explore.

NOTES: CHAPTER 4

1 Corr, II, 118: 'The thing that's atrociously difficult is the linking of the ideas, and making sure that they arise naturally from each other.'

2 Corr, II, 180: 'the linking of the sentiments is the devil of a job, and in this novel everything depends on that; for I maintain that one can amuse just as well with ideas as with facts, but for that to happen they must flow from each other as water flows from one waterfall to another, and they must pull

the reader along in this way amidst the trembling of the sentences and the bubbling of the metaphors'.

3 Corr, II, 361: 'a fling lasts a minute and we've longed for it for months! Our passions are like volcanoes; they grumble incessantly, but the eruption is only intermittent.'

4 Corr, II, 426: 'it's a tough section. I have *all* my characters acting and speaking, all mingled together, and over and above that there's a great, enveloping landscape all around them. But, if I succeed, it will be really symphonic' (original emphasis).

5 MBNV, p. 3: 'her poetic need for luxury'; 'the tradesmen's bills'.

6 MBNV, p. 4: 'gentle, sensitive spirit, upright, just and obtuse, with no imagination'. 'a long expectation of a passion and an event which do not come'.

7 MBVN, p. 6: 'with no artistic taste, she has little of the artist about her, but she is poetic'.

8 MBVN, p. 6: 'this first experience must provide the dominant colour for the whole affair – its reflection must always hang over their relationship'.

9 MBVN, p. 9: 'with a joke on his lips, and stirs her whole character vigorously'.

10 The question of the levels of language used is explored in Chapter 5, 'Voices'.

11 MBVN, p. 66: 'why is she not seized with love for Léon? – Too young, doesn't explore her feelings, true passions don't reveal themselves, like *organs* which have a protective membrane' (original emphasis).

12 MBVN, p. 26.

13 Corr, II, 452: 'the groundwork of my agricultural fair has to be laid again, I mean, my whole love dialogue, which I'm only half way through. I don't have any ideas. It's in vain that I dig into my brain, my heart and feelings, nothing bursts forth.'

14 Corr, II, 486: 'my Bovary is on the immediate point of being fucked.'

15 Corr, II, 483: 'what a delicious thing it is to write! not to be oneself any more, but to wander around in the world one's talking about. Today, for example, man and woman together, lover and mistress at the same time, I went riding through a forest.'

16 Corr, II, 544.

17 Corr II, 573.

18 Corr, II, 575.

19 Corr, II, p. 496: 'before the aforementioned passage, I need a link containing 8 lines, and it's taken me 3 days, and there is not one unnecessary word in it, and yet I have to redo it! again! because it is too slow'.

20 Corr, II, p. 473: 'it enhances the fair and makes it seem shorter, because it gives a summary of what has happened'.

21 'With three sweet nothings, she'd adore you, I'm sure of it! it would be tender! charming! Yes, but then how would I get rid of her?'

22 *Flaubert: The Uses of Uncertainty* (London: Paul Elek, 1974), p. 144.

23 For a recent survey see N. Wing's interesting, if at times over-ingenious, essay. 'Emma's stories: narrative, repetition and desire in *Madame Bovary*', in *The Limits of Narrative* (Cambridge: University Press, 1986), pp. 41–77.

24 'now not one of us could remember a thing about him'.

25 'he knew (and better than she herself did) the long history of these promissory notes, at first tiny, endorsed by various names, spaced out over long intervals and continually renewed, until the day when, gathering together all the bills, the merchant had charged his friend Vinçart to carry

out in his own name the necessary legal proceedings.'
26 '"Fifty-four years service! A silver medal! Twenty-five francs! For you!"'
27 See G. Genette, 'Silences de Flaubert' in *Figures* (Paris: Editions du Seuil, 1966), pp. 223–43.
28 See 'The Critical Response', pp. 164–5.
29 Corr, II, p. 147: 'gently tickle many a feminine wound'.
30 See Chapter 5.
31 See S. Freud, 'Creative writers and day-dreaming', in *Complete Psychological Works* (London: Hogarth 1959), IX, pp. 143–53 and compare F. Jameson, *The Political Unconscious*, pp. 174–5.
32 'had designed for his garden a lawn symbolizing the star of honour, with two little twists of grass setting out from the top to indicate the ribbon'.
33 *The Gates of Horn* (New York: Oxford University Press, 1966), p. 254.
34 *L'Idiot de la famille* (Paris: Gallimard, 1971), II, p. 1130: 'Gustave, thank God, never knew how to "make a plan": and as a result, the "composition" of this work is a surprising marvel'.
35 'she would sob, call Léon, and send him tender words and kisses which were lost on the wind'.
36 'a motley assortment of rags covered his shoulders, and an old, stove-in beaver hat in the shape of a basin hid his face; but, when he took his hat off he revealed, instead of eyelids, two gaping and blood-stained orbits.'
37 Compare the description of Emma's letter to Léon with their flowers, verses, moon and stars (288).
38 'he too, the wig-maker, lamented the fact that his vocation had been stopped short, bemoaned his lost future, and, dreaming of a shop in a city, like Rouen, for instance, on the port, next to the theatre, he would spend the entire day strolling up and down'.
39 For particularly stimulating studies see T. Tanner, *Adultery in the Novel* and M. Vargas Llosa, *The Perpetual Orgy*.
40 Tanner, p. 247.
41 *Nélida*, p. 49: 'and Timoléon fixed his intoxicated eyes on the eyes of the troubled girl; he dared to squeeze her supple waist gently; and his hand, without squeezing her own, held it and bound it through an inexplicable magnetism. As they swept across the floor, moving ever more swiftly, to the sound of music whose imperious rhythm tore Nélida away from herself, dazed her, filled her with a sense of giddiness, the girl, moved, palpitating, driven by an irresistible impulse in a whirl of light and sound, felt her brain filled with the perfidious perfume of jasmine.'
42 MBNV, p. 129: 'am I merely a character in a novel, the product of a delirious imagination, the invention of a little jackanapes whose birth I witnessed and who invented me to make people believe I don't exist.'
43 Here, too, joining a series of women from Saint Theresa to Balzac's Valérie.
44 'she felt she was still whirling about in the waltz, under the light of the chandeliers, in the vicomte's arms, and that Léon was close by, that he was going to come . . . and yet she still felt Rodolphe's head beside her.'
There are several similar passages: one occurs during Emma's relationship with Léon: 'les premiers mois de son mariage, ses promenades à cheval dans la forêt, le Vicomte qui valsait, et Lagardy chantant, tout repassa devant ses yeux . . .' (289): (the first months of her marriage, her rides in the forest, the Vicount waltzing, Lagardy singing, all passed before her eyes).
45 'A hundred times I've even wanted to leave, and I followed you and stayed.' 'Manure.' 'As I would stay this evening, tomorrow, the next days,

all my life!' 'To M. Caron of Argueil, a gold medal!' 'For never have I found in anyone else's company such complete charm.' 'To M. Bain, of Givry-Saint-Martin!' 'So I shall carry off with me the memory I have of you.''For a merino ram . . .' 'But you will forget me, I will have passed like a shadow.' 'To M. Belot, of Notre-Dame . . .' 'But no! I will be something, won't I, in your thoughts and in your life?' 'Pig class, equal first prize.'

46 'in my soul you are like a Madonna on a pedestal, in a high, solid, immaculate place . . . Be my friend, my sister, my angel!'

47 'it is impossible, don't you agree, to see a more perfect representation of the void'.

48 'the vaults bent down to gather up in the shadows the confession of her love, the windows glowed in order to illuminate her face, and the censers would burn so that she could appear like an angel in the smoke of their perfumes'.

49 'Léon fled, for it seemed to him that his love which, for almost two hours, had been immobilized in the church like the very stones, was now about to evaporate, like smoke, through the kind of broken-off pipe, that oblong cage, that open chimney, which ventures so grotesquely on the cathedral like the extravagant attempt of some over-imaginative coppersmith.'

50 Sartre, *L'Idiot de la famille* (Paris: Gallimard , 1971), II, p. 1284: 'in giving herself to the young clerk, Emma parodies herself; it's a caricature, this lovemaking, a hysterical imitation of the unique instant. That unique instant can never be recovered'.

51 T. Tanner, *Adultery in the novel*, p. 247.

52 'one of those indescribable ivory ornaments, which serve no purpose at all'.

53 *Flaubert: Madame Bovary* (London: Edward Arnold, 1962), p. 35.

54 See Amossy and Rosen, *Le Discours du cliché* (Paris: CDU et SEDES réunis, 1982) pp. 66–82.

55 'her soul sank ever deeper into that intoxication and drowned there, shrivelled up, like the duke of Clarence in his butt of malmsey wine'. A curious image used, more appropriately, of Musset in a letter Flaubert wrote to Louise Colet in 1852, to which he adds a comment recalling Homais's pharmacy: 'l'alcool ne conserve pas les cerveaux, comme il fait pour les foetus' (Corr, II, 119): 'alcohol does not preserve brains as it does foetuses'.

56 'he would go his way, ruminating on his happiness, like those who still savour after their dinner, the taste of the truffles they are digesting'.

57 'a work horse, turning constantly around in the same circle, eyes blinkered, unaware of what he crushes'.

58 Of course Flaubert is making use of something very much part of daily life at the time of his novel, but the motif certainly seems here to be fulfilling two roles, that of adding to the image of society and that of suggesting patterns in the text.

59 'her desires, her sorrows, the experience of pleasure and her ever-new illusions, had gradually developed her, in the same way that flowers are developed by manure, rain, wind and sun'.

60 'a great pink-feathered bird soaring in the splendour of poetic skies'.

61 'like the pigeons of the *Lion d'or* which dipped their pink feet and white wings in the gutters of the pharmacy'.

62 'a captive turtle-dove seeking to fly away again'.

63 'falling into the mud like wounded swallows'.

CHAPTER 5

Voices

The letters Flaubert wrote in the years he devoted to working on *Madame Bovary* offer particularly detailed information concerning his aesthetic convictions and his vision of art and literature. Throughout this period, he consistently repeats that what he demands of himself where style is concerned makes literary composition atrocious labour for him, a form of torment or monastic penance. The reason for this is that style, as he perceives it, is what creates the writer's own unique and absolute 'manière de voir les choses'.[1] Convinced that, however advanced and complex prosodic laws might be, those of narrative prose remained ill-defined and random, Flaubert nevertheless had in mind a style he considered ideal and for which he constantly strove:

> j'en conçois pourtant un, moi, un style: un style qui serait beau, que quelqu'un fera à quelque jour, dans dix ans, ou dans dix siècles, et qui serait rythmé comme le vers, précis comme le langage des sciences, et avec des ondulations, des ronflements de violoncelle, des aigrettes de feux, un style qui vous entrerait dans l'idée comme un coup de stylet, et où votre pensée enfin voguerait sur des surfaces lisses, comme lorsqu'on file dans un canot avec bon vent arrière.[2]

This desire for a rhythmical prose, beautiful and precise, musical and penetrating, is accompanied by a conviction that a finely written sentence will share with verse the property of being unchangeable. Moreover, for Flaubert, writers who fail to understand the anatomy of style will also fail to convey truth. This emphasis on the rationality demanded of a prose writer leads him to mistrust inspiration, which is perceived as mere delusion, and to search instead for the complicated mechanics that allows for the fusion of thought and expression. Yet he was fully aware of the other side of this problem, which might lead him to place so much emphasis on style that he could forget the ultimate aim of his work.

Madame Bovary, moreover, posed particular problems, especially where dialogue was concerned. In September 1853, for example, he complained to Louise Colet:

> quelle difficulté que le dialogue, quand on veut surtout que le dialogue ait du *caractère*! Peindre par le dialogue et qu'il n'en soit pas moins vif, précis et toujours distingué en restant même banal, cela est monstrueux et je ne sache personne qui l'ait fait dans un livre (original emphasis).[3]

The desire to create a means of conveying even the most banal and trivial of conversations in a style that would be rhythmical and precise dominates much of his thinking, and is the key to his manipulation of the subtleties of *style indirect libre*. Even the explanation of Emma's financial problems he seeks to put into rhythmical dialogue, encountering as a result such apparently insuperable problems that he confides to Louis Bouilhet that the novel has now become 'un véritable *pensum*'.[4]

As important as dialogue and posing problems just as serious is the question of narration. Flaubert, fully aware from an early stage of the gamble he was taking, asserts to Louise Colet that 'toute la valeur de mon livre . . . sera d'avoir su marcher droit sur un cheveu, suspendu entre le double abîme du lyrisme et du vulgaire'.[5] It was these two tendencies of the novel that he wanted to fuse into what he calls a narrative analysis.[6] For him, narration demanded drama, depiction or emotion, rather than declamation, and the psychological narration called for the same speed, clarity and drive as a purely dramatic narration.

All of this relied on the objectivity and impersonality of the narrating voice, because, as he affirms in a formula offering close parallels to Diderot's theories in *Le Paradoxe sur le comédien*, '*moins on sent une chose, plus on est apte à l'exprimer comme elle est*'(original emphasis).[7] This is both a practical and an aesthetic consideration, since too much involvement in a situation or emotion would lead to a clouding of the vision, a failure to perceive what it was one was experiencing, and would in any case run counter to Flaubert's dictum, preferring exposition to explanation: 'soyons *exposants* et non discutants'(original emphasis).[8]

Observation and documentation are, therefore, key terms in Flaubert's correspondence, spurring him to request information on club feet and on arsenic poisoning, and underlying his request to Bouilhet to provide suggestions for Homais to make regarding a cure for the blind man, but, of course, these are to be suggestions that will serve to show Homais's ignorance of such matters. From a very early stage in the preparation of the novel he described himself as observing closely the dullest details, training his eyes on what he depicts, with deftly evocative alliteration, as 'les mousses de moisissure de l'âme'.[9] Nevertheless, this does not, of course, lead to the undifferentiated representation of banal reality that the self-styled champions of 'Realism', mainly Champfleury and Duranty, were promoting in the very years that Flaubert was at work on his novel. Flaubert stresses rather an 'observation artistique',[10] which draws on the writer's imagination to transform external truth as if it were being perceived through a magnifying mirror.[11] The image here shows Flaubert actively participating in the contemporary aesthetic debate, in which so many writers and artists used the symbol of the mirror to convey the work of art. And throughout his correspondence he insists that creating truth is, as he puts it in a comment on Zola's novel *L'Assommoir*, less important than creating beauty.[12]

The sophistication with which Flaubert manipulates certain structural devices is matched by his experimentation with the techniques of narrative voice. Indeed, the reason why *Madame Bovary* opens so many questions about the way in which we respond to narrative lies not only in the nesting of tales within the text but also in the renowned slipperiness of the narrative positions adopted. Rejecting the assertion of omniscience found in Balzac or Stendhal, Flaubert combines passages of internal focalization, in which the narrator tells only what the characters know, with passages using a deliberately blinkered vision, recounting the tale through minds of limited understanding.[13] Moreover, some of the nested tales employ

external focalization, where the narrator's knowledge is not
as great as that of the central character: Félicité, for instance,
knows less than the central character in her tale about la
Guérine. The choice of narrative position inevitably raises
questions about the kind of language that can be used. Is
it possible, for instance, to convey the mentality of a child
through the finely wrought language that Henry James uses
when he attempts to recount adult behaviour through the mind
of the young Maisie? Is the ability to manipulate language the
only proof of either intelligence or sensitivity? Is the banality of
Charles's conversation an unquestionable proof of the quality of
his mind? Is it possible to use the novel to convey non-linguistic
indications of emotion or sensitivity? One of the challenges
Flaubert sets himself in *Madame Bovary* is that of exploring
minds incapable of giving sophisticated expression to their
inner feelings and yet to do so without claiming the kind of
omniscience that, for instance, Stendhal uses to justify Julien's
actions.

Flaubert's correspondence contains, in varying formulations,
several statements insisting that 'l'écrivain doit être comme
Dieu dans son œuvre, visible partout, mais présent nulle
part'.[14] The relative exclusion of authorial omniscience and
all that that involves in terms of the kind of language it makes
available to the writer is partly the result of a philosophical
position. The vision of a world devoid of meaning, where
the individual's awareness of her own nature and experience
is at best fragmentary, would be irrevocably undermined by
authorial interventions, with their suggestion of power and
pattern, of a rational teleology which may be inaccessible to
the character but which is evident to the reader. But it is
clear that Flaubert's decision is also a response to an aesthetic
challenge, corresponding to his desire to 'faire rêver', to open up
a space for meditation that would be instantly plugged by explicit
authorial comment. Above all, perhaps, the rejection of such
comments allows the text to raise central questions concerned
with the problematics of language. The inadequacy of language
is asserted at an early stage in the novel, when Emma is first
plagued by the boredom of her marriage: 'Peut-être aurait-elle
souhaité faire à quelqu'un la confidence de toutes ces choses.
Mais comment dire un insaisissable malaise, qui change d'aspect

comme les nuées, qui tourbillonne comme le vent? Les mots
lui manquaient.' (42)[15] Any attempt to express such a feeling in
words would inevitably alter it.

Moreover, the words she does possess seem to have no link
with life, to belong merely to the domain of books, into which
she can look but not enter: 'Emma cherchait à savoir ce que
l'on entendait au juste dans la vie par les mots de *félicité,* de
passion et *d'ivresse,* qui lui avaient paru si beaux dans les livres.'
(36) (original emphasis)[16] There seems to be little correlation
between words and emotions in Emma's perception of the
world, and any attempt to bridge the gap leads to distortion:
'la parole est un laminoir qui allonge toujours les sentiments'
(239).[17]

SPEAKING

One of the ways in which Flaubert points to the inadequacy
of language, or more precisely to the gaps between intention
and statement, and between statement and interpretation, is
through conveying directly the conversations of his characters.
The difficulty of such a solution is evident, and emphasized by
Flaubert himself in a letter written in 1853: 'Bien écrire *le médiocre*
et faire qu'il garde en même temps son aspect, sa coupe, ses mots
même, cela est vraiment diabolique'(original emphasis).[18] However much of a struggle it may have demanded, there is little
doubt that Flaubert relished the challenge, particularly, perhaps,
in regard to capturing the rhythm, images and expressions of the
peasants, as indeed Maupassant, who drew such inspiration from
Flaubert, was subsequently to do in far greater detail. Félicité's
retelling of la Guérine's story is only one example of Flaubert's
experimentation with the possibilities of the written language
in this regard. The conversation with the wet-nurse is not only
amusing in its far from sympathetic portrayal of Emma, longing
to be alone again with Léon and yet afraid of what might be
said if she dismisses Mme Rolet too abruptly, but it also
reveals the grasping nature of the peasant, eager to extract the
maximum benefit from the situation. The suggestion implicit in
the periphrasis, 'la paysanne', which presents her as typical of her
class, needs no further authorial comment. Flaubert experiments

here with a combination of reported and direct speech, together with a series of brief indications revealing the importance of both words and gesture:

> Alors la paysanne, la tirant à l'écart, derrière un orme, se mit à lui parler de son mari, qui, avec son métier et six francs par an que le capitaine. . .
> —Achevez plus vite, dit Emma.
> —Eh bien, reprit la nourrice poussant des soupirs entre chaque mot, j'ai peur qu'il ne se fasse une tristesse de me voir prendre du café toute seule; vous savez, les hommes . . .
> —Puisque vous en aurez, répétait Emma, je vous en donnerai! . . . Vous m'ennuyez!
> —Hélas! ma pauvre chère dame, c'est qu'il a, par suite de ses blessures, des crampes terribles à la poitrine. Il dit même que le cidre l'affaiblit.
> —Mais dépêchez-vous, mère Rolet!
> —Donc, reprit celle-ci faisant une révérence, si ce n'était pas trop vous demander . . . , -elle salua encore une fois, – quand vous voudrez, – et son regard suppliait, – un cruchon d'eau-de-vie, dit-elle enfin, et j'en frotterai les pieds de votre petite, qui les a tendres comme la langue (original ellipses) (96).[19]

Conveying the speech of the middle-class characters directly allows Flaubert to indulge his sardonic delight in the clichéd and hackneyed, drawing attention to the gap between the images the characters have of themselves and the image conveyed to others. Emma and Léon, each eager to impress the other with a show of artistic sensitivity, exchange the following remarks:

> —Et quelle musique préférez-vous?
> —Oh! la musique allemande, celle qui porte à rêver (84–5)[20]

thereby recalling, in a typically Flaubertian piece of irony, not merely the entries in the *Dictionnaire des idées reçues* where music is granted the power to make one 'penser à un tas de choses'[21] and Germans are depicted as a nation of dreamers, but also, most ironically, Flaubert's own desire to make his readers dream. Equally indicative of the threadbare nature of the Romantic phraseology that informs their conversation is Emma's linking of sunset and sea:

> —Je ne trouve rien d'admirable comme les soleils cou-
> chants, reprit-elle, mais au bord de la mer, surtout.
> —Oh! j'adore la mer, dit M. Léon (84).[22]

In all these exchanges what is revealed, indirectly but with particular clarity, is the human tendency to interpret as patterns of shared experience and sympathy what may be the mere product of cliché.

These social exchanges are so perfectly caught as to need no commentary, but at times the narrative voice makes its presence felt with a dry, deflating question. Emma and Léon, desiring each other but unable to find the courage to say so, discuss a company of Spanish dancers:

> —Vous irez? demanda-t-elle.
> —Si je le peux , répondit-il.
> N'avaient-ils rien autre chose à se dire? (97).[23]

Deflation, of both speaker and listener, can also be achieved by reporting or paraphrasing the speaker's comments and focusing on the emotional response of the listener. Thus, on meeting Léon again, Emma listens to his protestations of despair at their former parting: 'Madame Bovary, en l'écoutant, s'étonnait d'être si vieille; toutes ces choses qui réapparaissaient lui semblaient élargir son existence' (241).[24] The intensity of emotion Emma had imagined experiencing at such a moment, the sense of union with the other, all this is corrosively undermined by the narrator's assertion that what she feels is old and by her own limited control of language when all she can reply is 'Oui, c'est vrai! . . . c'est vrai! . . . c'est vrai' (original ellipses) (241).[25]

While the use of direct or paraphrased speech may reveal the inadequate control of language that leads Emma astray, it also shows that the best controllers of the spoken language are the representatives of bourgeois pragmatism, Homais, Lheureux and Lieuvain. With these characters in particular, therefore, the text forces us into an uncomfortable awareness of the manipulating power of language. It is often, however, their own use of language that serves to deflate these characters, rather than direct narrative intervention. The wonderfully named Lieuvain, singing the praises of the agricultural world, trips over his own pompous rhythms when he runs out of uses for the hen:

> Qui n'a souvent réfléchi à toute l'importance que l'on retire de ce modeste animal, ornement de nos basses-cours, qui fournit à la fois un oreiller moelleux pour nos couches, sa chair succulente pour nos tables, et des œufs (149).[26]

It is not only the broken rhythm that betrays him, but also the device of the rhetorical question, here revealed as particularly vacuous, for who, after all, does often cogitate upon the uses of the hen? And the unstoppable Homais, whose long sentences dominate conversations and whose written pieces reveal the power of the press, is caught out by his very intoxication with words when he describes the climate at Yonville and in his desire to bring in centigrade, Réamur and Fahrenheit ('mesure anglaise') comes to grief over his arithmetic (83). Elsewhere the narrative voice pulls the rug from his feet, as when he hears of the bankruptcy of the *Café français*: 'quelle épouvantable catastrophe! s'écria l'apothicaire, qui avait toujours des expressions congruantes à toutes les circonstances imaginables.'(138)[27] Here again, as so often with Homais, there are parallels with the *Dictionnaire des idées reçues*. In this case, the comparison is with the comment under the heading 'accident': 'Toujours déplorable ou fâcheux (comme si on devait jamais trouver un malheur une chose réjouissante. . .)'.[28]

The dialogue between the narrative voice (or voices) and the characters is further highlighted by the device of paraphrasing conversations while indicating the tone and nature of the speech used through the insertion of brief italicized quotations, islands of discourse reminding us of Bakhtin's assertions about the dialogic nature of the novel.[29] As C. Duchet remarks: 'l'italique introduit, avec sa dissonance, une opposition discursive jusqu'à l'intérieur de l'énoncé cité, et socialise le texte en y faisant entendre la voix du discours social'.[30] In this way is captured the jargon of the school yard in the opening passages of the novel (*nouveau, genre*), Homais's bumbling attempts to use the colloquialisms of the day (*turne, chicard, Breda-Street*), the collective wisdom of the cliché ('*avec du toupet, un homme réussit toujours dans le monde*').[31] What we are being shown here is the way in which society uses language to impose preconceived ideas and accepted judgements, forcing the individual into linguistic categories: Charles reduced to 'a new boy' for instance, or Homais trying to cross the boundary between bourgeois and working-class but remaining within a strictly delineated category. Emma's attempt to impose on the chaos of existence the grid provided by her favourite reading matter is only the most evident symptom of a constant disease, in which the individual is continually pushed into patterns of perception. As Amossy and Rosen argue in their study of cliché, 'la modulation incessante de la parole de l'Autre, envahissant toutes les "voix" romanesques et s'infiltrant dans tous les régistres, transforme le texte en ce phénomène d'écho si spécifiquement flaubertien que l'on peut qualifier de chœur social ou de ressassement anonyme'.[32]

WRITING

The power of language to deceive is also revealed through the characters' manipulations of the written word. Emma's letters to Léon, through which she tries to convince herself of the intensity and uniqueness of their passion, are reduced to the level of empty pastiche when the narrative voice paraphrases them and adds its own gloss: 'dans les lettres qu'Emma lui envoyait, il était question de fleurs, de vers, de la lune et des étoiles, ressources naïves d'une passion affaiblie' (288).[33] Rodolphe's letter breaking off his affair with Emma shows with particularly crude intensity the gulf between word and truth: '"O mon Dieu! non, non, n'en accusez que la fatalité!" – Voilà un mot qui fait toujours de l'effet, se dit-il.' (208).[34] But it is perhaps in Homais's newspaper articles that we are made most sharply aware of the power of the written or spoken word to create a version of reality that is entirely a product of language, and that therefore throws into doubt our beliefs about what we perceive as external reality. The narrator's version of the firework display at the end of the agricultural show may speak of dampened fireworks producing nothing but an occasional roman candle (156); Homais, however, paints an entirely different picture: 'le soir, un brillant feu d'artifice a tout à coup illuminé les airs. On eût dit un véritable kaléidoscope, un vrai décor d'Opéra.' (158)[35]

'Véritable, vrai', locked together with those manipulators of vision, the kaleidoscope and the opera set: the effect of Homais's piece is to reveal the ability of language to manipulate objective truth, and to undermine what J. Culler has described as 'the basic enabling convention of the novel as a genre [:] confidence in the transparency and representative power of language'.[36] On other occasions, however, the written word is shown to have a particular transparency; this is the case, for instance, with the letter Emma receives from her father. Despite the spelling mistakes and the humdrum nature of the words, we are told, Emma has not the slightest difficulty in pursuing 'la pensée douce qui caquetait tout au travers comme une poule à demi cachée dans une haie d'épines' (177).[37] She is instantly reminded of her moments of happiness and pleasure in the period of her life spent on the farm, and even in its blank spaces the letter, for all its clumsiness and lack of sophistication, speaks directly to her: having referred to his difficulties in leaving the farm now that he is alone, he leaves a gap of a few lines, as if he had dropped his pen and dreamed for a while (177), in a dream Emma is perfectly able to share. Moments like these clearly reaffirm the power of language, of gesture and of silence to communicate.

STYLE INDIRECT LIBRE

Flaubert's main means of giving expression to those whose powers of articulation are limited is through *style indirect libre*, sometimes known in English as 'free indirect discourse', the device of presenting the character's thoughts and speech in the guise of the narrator's discourse.[38] It had been used before in French literature, but it is Flaubert who first exploits it systematically and who refines it into such a powerful and subtle technique. Frequently expressed in the imperfect, it has the effect, as Dorrit Cohn points out, of 'revealing a fictional mind suspended in an instant present, between a remembered past and an anticipated future'.[39] Emma's conviction that nothing in her life changes and that nothing can change, is intensified for us as readers by the vision of her caught in those open-ended imperfect tenses.

Style indirect libre enables the thoughts and speech of a character to be translated into a form of expression in harmony with the narration itself, and on the same linguistic level, while still conveying, through imagery and, at times, through the choice or register of vocabulary, the personality of the individual concerned. The pompous verbosity of a Homais, for instance, erupts into the more sober narrative style when he explains his choice of name for his daughter Athalie as 'un hommage au plus immortel chef-d'œuvre de la scène française' (92):[40] only Homais and his sort would think of qualifying immortality! Moreover, in phraseology that parodies the gothic novel, Emma's boredom after the departure of Léon is suggested in the rhythms of narrative discourse:

> Tout lui parut enveloppé par une atmosphère noire qui flottait confusément sur l'extérieur des choses, et le chagrin s'engouffrait dans son âme avec des hurlements doux, comme fait le vent d'hiver dans les châteaux abandonnés (126).[41]

Through *style indirect libre*, therefore, Emma's reading impinges on the narrative texture of the novel, forcing us as readers either to participate in it or to make a positive act of recuperation. What makes that recuperation both necessary and difficult is that Flaubert slips so subtly from narrative discourse to *style indirect libre*. In the moments following Emma's seduction, for example, the movement from external to internal narration is indicated merely by the sudden introduction of an alien image:

> Les ombres du soir descendaient; le soleil horizontal, passant entre les branches, lui éblouissait les yeux. Çà et là, tout autour d'elle, dans les feuilles ou par terre, des taches lumineuses tremblaient, comme si des colibris, en volant, eussent éparpillé leurs plumes (165).[42]

The Florida of Chateaubriand's *Atala* or of his *Mémoires d'Outre-Tombe*[43] seems to have imposed itself on Emma's vision of Normandy. Significantly, there is no need for Rodolphe's mind to be entered here: an external description of him, cigar clenched between his teeth as he repairs one of the bridles, is enough to reveal the gulf between Emma's response and his. Elsewhere in the text, however, *style indirect libre* is used to convey Rodolphe's mentality. Here again there is no visual signal to indicate a shift from narrative viewpoint to that of Rodolphe, nothing

analogous to the conventional punctuation marks which mark
direct speech. Nor is there any interpolation of 'he thought'
or 'he said'. Embedded directly into the text is the following
comment:

> Emma ressemblait à toutes les maîtresses; et le charme de
> la nouveauté, peu à peu tombant comme un vêtement,
> laissait voir à nu l'éternelle monotonie de la passion, qui
> a toujours les mêmes formes et le même langage (196).[44]

The privileged position the reader occupies through those passages of narrated monologue that allow us to enter Emma's mind
prevents us from reading this cynicism as entirely that of the
narrator: moreover, the imagery used, monotony as a stripper
slowly divesting herself of novelty, is very much in the idiom
of the roué. And yet, the second half of the statement, frequently
quoted in studies on Flaubert, offers no hint of whether or
not this is a moment when narrator's discourse and narrated
discourse meet, whether, that is, Rodolphe's thoughts and those
of the narrator coincide. The narrative voice does, however,
add a gloss which quite unambiguously dissociates itself from
certain aspects of Rodolphe's position: 'il ne distinguait pas, cet
homme si plein de pratique, la dissemblance des sentiments sous
la parité des expressions' (196).[45] Yet again, it is the inadequacies
of language, or, at least, of our awareness of language, that are
centrally at issue here.

Narrative interventions can, therefore, be associated with *style
indirect libre*, either by conveying a particular position in a way
that makes it impossible to decide whether this position is held
only by the character or by both character and narrator, or
in the form of a gloss commenting on a passage of narrated
discourse. Such intervention may not, of course, transgress
Flaubert's proclaimed law of authorial invisibility, given that
narrative and authorial voice may not be one and the same:
nevertheless, they do suggest that certain moral or pragmatic
positions are taken as axiomatic. The gulf between Charles's
image of the prestige of domino-playing and that of the narrator
is evident in the very choice of vocabulary and image, needing
no direct interventionary comment:

> S'enfermer chaque soir dans un sale appartement public,
> pour y taper sur des tables de marbre de petits os de

mouton marqués de points noirs, lui semblait un acte
précieux de sa liberté, qui le rehaussait d'estime vis-à-vis
de lui–même (11).[46]

Here, as in so many passages concerning Emma, what Flaubert
reveals with such remarkable subtlety is both the hackneyed
nature of the experience or the ideal and its appeal to the
individual. This suggestion of two responses is produced by
the simultaneous presence of two voices, that of the character,
and that of the glossing narrator. The ease with which the
narrating voice can make way for *style indirect libre* is illustrated
by a commentary on Emma's false interpretations:

> Elle confondait, dans son désir, les sensualités du luxe avec
> les joies du cœur, l'élégance des habitudes et les délicatesses
> du sentiment. Ne fallait-il pas à l'amour, comme aux
> plantes indiennes, des terrains préparés, une température
> particulière? (60–1).[47]

SIL

The ability to make these distinctions having been denied in
Emma, they must be the product of a narrative voice: but the
presuppositions in the question leading on from them indicate
that it at least is created by Emma. Here narrative discourse
gives way with such subtlety to *style indirect libre* that the reader
is forced to focus more sharply than in habitual modes of
reading on the interplay of different voices. A more immediately
recognizable moral intervention is provided after an account of
Emma's reverie about eloping with Rodolphe: 'dans tout cela,
jamais il n'était question de son enfant' (202),[48] yet even here we
cannot be sure that this sentence is not Rodolphe's thought since
it is immediately followed by a reference to him.

Occasionally the narrative voice provides a Balzacian gener-
alization – 'chaque notaire porte en soi les débris d'un poète'
(296)[49] – or raises questions about the interpretation to be
placed on acts or gestures – 'était-ce sérieusement qu'elle parlait
ainsi? Sans doute qu'Emma n'en savait rien elle-même.' (242)[50]
Yet again, what is evident in such authorial interventions is
Flaubert's interest in the workings of the mind, the conscious
and subconscious forces that determine individual responses. A
more subtle device that achieves similar results, and shows just
how much can be achieved by suggestion rather than statement,

can be found in the passages where Emma is shown looking at herself in the mirror and which are followed by the narrator's description of her.

But in general, although guide-lines may be deduced from the text, they are oblique or covert, and the use of *style indirect libre* in passages where the narrative voice falls silent led to the problems Flaubert experienced with the censors, for if he expresses through narrated discourse Emma's discovery of the 'souillures du mariage' and the 'désillusion de l'adultère' (230),[51] he refuses to add any moralistic gloss in the narrative voice, thereby making it possible to argue that these are his own convictions.[52]

In a perceptive comparison between the techniques of Flaubert and those of Henry James, F. Jameson argues that 'what is essential to the production of [*Madame Bovary*] is not, as in James, the construction of a central observational and psychic perspective within which one may for a time remain, but rather the quite different matter of inventing modulations, chromatic bridge-passages, cinematographic fadeouts or montages, which allow us to slip from one point of view to another'.[53] The shifting viewpoints in *Madame Bovary*, with the translation of individual discourse into a general narrative style, result, despite the variations in imagery and vocabulary for certain characters, in a remarkable unity of tone and of rhythm, which allows the novel to enact that eternal monotony that lies at the heart of its diegetic world. And it is this device, too, that enables Flaubert to recreate what he so admired in *Don Quichotte*: 'cette perpétuelle fusion de l'illusion et de la réalité qui en fait un livre si comique et si poétique'.[54]

PARODY AND PASTICHE

The richness of these mingled viewpoints and voices in the novel is intensified by Flaubert's frequent use of parody and pastiche.[55] *Madame Bovary* so clearly includes among its central concerns a preoccupation with the linguistic patterns of Romanticism and those of the rising middle classes that it is hardly surprising to find it contains so many embeddings recalling other writers, including those whose works were published in the form of serialized novels in newspapers

and who are now largely forgotten. Though at times these
border on parody, on a deliberate exaggeration of stylistic
feature or thematic content, there are certainly passages where
mockery does not seem to be at issue. Rather, the exploration
of various stylistic devices and linguistic registers is a central
analytical tool.

Obviously parodic is the evocation of the keepsakes read with
such furtive pleasure in the convent, where Flaubert, as so often,
brings into play the Rabelaisian device of the list to suggest the
limited number of themes and plots, and introduces a series
of comparisons whose hackneyed nature offers a magnified
reflection of the clichés, both linguistic and visual, in the works
under attack :

> ce n'étaient qu'amours, amants, amantes, dames per-
> sécutées s'évanouissant dans des pavillons solitaires,
> postillons qu'on tue à tous les relais, chevaux qu'on
> crève à toutes les pages, forêts sombres, troubles du cœur,
> serments, sanglots, larmes et baisers, nacelles au clair de
> lune, rossignols dans les bosquets, *messieurs* braves comme
> des lions, doux comme des agneaux, vertueux comme on
> ne l'est pas, toujours bien mis, et qui pleurent comme des
> urnes (original emphasis) (38).[56]

Yet here again Flaubert is able to reveal both the clichéd nature
of the images and scenarios, and the lyrical attractions of such
works for Emma, a double-handedness reminiscent of his own
duality.

More exploratory of the ways in which language is manipulated are the newspaper articles Homais pens with such
enthusiasm. Anyone familiar with the daily or weekly press of
the mid-nineteenth century will recognize the inflated rhetoric,
the over-worked periphrases, the self-righteous moralizing.[57]
Yet this is not so much – perhaps not even – a question
of outright parody, but rather a flexing of literary muscles,
an attempt to meet the challenge of imitating a particular
style, just as Baudelaire does in his literary criticism and
Proust in his pastiches. As a result, the opening paragraph
of Homais's description of the *comices agricoles*, for all its
predictable use of rhetorical questions, its redundancies –
'festons, fleurs, guirlandes' are all near-synonyms – its mixed

metaphor of a wild sea under the torrents of a tropical sun
and its shop-soiled similes and epithets, nevertheless suggests
the excitement Homais felt as he dashed it off, 'de verve',
the day after the show: 'Pourquoi ces festons, ces fleurs, ces
guirlandes? Où courait cette foule, comme les flots d'une mer
en furie, sous les torrents d'un soleil tropical qui répandait sa
chaleur sur nos guérets?' (158).[58] Whereas Balzac's reaction to
journalistic criticism, expressed, for example, in *Illusions perdues,*
bristles with constant hostility, Flaubert presents Homais, at this
stage of his career, with more ambivalence. The narrative voice
is used to increase the mockery by lifting from the article isolated
clichés that float in the narrative discourse like icebergs: 'il
n'oubliait point "l'air martial de notre milice", ni "nos plus
sémillantes villageoises",' nor indeed the old soldiers, whose
hearts are set beating in time to the virile sound of the drums
(158).[59] Later, as Homais's motives become considerably less
pure, the parody becomes more cutting. When he writes an
account of the operation on Hippolyte, the heavy-handedness
of the exclamations, the predictability of the categories in need of
assistance, and the self-congratulatory tone have few redeeming
features: 'Honneur! Trois fois honneur! N'est-ce pas le cas de
s'écrier que les aveugles verront, les sourds entendront et les
boiteux marcheront!' (183).[60] Of course Homais himself is
dealing in pastiche here, deliberately setting up Biblical echoes to
suggest that true progress demands science, not miracles. At issue
here is the contemporary belief in the inexorable forward march
of progress, so sardonically ridiculed by Baudelaire, for example,
in 'Les Yeux des pauvres' and 'Assommons les pauvres'. Later
still, when his failure to cure the blind beggar leads to the latter
accusing him in public, Homais's use of the newspaper to have
the man jailed reflects his growing awareness of the personal
power he can wield through the medium, and lends a particularly
unpleasant tone to the inflated terminology and the pompous
syntax: 'Malgré les lois contre le vagabondage, les abords de
nos grandes villes continuent à être infestés par des bandes de
pauvres. On en voit qui circulent isolément, et qui, peut-être,
ne sont pas les moins dangereux. A quoi songent nos édiles?'
(350).[61] Where Homais's journalism is concerned, therefore,
parody becomes partly a means of expressing, indirectly, a
moral judgement, through which can be inferred a code of

values structuring the text without being expressed at a primary
level, and partly Flaubert's amazed and amused response to the
linguistic manipulation practised by his contemporaries.

In terms of evident parody, Flaubert's fascination with the
use of language in numerous spheres, not just that of fiction
and the press, is also obvious when Homais chooses an
epitaph for Emma's tomb. The language used to convey
human relationships and to express mortal man's longing
for immortality in monuments to the dead lends itself almost
too easily to parody: Homais's ransacking of his imagination
produces, again, perhaps, predictably, 'sta viator amabilem
conjugem calcas' (352).[62]

Yet, however important the parodies embedded in the
narrative, the more subtle mockery, and at times the sense
of fascination at linguistic possibilities that can be conveyed
through pastiche, are perhaps more central to the novel's
characteristic ambivalence, that constant sense of a guffaw
followed by a 'yes, but'. The echoes of Chateaubriand are a
case in point. Some of the youthful fascination Flaubert felt
for Chateaubriand may have dissipated well before *Madame
Bovary*, yet the text retains the memories of those persistent
rhythms and sumptuous metaphors in passages poised on a
knife-edge between rejection and 'pastiche d'admiration'.[63]
Emma, like René, conceives of love as a mighty and
overwhelming storm, whirling the individual away against
will and reason, in an emotion where the secular and the
religious are indistinguishable: the narrative voice confronts
this vision with the implacable rhythms and images of every-day
existence:

> l'amour, croyait-elle, devait arriver tout à coup, avec de
> grands éclats et des fulgurations, – ouragan des cieux qui
> tombe sur la vie, la bouleverse, arrache les volontés
> comme des feuilles et emporte à l'abîme le cœur entier.
> Elle ne savait pas que, sur la terrasse des maisons, la pluie
> fait des lacs quand les gouttières sont bouchées (103).[64]

René, externalising his passions in the fire of Etna, stripping
a willow branch of leaves and investing each with an idea,
'appelant de toute la force de [ses] désirs l'idéal objet d'une
flamme future',[65] is no match for the dour tones of pragmatics,

just as Emma strikes Rodolphe as 'bien sentimentale' when she evokes, in dull echo of Chateaubriand, the evening bells and the voices of nature (174). The slipperiness of the narrative viewpoint is all the greater, therefore, when what appears to be a narrative, even an authorial, judgement, is couched in what seems to be yet another pastiche of Chateaubriand: 'la parole humaine est comme un chaudron fêlé où nous battons des mélodies à faire danser les ours, quand on voudrait attendrir les étoiles' (196);[66] 'notre cœur est un instrument incomplet, une lyre où il manque des cordes, et où nous sommes forcés de rendre les accents de la joie sur le ton consacré aux soupirs'.[67]

A detailed survey of the way in which the works devoured by the characters in *Madame Bovary* invade both their concept of the world and their modes of expression would demand and reward more space than is available here,[68] but no study of the use of pastiche in the novel can ignore the moments when the narrative voice itself confronts that of the acknowledged master of the novel form in Flaubert's day, Balzac. Clearly fascinated by the Protean author of *La Comédie humaine*, Flaubert attempts in a letter to Louise Colet to come to terms with his strengths and weaknesses: 'quel homme eût été ce Balzac, s'il eût su écrire! Mais il ne lui a manqué que cela. Un artiste, après tout, n'aurait pas tant fait, n'aurait pas eu cette ampleur.'[69] That 'ampleur,' summed up by Baudelaire as a desire to 'tout voir, de tout faire voir, de tout deviner, de tout faire deviner',[70] is in part a product of the many characteristic digressions in Balzac's novels, the descriptions included primarily because of exuberant delight at capturing in language the fleeting and changing aspects of contemporary life. Pons's hazel-coloured spencer, Flicoteaux's restaurant, the old, decaying *quartier* around the Louvre where Bette lives, may all externalize the character of the person associated with them, but the intensity with which they are described suggests a joyous relish in the power of language that far outweighs any structural or metaphorical concerns. That delight is both echoed, and, apparently, shared, in the description of the *cheminots* Homais brings back from Rouen for his wife:

dernier échantillon des nourritures gothiques, qui remonte peut-être au siècle des croisades, et dont les robustes Normands s'emplissaient autrefois, croyant voir sur la

table, à la lueur des torches jaunes, entre les brocs
d'hypocras et les gigantesques charcuteries, des têtes de
Sarrasins à dévorer (305).[71]

Here is undoubtedly a moment when Flaubert, quite clearly for
the sheer challenge and pleasure of doing so, reveals the same
kind of fascination with food that Emma displays when faced
with the lobsters and pineapples at the Vaubyessard ball.

READING

It is hardly surprising that such echoes – parodic or eulogistic,
conscious or unsuspected – should filter into a novel whose
characters are such obsessive readers and where images of
reading recur with such significant frequency. One example is
particularly memorable:

Le feu se mourait dans les cendres; la théière était vide;
Léon lisait encore. Emma l'écoutait, en faisant tourner
machinalement l'abat-jour de la lampe, où étaient peints
sur la gaze des pierrots dans des voitures et des danseuses
de corde, avec leurs balanciers. Léon s'arrêtait, désignant
d'un geste son auditoire endormi; alors ils se parlaient à
voix basse (101–2).[72]

There are subdued echoes here of Paolo and Francesca reading
together, but the love scene that followed the reading in Dante's
verse is ironically replaced in this case by a quiet conversation
chaperoned by sleeping pharmacist and husband. Perhaps what
is most significant, however, is the image of reading conveyed
to us, where Emma, ever one to dream between the lines, cannot
even concentrate on what is being read to her but fiddles at the
same time with another means of representation, the figures on
the lampshade which are part of a central nineteenth-century
topos, the pantomime and the circus performer.[73] Symbols of
escapism and pretence, they also slyly categorize Emma as
tightrope walker and Léon as Pierrot, the pale-faced clown
whose Columbine prefers Harlequin. Even the placing of the
pierrots in 'voitures' offers a brief foretaste of the scene in the
cab at Rouen. But there is a further aspect to this image that
needs attention. The way in which Emma's image of the world
is shaped and controlled by her reading is of course central, but

the visual representation of reality is also important,[74] however much it may be overshadowed by the fact that those who surround her privilege the written word, upholding Victor Hugo's famous dictum in *Notre-Dame de Paris* concerning the printed word's modern domination over the visual images – engravings, stained glass windows, tapestries etc. – which had previously fed the minds of the illiterate masses. The decision taken to prevent Emma from reading novels, based in the final version on Mme Bovary mère's image of them as works that are against religion (129), was in an earlier version the result of a long, hilarious conversation between Homais and 'la bonne dame', with Charles interspersing the odd 'But since it amuses her',[75] in a scene that seems an elaboration of the item in the *Dictionnaire des idées reçues* under the heading 'jeune fille': 'éviter pour elles toute espèce de livres'.[76] Charles's mother argues that books simply confuse the female mind, which is incapable of decoding them: 'elle ne sait pas le latin! il lui est impossible de peser le pour et le contre; et moi je soutiens qu'à force de se tourmenter toujours, afin de vouloir en apprendre davantage on finit par se rendre malade.'[77] For his part, Homais offers an argument that is both physiological – 'l'inertie musculaire qui est trop complète ne balance pas l'action céphalique qui est trop violente'[78] – and hermeneutic:

des cavernes, . . . des spectres, des ruines, des cimetières, des faux-monnayeurs, des clairs de lune; que sais-je? toutes sortes de tableaux lugubres et qui prédisposent singulièrement à la mélancolie. Puis ajoutez que ces produits fiévreux d'imaginations en delire sont entachés de néologismes, d'expressions barbares, de mots baroques si bien qu'on est obligé de se casser la tête pour les comprendre.[79]

To which horrendous vision Mme Bovary mère adds, in a delightful non-sequitur, the clinching comment: 'tous ces livres . . . font voir l'existence en beau, puis quand on arrive à la réalité, on trouve du désenchantement'.[80]

Of course, images of people misled or corrupted by their reading are almost as old as the novel form itself. *Don Quixote*, the first book Flaubert had read to him[81] and which, as his correspondence reveals,[82] he so fervently admired, is merely the

great ancestor of a long line of such works, which would include
Rousseau's *Julie ou la nouvelle Héloïse*, Richardson's *Clarissa*,[83]
Stendhal's *Le Rouge et le noir*, and in a different way, Nerval's
Sylvie. Even *Paul et Virginie*, the first book Emma is reported
to have read, depicts Paul selecting and reading novels in the
same way that Emma herself does: to history Paul prefers 'des
romans, qui, s'occupant davantage des sentiments et des intérêts
des hommes, lui offraient quelquefois des situations pareilles à
la sienne . . . il fut bouleversé par la lecture de nos romans
à la mode, pleins de mœurs et de maximes licencieuses; et
quand il sut que ces romans renfermaient *une peinture véritable
des sociétés de l'Europe* il craignit . . . que Virginie ne vînt à s'y
corrompre' (my emphasis).[84] Indeed, one could well consider
that the theme of fiction regarded as truth is so much of a
cliché in literature that Flaubert's own use of it is parodic,
yet another of the ironic devices with which he questions the
reader's expectations. Although he decided to excise the long
conversation about novels quoted above, the very brevity of
the expression, 'donc il fut résolu que l'on empêcherait Emma
de lire des romans' (129)[85] and the underlying assumption that
so simple a gesture will cure so complex a state of mind are
surely meant to be comic, part of the narrative voice's continual
mockery of the bourgeois. One cannot help feeling that J. Culler
is astray when he claims: 'if there is anything that justifies our
finding [the novel] limited and tendentious it is the seriousness
with which Emma's corruption is attributed to novels and
romances'.[86] L. Bersani, too, argues that 'much of the force
of the potential argument in *Madame Bovary* against literature's
violation of experience is lost because experience hardly seems
worth the trouble':[87] if it were otherwise Emma would indeed
simply be the 'silly woman' that so many (male) critics have
dismissed her as. Yet Flaubert's point is surely more subtle and
complex than either critic is willing to admit. What needs to be
stressed is first that Flaubert puts that argument against literature
in the mouths of characters with whom we have little sympathy
and, secondly, that, as usual, he emphasizes the extent to which
both sides of the argument are riddled with *idées reçues*.

The double-sidedness of the narrative position is revealed
in various passages exploring the role of Emma's reading.
The beauty of Romantic phraseology and imagery, its ability

to play on the emotions, and the promise it offers of an existence where inner and outer worlds are in perfect harmony are brilliantly conveyed in a passage where the very rhythms also suggest how quickly this palls in the face of everyday reality: 'Comme elle écouta, les premières fois, la lamentation sonore des mélancolies romantiques se répétant à tous les échos de la terre et de l'éternité! . . . Mais elle connaissait trop la campagne; elle savait le bêlement des troupeaux, les laitages, les charrues' (37).[88] The typically Flaubertian ability to suggest both sides is also demonstrated in his description of the romances Emma sang in the convent: 'pacifiques compositions qui lui laissaient entrevoir, à travers la niaiserie du style et les imprudences de la note, l'attirante fantasmagorie des réalités sentimentales' (39).[89] The point here is not so much that literature has violated experience or that Emma's corruption can be simplistically attributed to her reading, but that literature and art are indeed potent means of awakening human emotions and exploring psychological truths. After all, as V. Brombert has asserted and as Flaubert's correspondence makes so abundantly plain, 'if he held one consistent belief it was indeed the priority of Art over life'.[90] The problem for Emma is more that she is a continual consumer of art and life, wanting to deal equally with both, unable to replace the consumption of life with the creation of art, which was Flaubert's own route.

Moreover, we need to avoid falling into the trap of assuming too much about Emma's reading matter: although the final narrative withholds from us titles and authors in all but a few cases, several critics enter into lengthy arguments based on the way in which the works they suppose Emma reads deliberately mislead their readers. L. Czyba, for example, asserts that 'les lectures d'Emma sont moins "romantiques" qu'on ne le croit traditionnellement: à part Chateaubriand, Lamartine et Walter Scott, il s'agit surtout de stéréotypes du XVIIIe siècle et d'infra-littérature.'[91] Yet this description omits Balzac, George Sand and Suë, as well as Bernardin de Saint-Pierre, who can scarcely be relegated to the category of 'stereotype'. Equally questionable is L. Bersani's affirmation that 'the realistic claims of Emma's favourite novels depend on their ignoring their own mediating processes, on their attempt to hide the differences between the nature of the intensities they seem to exalt and that of the exalting narrative itself'.[92] It is difficult to place much reliance on such sweeping assertions when they make no reference to actual works making these 'realistic claims', and, indeed, such claims were certainly far from the minds of several of the writers Flaubert does mention. George Sand, for instance, specifically sought to portray not truth as it existed but truth as it ought to be. Literature, Flaubert suggests, posits a reality that is merely a product of literature: but what if the literature referred to in literature exists only within the literary domain? A Balzac or a Walter Scott so altered after passing through Emma's imagination that they bear little relationship to their namesakes in literary history? What *Madame Bovary* reveals in particular, so it seems to me, is that reading novels is metonymic for the reading of existence, and that the way in which the individuals in the novel interpret the world is almost invariably simplistic, not because of claims made either by literature or by the world, but simply because of the nature of existence, and of the individuals at issue.

 The reading of books and the imposition of fictional images on to the external world is a dominant and obvious theme. Even something which we might consider natural and spontaneous, maternal love,[93] is presented as being copied, at least where Emma is concerned, from Hugo's *Notre-Dame de Paris* from which she borrows an emotion–charged, highly romantic image of motherhood. This image founders, predictably enough, on the reality of Berthe's physical presence: her tears, her saliva, her blood, cannot be contained within the fictional framework. This is hardly surprising, for Flaubert has chosen as his archetypal fictional image of motherhood a woman whose intense maternal love stems from her child's absence and draws sustenance from the fanatical belief that she has been stolen by gypsies. Moreover, Sachette's discovery of her daughter leads, ironically and almost instantaneously, to Esmeralda's death.

The fictional works that supply such images range from the sensual, through the lyrical to the exotic. Moreover, the works specifically mentioned in the text are frequently those that have exerted considerable influence, not only upon Emma, but upon the major writers of the nineteenth century. Bernardin de Saint-Pierre's *Paul et Virginie*, in which the portrayal of luxuriant and unspoiled tropical forests feeds

Emma's mental landscapes, was described by Gautier as the most corrupting novel he had ever read, although Baudelaire, in 'De l'essence du rire', referred to the heroine as a great archetypal figure who perfectly symbolizes absolute purity and naivety.[94] Certainly, the portrayal of Virginie's awakening sensuality as she enters puberty is remarkably intense in its eroticism, and all the more so if we place it in the sober company of the great majority of eighteenth-century novels. No wonder Emma, like so many of her contemporaries, was drawn to the beauty of its descriptions of tropical landscapes, the spontaneity of the relationship between the two adolescents, and the powerful depiction of the blossoming of their sexual personalities. The Romantic lyricism of Chateaubriand's *Génie du christianisme* also shapes her consciousness, although here, as we have seen, the beauty of nature conveyed in the work, indeed, according to the narrative voice, created by the work, collides with the everyday experience of bleating sheep, milk yards and farm carts. Walter Scott, whose fictionalized Scotland makes an unexpected entry into rural Normandy when Emma wishes she could lock her sorrows away in a Scottish cottage (42), also exerted considerable influence, inspiring Hugo and the young Balzac, among others, and awakening a sense of the attractions and excitement of the historical past. If her image of history is largely a creation of Walter Scott, producing as heroines a curious amalgam of saints, queens and king's mistresses, her vision of contemporary Parisian life is drawn from Balzac, George Sand and Eugène Suë (59), the last mentioned being read primarily for his descriptions of furniture, adds Flaubert in a piece of buffoonery, for although such passages can indeed be found in his novels, he is best-known for his ability to create racy adventure stories. Certainly Balzac's vision of Paris, his tendency to classify and stratify its population and his ability to evoke the apparently sophisticated attraction of salon entertainments leaves an indelible mark on Emma's mind. George Sand's images of passion, particularly of women finding physical satisfaction in adulterous relationships, whatever the unhappiness the author suggests lies in wait for such women, offer Emma a means of brief escape from the dull reality of existence.

In addition there are the keepsakes, the romances sung in the convent music classes, and the women's magazines, *Le*

Sylphe des salons and *La Corbeille*, in the second of which she
could have found advice on the cold-cream of which she is
so prodigal, and the name of her daughter in the play by
Barrière and Louin, *Le Piano de Berthe*.[95] Later we find her
turning to stronger stuff, spending her days in an improvised
Oriental harem and her nights reading extravagant books with
orgiastic tableaux and gory situations(295). This seems to me to
be one of the moments when the text opens an especially ironic
window into a world external to it, for such a description fits
with parodic aptness Flaubert's own *Tentation de Saint-Antoine*, or
indeed some of his youthful works, notably 'Quidquid volueris',
where the influence of Sade is particularly in evidence.[96]

If accretion rather than selection seems to dominate Emma's
choice of reading matter, the same principle is at work when
others choose for her. Bournisien, at a loss to reach her heights of
spiritualism in the days when she is recovering after Rodolphe's
departure, turns to books as a kind of multi-vocal repository of
wisdom. The passage describing what results from his request
for *'quelque chose de fameux pour une personne du sexe, qui
était pleine d'esprit'* (219) (original emphasis)[97] is a ferociously
witty evocation of the religious book trade, ranging from the
self-seeking commercialism of the bookseller, to the pretentious
humility of the author of *L'Homme du monde aux pieds de Marie*,
who signs himself 'M. de ★★★, décoré de plusieurs ordres' (220).

Although Emma's reading is constantly thrust into the
foreground in *Madame Bovary*, she is far from being the only
one to read in a society in which there were, after all, few other
entertainments. Léon's response to literature echoes Emma's
own, yet another in the interminable series of repetitions:

> On se promène immobile dans des pays que l'on croit voir,
> et votre pensée, s'enlaçant à la fiction, se joue dans les
> détails ou poursuit le contour des aventures. Elle se mêle
> aux personnages; il semble que c'est vous qui palpitez sous
> leurs costumes.
> —C'est vrai! c'est vrai!, disait-elle. (85)[98]

And for Léon, like Emma, thought becomes so entwined with
fiction that when she becomes his mistress each is incapable of
perceiving the other except through the looking-glass of cliché

and literature. The cliché is conveyed through the italics as Léon exults: 'n'était-ce pas *une femme du monde*, et une femme mariée! une vraie maîtresse enfin?' (271) (original emphasis)[99] and is parodically echoed in the anonymous letter his mother receives, warning her that her son '*se perdait avec une femme mariée*' (295) (original emphasis).[100] The way in which Léon fictionalizes Emma (rather as Swann is to transform Odette in *A la recherche du temps perdu*) is concisely summed up when he sees her as 'l'amoureuse de tous les romans, l'héroïne de tous les drames, le vague *elle* de tous les volumes de vers' (271) (original emphasis).[101] Emma, too, sees Léon in terms of literary heroes when she writes to him: 'en écrivant, elle percevait un autre homme, un fantôme fait de ses plus ardents souvenirs, de ses lectures les plus belles, de ses convoitises les plus fortes' (296–7).[102]

Homais himself, prosaic though he may seem, and regardless of the difficulties modern novels may pose him, has a library consisting of what he terms the best authors: Voltaire, Rousseau, Delille, Walter Scott, *L'Echo des feuilletons* (86), the humour here arising from the clash of tendency and quality of those listed. Above all, he is an avid reader of newspapers, as he reveals when he quotes 'That is the question', adding: 'As I read recently in the newspaper' ('Comme j'ai lu dernièrement dans le journal'(214)). (The Shakespearian tag is indeed quoted *ad nauseam* in the mid-nineteenth-century press.) Again one notes the delight Flaubert takes in capturing, even in such tiny ways as this, the detail of contemporary life. Homais, too, provides us with an individual mode of reading, one which is no less (and no more) parodically treated than Léon's escapism. In a passage conveyed through *style indirect libre*, where the carefully balanced and rounded periods of Homais's spoken style elbow their way into the narrator's discourse, the pharmacist reveals a method of reading that epitomizes the duality of his personality and the ease with which he has absorbed contemporary responses:

> ses convictions philosophiques n'empêchaient pas ses admirations artistiques, le penseur chez lui n'étouffait point l'homme sensible; il savait établir des différences, faire la part de l'imagination et celle du fanatisme. . . Lorsqu'il lisait les grands morceaux, il était transporté;

> mais, quand il songeait que les calotins en tiraient avantage
> pour leur boutique, il était désolé, et dans cette confusion
> de sentiments où il s'embarrassait, il aurait voulu tout à
> la fois pouvoir couronner Racine de ses deux mains et
> discuter avec lui pendant un bon quart d'heure (92).[103]

The vision of literature as reducible to a series of excerpts,
the 'grands morceaux', and the traditional response to them
– 'transporté' – together with the typical inability to separate
writer from social persona, book as product of the mind and
book as a means of propaganda, are brilliantly captured in this
witty evocation of received readerly wisdom. The phraseology
Homais uses also reveals Flaubert's gift for parody: the blend
of elevated language and colloquialisms, the shift from
'admirations artistiques' to 'calotins', from 'l'homme sensible'
to 'boutiques'. Equally typical of Homais is the mixture of
admiration and the conviction of his own personal value, the
certainty that if he only had the chance he could convert Racine
to his own way of thinking.

Charles, too, attempts to extend his knowledge through the
printed word, and reveals yet another response when he leafs, in
desultory fashion, through *Anacharsis*, or lets Emma discover that
the pages of his *Dictionnaire des sciences médicales* have not been
cut, or falls asleep over a volume of *La Ruche médicale*, thereby
suggesting an antithetical image of an ideal husband studying
into the night and filling the bookshops and newspapers with his
name. Even Justin, in the torments of his calf-love for Emma,
turns for some form of enlightenment to *L'Amour conjugal*
(255–6), a work Flaubert claims to be a current best-seller and
which, unlike Homais, he judges inept.[104]

Whether Rodolphe reads novels is less certain. He may know
enough to parody the language of romanticism when he wants
to seduce Emma, but that may merely be through the absorption
of contemporary clichés overheard in the club or picked up
casually from a newspaper. Our main image of Rodolphe
reading concerns not books but letters, which, as we have
seen, form a further chorus of voices amid all the other voices
of the novel. As he leafs through the love letters and tokens
(kept, as the narrative voice adds in one of those moments of
particularly sharp focus on an object, in an old biscuit box from

Reims) the lyrical legion of adulteresses (167) who had sung in
Emma's mind like sisters are reduced to a pack of cards:

  ces femmes, accourant à la fois dans sa pensée, s'y gênaient
  les unes les autres et s'y rapetissaient, comme sous un même
  niveau d'amour qui les égalisait. Prenant donc à poignée
  les lettres confondues, il s'amusa pendant quelques minutes
  à les faire tomber en cascades, de sa main droite dans sa
  main gauche (207).[105]

Pleasure itself leaves no trace in Rodolphe's memory, nothing
that can be recuperated. In him we find the most reductive
of all images of reading, for, instead of projecting himself or
his beloved into the multiple variety of the written texts, he
reduces all texts and all pleasures to the eternal repetition of a
single moral: 'quel tas de blagues!' (207).[106]

Throughout the novel, therefore, to the voices of the
characters and the narrator are added the voices of inherited
stereotypes, both through the kinds of allusion examined
above and through the use of parody. Nevertheless, however
important the printed word may be in the way in which
it manipulates, filters and distorts the comprehension of a
reality external to it, however strong the suggestion that the
written word is less concerned with commenting on than with
creating that external reality, other forms of representation are
also central to that manipulation. Emma's tendency to dream
between the lines indicates clearly enough that an even more
powerful source of distortion may be pictorial representations,
whose impact is more immediate. Paintings, engravings and
decorations, like mirrors and windows, create a version of reality
that reduces and tames it, keeping it safely within a restricted
framework.

Almost the first thing Emma sees on her way to the convent,
that factory of her later illusions,[107] is a pictorial representation
of the history of Mademoiselle de la Vallière, reproduced on
the dinner plates. Art and history, the passion of kings and the
triumph of the church are mercilessly reduced here to serve the
needs of didacticism and utility. And it is utterly typical not only
that the message they convey is partly eradicated by the scraping
of knives across their surface, but also that it offers no hierarchy
of values, glorifying indifferently 'la religion, les délicatesses du
cœur et les pompes de la Cour' (36).[108] The pious illustrations

with their blue borders (37) take priority over the words of
the mass and the keepsakes are memorable above all for their
engravings, the texture of whose silken protective paper is
admirably captured in a sentence intimating that the gesture of
revealing the engraving has acquired for Emma almost mystic
(and therefore erotic) status: 'elle frémissait, en soulevant de son
haleine le papier de soie des gravures, qui se levait à demi plié
et retombait doucement contre la page' (39).[109] For Léon, too,
love is a product as much of pictorial as of literary sources:
much of his pleasure in Emma's beauty stems from his ability
to discern correspondences between it and paintings. Thus, 'il
retrouvait sur ses épaules la couleur ambrée de l'*odalisque au
bain*; elle avait le corsage long des châtelaines féodales; elle
ressemblait aussi à la *femme pâle de Barcelone*, mais elle était
par–dessus tout Ange!' (271) (original emphasis).[110] Again, what
undermines this imposition of the pictorial on life, is less the
individual details than the cumulative effect, the Orient and
Spain, odalisque and angel, Romantic middle ages and Romantic
present, suggesting fragmentation rather than harmony. Even
the titles, far from referring to specific works, evoke a series
of paintings and poems all repeating the modish themes of
the mystic east and melancholy Spain.[111] Emma's uniqueness
is again implacably reduced to cliché. There are, moreover,
sinister echoes here of Rodolphe, gazing at a miniature of
Emma and finding that 'à force de considérer cette image et
d'évoquer le souvenir du modèle, les traits d'Emma peu à peu
se confondirent en sa mémoire, comme si la figure vivante
et la figure peinte, se frottant l'une contre l'autre, se fussent
réciproquement effacées' (206).[112] Any attempt we make, this
passage tells us, to fix the transient, to transpose life into art,
leads to a dulling rather than a heightening of the experience
we want to preserve. Here, too, however, Flaubert suggests the
other side of the coin, the frequency with which lovers do seek
images and echoes of the beloved in works of art, and attempt
to find our personal experience captured and celebrated by the
creators of plastic beauty, and the way in which by doing so we
refine our perceptions of both art and life.

Two other devices throw into question passive responses
to art. The first of these is the series of gaps created by
Emma's inability or refusal to read the whole of what is set

before her, a tendency parodically echoed by Charles's uncut pages. As we have seen, the legends on the La Vallière plates, for instance, are incomplete, worn away by cutlery; weary of staring at the map of Paris Emma turns away and dreams instead; and she leaves the performance of *Lucia de Lammermoor* before the mad scene suggests the results of frustrated passion.[113] Above all, we are informed, her reading was rather like her tapestries, which had all been begun but which now cluttered her wardrobe unfinished(128). The inability to conclude is partly the result of being overwhelmed by a multiplicity of desires, but it is also a concomitant of Emma's image of desire, which, as her experience with Charles, Rodolphe and Léon reveals, risks degeneration or destruction if the object of desire is attained. The second device results from an appearance of realism that is suddenly rent asunder to reveal the supernatural: as Alison Fairlie writes: 'Flaubert, même dans ses romans les plus "réalistes" vise des effets fantastiques, obsédants, vertigineux.'[114] If Rouen is so carefully described and so meticulously transformed into a painting, circumscribed and tamed by the narrator,[115] both when Charles lives in it as a student and when Emma travels to it for her rendezvous with Léon, it is in order to make the irruption of the fantastic all the more powerful. The cab's Rabelaisian progress through the city offers a perfect example of this technique, where the long list of place names, however much they may correspond to the contemporary topography of the city, does not convey a sense of realism so much as turn them into mere cacophonous sounds, and where the occasional intervention of specific detail – the terrace with its green mantle of ivy, for example – is so arbitrary as to offer a sly commentary on realism's claims to significant selection:

elle passa par Saint-Sever, par le quai des Curandiers, par le quai aux Meules, encore une fois par le pont, par la place du Champ-de-Mars et derrière les jardins de l'hôpital, où des vieillards en veste noire se promènent au soleil, le long d'une terrasse toute verdie par des lierres . . . On la vit à Saint-Pol, à Lescure, au mont Gargan, à la Rouge-Mare, et place du Gaillard-bois; rue Maladrerie, rue Dinanderie,

devant Saint-Romain, Saint-Vivien, Saint-Maclou, Saint-
Nicaise, – devant la Douane, – à la basse Vieille-Tour, aux
Trois-Pipes et au Cimetière Monumental (250).[116]

The endless procession of sounds suggests repetition through
rhymes – Maladrerie, Dinanderie and the seemingly
unquenchable tide of saints – and reveals in its constant circling
yet another version of the Dance of Death, intensified here
both by the reference to the cemetery and by the comparison
between the cab and, on the one hand, a tomb and, on the
other, a ship (that of Charon, perhaps, whose name appears in
the final hours of Emma's life?).[117] A similar result is achieved
when Emma's tendency to impose the imaginary on the real is
changed from a source of pleasure to an uncontrollable torment
at the moment when she realizes there is no way out of her
financial predicament. The familiar landscape around Yonville,
so meticulously described by the narrative voice and so pitilessly
reduced to statistics by Homais, is transformed into a turbulent
ocean lit by fiery balls of light and overlaid with a succession of
images from the past:

> Il lui sembla tout à coup que des globules couleur de
> feu éclataient dans l'air comme des balles fulminantes
> en s'aplatissant, et tournaient, tournaient, pour aller se
> fondre sur la neige, entre les branches des arbres. Au
> milieu de chacun d'eux, la figure de Rodolphe apparaissait.
> Ils se multiplièrent, et ils se rapprochaient, la pénétraient;
> tout disparut. Elle reconnut les lumières des maisons, qui
> rayonnaient de loin dans le brouillard (319–20).[118]

Gaps, indecipherable objects, the abrupt intervention of the
fantastic into the fabric of the everyday, all these tear apart
the conviction of Flaubert's characters that the world has
a comprehensible meaning of which literature and art are
metonymic, framed and discrete illuminations of an accessible
simplified truth. There is nothing tendentious in the irony of this
grim joke.

NOTES: CHAPTER 5

1 Corr, II, 31: 'way of seeing things'.
2 Corr, II, 79: 'yet I myself can imagine a style: a style which could be

beautiful, which someone will achieve one day, in ten years time, or in ten centuries, and it will be as rhythmical as poetry, as precise as scientific language, undulating, with the throb of a cello, with plumes of fire, a style which will pierce your mind like a stiletto, and in which your thought will at last sail on smooth surfaces, as when one glides in a canoe with a good tail wind'.

3 Corr, II, 444: 'how difficult the dialogue is, when what you want above all is that it should have *character*! Using dialogue to depict, and making that depiction no less lively, precise and constantly refined, even while it remains banal, that's monstrous, and I don't know any one who has done it in a book.'

4 Corr, II, 596: 'a real detention chore'.

5 Corr, II, 57: 'the whole value of my book will have been to succeed in walking straight along a knife edge, hung over the twin abysses of the lyrical and the vulgar'.

6 ibid.

7 Corr, II, 127: 'the less one feels a thing, the better able one is to express it as it really is'.

8 Corr II, 302: 'let's *reveal* and not disuss'.

9 Corr, II, 143: 'the mossy mildews of the soul'.

10 Corr, II, 349.

11 See Corr, II, 463. For the image of the mirror in contemporary aesthetic debates see U. Schöning, *Literatur als Spiegel*, and M. Iknayan, *The Concave Mirror*.

12 Letter of 14 January 1880.

13 The technique of internal focalization can best be illustrated by the novels of Simone de Beauvoir: Faulkner, in *The Sound and the Fury*, resorts to a blinkered vision, a technique also used in such films as *Shane* and *The Fallen Idol*.

14 Letter of 10 August 1862. 'The writer must be like God in his work, present everywhere but visible nowhere'.

15 'Perhaps she would have liked to confide in someone about all these things. But how can you express a vague malaise, as changeable as the clouds, eddying like the wind? She couldn't find the words.'

16 'Emma tried to discover what precisely was meant by the words *happiness, passion, intoxication*, words which she had found so beautiful in books.'

17 'the word is a rolling mill which always draws emotions out'.

18 Corr, II, 429: 'To do a good job of writing *the mediocre* and yet make it retain its aspect, its rhythm, even its words, now that's really devilish.'

19 'Then the peasant woman, drawing her aside, behind an elm, began to talk about her husband, who, with his trade and the six francs that the captain ... "Get on with it", said Emma. "Well", the nurse went on, sighing between every word, "I'm afraid he'll be put out seeing me take coffee all on my own; you know what men are like . . ." "Since you'll have some", Emma repeated, "I'll give you enough! . . . What a nuisance you are!" "Alas, my poor, dear lady, the thing is that as a result of his wounds, he gets terrible cramps in the chest. He's even saying that cider weakens him." "Do get a move on, Mother Rolet!".

"So", continued the latter with a courtsy, "if it weren't asking too much of you. . . " she bowed again, "whenever it's convenient", and her gaze pleaded with Emma, "a jug of brandy", she said at last, "and I'll rub your little one's feet with it, she's got feet as soft as a tongue."'(original ellipses)

20 ' "What kind of music do you prefer?" "Oh! German music, the sort that makes you dream." '

21 'think of lots of things'.

22 ' "There's nothing so admirable as sunsets", she replied, "but at the seaside especially." "Oh! I adore the sea", said M. Léon.'

23 ' "Are you going?" she asked. "If I can", he replied. Was there nothing else they wanted to say to each other?'

24 'Madame Bovary, as she listened to him, was amazed to find herself so old; all these things which reappeared seemed to her to extend her existence.'

25 'Yes, it's true!. . . it's true!. . . it's true.' (original ellipses).

26 'Who has not often reflected on all the importance we extract from this modest animal, the ornament of our farmyards, which provides at once a soft pillow for our couches, its succulent flesh for our tables, and eggs.'

27 ' "What a terrible catastrophe", cried the apothecary, who always had the right expression for every conceivable occasion.'

28 'Always deplorable or regrettable, (as if there were ever likely to be something delightful in a misfortune)'.

29 M. Bakhtin, *The Dialogic Imagination* (Austin, Tex.: University of Texas Press, 1981).

30 'Signifiance et in-signifiance', *La Production du sens chez Flaubert* (Paris: Union générale d'édition, 1975), p. 366: 'the italics introduce, through their dissonance, a discursive opposition within the very centre of the quoted enunciation, and socializes the text by allowing us to hear the voice of social discourse'.

31 'with a bit of cheek a man can always get on in the world'.

32 *Le Discours du cliché* (Paris: CDU et SEDES réunis, 1982) p. 67: 'the incessant modulation of the language of the Other, invading all the novelistic "voices" and infiltrating all the linguistic registers, transforms the text into that echo phenomenon which is so specifically Flaubertian and which one can describe as a social chorus or an anonymous recapitulation'.

33 'in the letters Emma sent him, there was talk of flowers, poetry, the moon and the stars, those naïve resources of weakened passion'.

34 ' "Oh, ye gods! No, no, accuse fate alone!" Now there's a word which is always effective, he said to himself.'

35 'in the evening a brilliant firework display suddenly illuminated the skies. You would have called it a real kaleidoscope, truly a set for an opera.'

36 J. Culler, *Flaubert* (London: Paul Elek, 1974), p. 78.

37 'the gentle thought that clucked all through it, like a hen half-hidden in a thorn hedge'.

38 This device has been explored by many critics: see especially A. Banfield, *Unspeakable Sentences* (London: Routledge and Kegan Paul, 1982); D. Cohn, *Transparent Minds* (Princeton, NJ: Princeton University Press, 1978); M. Lips, *Le Style indirect libre* (Ann Arbor, Mich.: University microfilms International, 1979: first published 1926); R. Pascal, *The Dual Voice* (Manchester: Manchester University Press, 1977); F. K. Stanzel, *A Theory of Narrative*, translated C. Goedesche (Cambridge: Cambridge University Press, 1984); S. Ullmann, *Style in the French Novel* (Cambridge: Cambridge University Press, 1957).

39 Cohn, *Transparent Minds*, p. 126.

40 'a homage to the most immortal masterpiece of the French stage'.

41 'Everything seemed to her to be enveloped in a black cloud which floated randomly over the surface of objects, and despair swept into her soul as the winter wind sweeps into abandoned castles.'

42 'The evening shadows were falling; the horizontal rays of the sun, passing between the branches, dazzled her eyes. Here and there, all around her, in the leaves or on the ground, luminous patches trembled, as if hummingbirds, as they flew, had scattered their feathers.'

43 Which Flaubert had read while working on his novel and which prompted the comment, important in the light of Flaubert's own struggle against his lyrical tendencies: 'Quel homme c'eût été sans sa poétique! Comme elle l'a rétréci!' (What a man he would have been had it not been for his poetics! How they diminished him!), Corr, II, 86.

44 'Emma resembled all mistresses; and the charm of novelty, gradually falling like a garment, revealed in all its nudity the eternal monotony of passion, which always uses the same forms and the same language.'

45 'he did not distinguish, this man so rich in practical experience, the difference of feelings under the similarity of expressions'.

46 'Shutting oneself away each evening in a dirty public room, in order to clatter on the marble tables with little sheep's bones marked with black spots, seemed to him to be a precious act of liberty, which raised him in his own esteem.'

47 'In her desire she conflated the sensualities of luxury with the joys of the heart, the elegance of customs with delicacy of sentiment. Did not love, like Indian plants, need specially prepared ground, a particular temperature?'

48 'and in all that, there was never any mention of her child'.

49 'every notary carries within him the remains of a poet'.

50 'was she serious in speaking like this? Probably Emma herself did not know.'

51 'the stains of marriage and the disillusion of adultery'.

52 This was one of the passages cited by the prosecuting attorney in the trial of *Madame Bovary*.

53 *The Political Unconscious*, pp. 222–3.

54 Corr, II, 179: 'this perpetual fusion of illusion and reality which makes it so comic and so poetic a book'.

55 On the subject of pastiche and parody see L. Hutcheon, *A Theory of Parody* (London: Methuen, 1985).

56 'there was nothing but romance, lovers, persecuted ladies swooning in lonely pavilions, postilions murdered at every staging post, horses killed on every page, dark forests, troubles of the heart, vows, sobs, tears and kisses, barks floating in moonlight, nightingales singing in thickets, *gentlemen* as brave as lions, gentle as lambs, virtuous as no one really is, always well dressed, men who weep like urns'.

57 For studies of the French press at the time see C. Bellanger (ed.), *Histoire de la presse française* II (Paris: Presses universitaires de France, 1969), J. and M. Lough, 'The writer and his public', in *An Introduction to Nineteenth Century France* (London: Longman, 1978), pp. 210–78, and T. Zeldin, 'Newspapers and corruption', *France*, II (Oxford: Oxford University Press, 1977), pp. 492–573.

58 'Why these festoons, these flowers, these garlands? Whither ran that crowd, like the water of a furious sea, under the torrents of a tropical sun which poured its warmth on our fields?'

59 'he did not forget to include "the martial air of our militia", or "our most vivacious village maidens"'.

60 'Honour! Cry honour thrice! Is it not the case to cry that the blind will see, the deaf will hear and the lame will walk!'

61 'Despite the laws against vagrancy, the outskirts of our cities continue to be infested by bands of the poor. Some can be seen moving about on their own and these perhaps are not the least dangerous. What can our city fathers be thinking of?'
See the *Dictionnaire des idées reçues* under the head 'édiles': 'tonner contre à propos du pavage des rues. "A quoi songent nos édiles"': 'thunder against them as regards street paving. "What can our city fathers be thinking of?"'

62 P. Ariès, in *Images de l'homme devant la mort* (Paris: Editions du Seuil, 1983), explores this area with the aid of a fascinating iconography.

63 The expression is used by C. Pichois in reference to Baudelaire, but is clearly extendible to Flaubert, particulary, for instance, in his 'Rabelaisian' letter to Bouilhet of 26 December 1852. On Flaubert's early enthusiasm for Chateaubriand see H. Redman, 'Aux pieds du maître', *Nineteeth-Century French Studies*, vol X, nos 3 and 4 (Spring – Summer 1982), pp. 291–300.

64 'love, she believed, should arrive suddenly, with great thunderclaps and lightning bolts, – a hurricane from the heavens that falls on life, overthrows it, tears away will-power like leaves and carries the entire heart to the abyss. She did not know that, on the terraces of houses, rain creates lakes when the gutters are blocked.'

65 Chateaubriand, *Atala. René* (Paris: Garnier-Flammarion, 1964), p. 158: 'summoning with all the strength of his desires the ideal object of a future passion'.

66 'human speech is like a split cauldron on which we beat melodies to make bears dance, when we would like to move the stars'.

67 *Atala*, p. 159: 'our heart is an incomplete instrument, a lyre with strings missing, and on which we are forced to give expression to accents of joy in the tone consecrated to sighs'.

68 To my knowledge no detailed study of this exists as yet.

69 Corr, II, 209: 'what a man that Balzac would have been, if he had known how to write! But that's the only thing he lacked. An artist, after all, would not have done as much, would not have had that sweep.'

70 Baudelaire, *Œuvres complètes* (Paris: Pléiade, 1976), II, p. 120: 'see everything, make his reader see everything, guess everything, make his reader guess everything'.

71 'the last example of that Gothic fare, which may perhaps go back to the century of the crusades, and with which the robust Normans fed themselves in days gone by, believing that they had before them on the table, in the yellow torchlight, between the jars of mulled wine and the gigantic servings of meats, heads of Saracens for them to devour'.

72 'the fire would be dying in the embers, the tea-pot would be empty, Léon would go on reading. Emma would listen to him, mechanically turning the lampshade on the gauze of which were painted clowns in carriages, and tight-rope walkers with their balancing rods. Léon would stop and point to his audience who had fallen asleep. Then they would talk quietly together.'

73 See J. Starobinski, *Portrait de l'artiste en saltimbanque* (Geneva: Skira, 1970) and G. Storey, *Pierrots on the Stage of Desire* (Princeton, NJ: Princeton University Press, 1985), pp. 152–79.

74 On this topic see J. Pommier, 'Flaubert et Alfred de Dreux', *Les Amis de Flaubert*, no. 2-3 (1951); J. Seznec, 'Flaubert and the graphic arts', *Journal of the Warburg and Courtauld Institute, 1945*; J. Seznec, 'Madame Bovary et la puissance de l'image', *Médecine de France* VIII (1949).

75 MBNV, pp. 396–97.

76 'avoid letting them read any kind of book'.

77 'she doesn't know Latin! It's impossible for her to weigh up the pros and the cons: and I personally maintain that by constantly tormenting yourself in wanting to learn more, you end by falling ill.'

78 'the muscular inertia is too complete and does not balance the cephalic action which is too violent'.

79 'Caves, ghosts, ruins, cemeteries, forgers, moonlight; and goodness knows what else, all sorts of lugubrious scenes that are wonderfully conducive to melancholy. Added to which these feverish products of delirious imaginations are dotted with neologisms, barbaric expressions, baroque words to such an extent that you are forced to rack your brains to understand them.'

80 'all these books make you see existence through rose-coloured glasses and when you come to reality you're disappointed '.

81 See, for instance, J. Bruneau, *Les Débuts littéraires de Gustave Flaubert* (Paris: Armand Colin, 1962) p. 24.

82 See C. Carlut, *La Correspondance de Flaubert: étude et répertoire critique* (Columbus, Ohio: Ohio State University Press, 1968); H. Hatzfield, 'Don Quijote und Mme Bovary', *Jahrbuch für Philologie*, II (1927), pp. 54–70 and 116–31; H. Hatzfield, 'Le Réalisme moderne dans *Don Quichotte et Madame Bovary*', in *Essais sur Flaubert*, ed. Carlut, pp. 271–84; H. Levin, *The Gates of Horn* (New York: Oxford University Press, 1963), pp. 246–69, and M. Robert, *Roman des origines et origines du roman* (Paris: Gallimard, 1972), pp. 131–234.

83 'Those confounded poets, with their terrenely celestial descriptions, did as much with me as the lady; they fired my imagination and set me upon a desire to become a goddess-maker', *Clarissa*, p. 213.

84 *Paul et Virginie* (Paris: Gallimard, 1984), pp. 183–4: 'novels which, by concentrating more on human sentiments and interests, offered him at times situations similar to his own. He was overwhelmed by his reading of our fashionable novels, full of licentious behaviour and maxims; and when he discovered that these novels included *a true painting of European societies,* he feared that Virginia might be corrupted there' (my emphasis).

85 'therefore it was resolved to prevent Emma from reading novels'.

86 J. Culler, *Flaubert*, p. 146.

87 L. Bersani, 'Emma Bovary's dangerous fusions', *Novel (Fall 1974), p. 25*.

88 'How she listened, the first times, to the sonorous lamentation of Romantic melancholy, repeated by all the echoes of the earth and of eternity! . . . But she knew the countryside too well; she knew the lowing of the herds, the milking, the carts.'

89 'peaceful compositions which allowed her to perceive, through the silliness of the style and the vagueness of the music, the seductive phantasmagoria of the realities of sentiment'.

90 V. Brombert, *Flaubert*, p. 4.

91 *La Femme dans les romans de Flaubert*, p. 67: 'Emma's reading is less "romantic" than is traditionally thought. Apart from Chateaubriand, Lamartine and Walter Scott, it consists above all of eighteenth-century stereotypes and of infra-literature.'

92 'Emma Bovary's dangerous fusions', p. 26.

93 But see A. Rich, *Of Woman Born* (New York; W.W. Norton and Co., 1976) and E. Badinter, *L'amour en plus* (Paris: Livre de Poche, 1980).

94 *Œuvres complètes* (Paris: Gallimard, 1976), II, p. 528.

95 *La Corbeille*, vol XII, 1852. On this magazine see A. Kleinert, 'Ein Modejournal und seine Leserin', *Romanische Forschungen*, vol. 90, 1978, pp. 458-77.

96 On Sadean influences in Flaubert see C. L. Tondeur, 'Flaubert et Sade', in *Nineteenth-Century French Studies*, vol. 10 (1981-82), pp. 75-84, and J. Ferguson, 'The Comices and the Fête', in *French Studies Bulletin*, no. 19 (Summer 1986), pp. 10-12.

97 'something splendid for a lady who had a very fine mind'.

98 '"You wander about, immobile, in countries you think you can see, and your thought, weaving into the fiction, delights in the details or pursues the contours of the adventures. It mingles with the characters; you feel that it's you who palpitates under their costumes."
   "It's true, it's true", she said.'

99 'was she not a *woman of the world,* and a married woman, a real mistress, in a word?'

100 '*was destroying himself with a married woman*'.

101 'the woman in love one finds in all novels, the heroine of all plays, the vague "She" of all volumes of verse'.

102 'as She wrote she perceived another man, a phantom made of her most ardent memories, the most beautiful books she had read, her strongest desires'.

103 'his philosophical convictions did not impinge on his admiration for certain artists, the thinker in him did not stifle the sensitive spirit; he was capable of establishing differences, making allowance for imagination and for fanaticism . . . When he read the great passages, he was transported; but, when he thought that bigots took advantage of them for their own purposes, he was desolate, and in that confusion of his feelings in which he became entangled, he would have liked both to be able to crown Racine with his own hands, and debate with him for a good long moment.'

104 Corr, II, 179.

105 'these women, rushing all together into his thoughts, hampered each other and were diminished, as if all brought down to a common denominator under a standard level of love. So taking handfuls of the letters, all jumbled together, he amused himself for a few moments by making them cascade down from his right hand into his left hand.'

106 'what a load of nonsense'.

107 Compare Balzac's statement in *Béatrix*: 'la vie de couvent, où s'enflamment les imaginations des jeunes filles' (Paris: Garnier-Flammarion, 1979), p. 99: 'convent life, which inflames young girls' imaginations'.

108 'religion, the delicacies of love and the ceremonies of the court'.

109 'she trembled, as she blew on the silk paper of the engravings to lift them up, and watched them rise up half folded and fall back gently on the page'.

110 'he discovered on her shoulders the amber colour of the "Bathing Odalisque"; she had the long waist of feudal chatelaines; she reminded one of the "pale woman of Barcelona", but above all she was the Angel!'

111 While we can, of course, identify the 'Odalisque au bain' as Ingres' painting and locate the pale woman in Musset, to do so misses, I believe, the point of the tendency lesser figures had to copy greater ones. Moreover, a draft of this passage describes this 'Odalisque au bain' in terms that make it quite clear that it is *not* Ingres' painting (see Ebauches II, p. 364-5).

112 'as a result of gazing at this picture and recalling the memory of the model,

he found Emma's features gradually blurred in his memory, as if the living
face and the painted face were each rubbing the other out'.
Compare the way in which after Emma's death, Charles finds that, no
matter how hard he thinks about her, her image fades from his memory.

113 On the subject of the opera see G. Daniels, 'Emma Bovary's Opera',
French Studies, XXXII (1978), pp. 285–303, and K. Ringger, '"Lucia de
Lammermoor" ou les regrets d'Emma Bovary', *Littérature et Opéra*, ed.
P. Berthier and K. Ringger (Grenoble: Presses universitaires de Grenoble,
1987), pp. 69–80. On the general topos of the night at the opera, see J.
M. Bailbé, *Le Roman et la musique en France sous la monarchie de juillet*
(Paris: Minard, 1969) and P. Michot, 'La Soirée à l'opéra: étude d'un
thème littéraire', *L'Opéra au XVIIIe siècle* (Aix-en-Provence: Publications
Université de Provence, 1982), pp. 559–78.

114 'Flaubert et la conscience du réel', in *Imagination and Language* (Cambridge:
Cambridge University Press, 1981), p. 329 (paper presented in 1966): 'Even
in his most "realist" novels, Flaubert aims for effects which are fantastic,
obsessive, vertiginous.'

115 See Corr, II, p. 575: 'j'ai la prétention de *peindre* Rouen' (original emphasis):
'I claim to *paint* Rouen'.

116 'it went by Saint-Sever, along the quai des Curandiers, by the quai aux
Meules, once again over the bridge, by Champ-de-Mars square, and behind
the hospital gardens, where old folk in black coats stroll in the sunshine
behind a terrace turned entirely green with ivy . . . It was seen at Saint-Pol,
at Lescure, at Gargan Mount, at the Rouge-Mare, at Gaillard-bois square;
at rue Maladrerie, rue Dinanderie, in front of Saint Romain, Saint-Vivien,
Saint-Maclou, Saint-Nicaise – in front of the customs house, – at the lower
old tower, at the "Three Pipes" and at the monumental cemetery.'

117 Mme Caron is one of those who watch Emma's attempt to raise money
from Binet (311).

118 'It suddenly seemed to her that globules the colour of fire were bursting in
the air like fulminating balls, which flattened out, turning and turning, and
finally melted on the snow between the branches of the trees. In the middle
of each of them, Rodolphe's face appeared. They multiplied, and came
closer to her, penetrating her; everything disappeared. She recognized the
lights of the houses, which floated far out in the fog.'

CHAPTER 6

Space and time

Elle s'acheta un plan de Paris, et, du bout de son doigt, sur la carte, elle faisait des courses dans la capitale. Elle remontait les boulevards, s'arrêtant à chaque angle, entre les lignes des rues, devant les carrés blancs qui figurent les maisons . . . Paris, plus vague que l'Océan, miroitait donc aux yeux d'Emma dans une atmosphère vermeille. La vie nombreuse qui s'agitait en ce tumulte y était cependant divisée par parties, classée en tableaux distincts. Emma n'en apercevait que deux ou trois qui lui cachaient tous les autres et représentaient à eux seuls l'humanité complète.(59–60)[1]

The world of *Madame Bovary*, the time and space created within the text, has as its centre a gap: however much her dreams may revolve around it, Paris, for Emma, is never anything more than a place created by literature and by maps. Here, through the depiction of Emma exploring the capital by means of its paper representation, Flaubert again offers an image of the way in which we read, mediated, moreover, by the intertext provided by his parody of Balzac. Balzac's imagery, in both *Le Père Goriot* and *Illusions perdues,* of Paris as ocean, unfathomable in its depth and unstable in its substance, as well as his categorization of Parisians in *La Fille aux yeux d'or,* combine with Emma's conviction of the mimetic function of the map ('les carrés blancs qui figurent les maisons', Flaubert writes, ironically choosing to depict the houses with white or blank spaces) to reveal how signifier is conflated with signified, the part assumed to be the whole. Above all, the imagined space of Paris assumes a reality that deprives the world in which Emma exists of any savour:

quant au reste du monde, il était perdu, sans place précise, et comme n'existant pas. Plus les choses, d'ailleurs, étaient voisines, plus sa pensée s'en détournait. Tout ce qui l'entourait immédiatement, campagne ennuyeuse, petits bourgeois imbéciles, médiocrité de l'existence, lui semblait une exception dans le monde, un hasard particulier où elle se trouvait prise, tandis qu'au delà s'étendait à perte de vue l'immense pays des félicités et des passions (60).[2]

Since what is close to her is constantly rejected ('plus les choses, d'ailleurs, étaient voisines, plus sa pensée s'en détournait'), Emma is led constantly to substitute for reality visions created by her imagination. On to the vast plain that surrounds her, therefore, she imposes an endless landscape of pleasure, a country of the mind which demands, in order to exist, the suppression of the physical world, and which can continue to exist only if its centre is always elsewhere: Emma can merely circle continuously around it, trapped more by its centrifugal force than by the reality in which she believes herself to be imprisoned. Thus, as she listens to the carts of the market-gardeners heading for Paris, she attempts to imagine their journey, but 'au bout d'une distance indéterminée, il se trouvait toujours une place confuse où expirait son rêve' (59).[3] One of the richest sources of suggestion in *Madame Bovary* is the movement between countries of the mind and the country of the narrative, a movement that is in part a product of the shifting voices and viewpoints of the text.

THE SENSE OF PLACE

Emma's vision of the world is one which constantly oscillates between images of enclosure and images of extension, or as G. Poulet puts it, 'ce que Flaubert a voulu montrer dans *Madame Bovary*, c'est une existence qui tantôt se replie et tantôt se déploie'.[4] The world of the novel moves from the enclosed space of the school and the convent, to the land around père Rouault's farm, Les Bertaux, captured in a crisply focused image which, for all its brevity, suggests Flaubert's sensitivity to pattern and shade: 'la plate campagne s'étalait à perte de vue, et les bouquets d'arbres autour des fermes faisaient, à intervalles éloignés, des taches d'un violet noir sur cette grande surface grise, qui se perdait à l'horizon dans le ton morne du ciel' (14).[5] It then proceeds through Tostes to Yonville, situated in a 'contrée bâtarde où le langage est sans accentuation, comme le paysage sans caractère' (72).[6] Yet these are lands on which Emma constantly superimposes images drawn from her reading, which, like the categories she imagines in Paris, hide from her any awareness of reality or beauty in her situation. Moreover, the two centres change in size and population according to the needs of the plot and the state of Emma's emotions, Yonville's inhabitants swelling from a mere handful to thronging masses during the agricultural fair, for example. In the vast spaces of Tostes Emma imagines the world of the cities as infinitely expandable: 'des existences où le cœur se dilate, où les sens s'épanouissent' (46)[7] in sharp contrast to her own life, in which her heart is constricted by the threads of the silent spider, boredom. Enclosure in *Madame Bovary*, however, does not always have negative associations: Charles may look back in disgust at the enclosed world of the school, when he had been 'enfermé entre ces hauts murs' (35), but he finds perfect happiness in a life delimited by his love for Emma: 'l'univers, pour lui, n'excédait pas le tour soyeux de son jupon' (35).[8] For Emma, too, enclosure may also be a source of delight and a synonym for pleasure: the hotel room in which Léon declares his love for her, we are told, 'semblait petite, tout exprès pour resserrer davantage leur solitude' (238)[9] and of course, the cab in which the two make love on that Rabelaisian circuit of Rouen provides yet another example of the enclosed as privileged space of pleasure.

The dichotomy set up between expansion and enclosure is only one aspect of the presentation of space in *Madame Bovary*. Even more important is the confrontation between physical landscape and imaginary landscape. Indeed, one of the sources of irony in the text is the conflict between the romantic description of landscape provided by Emma's reading and the narrative's description of the landscape in which she exists. The keepsakes read in the convent create, through their engravings, scenery that is every bit as much of a hotch-potch as Charles's schoolboy cap, or the cake at their wedding:

paysages blafards des contrées dithyrambiques, qui souvent nous montre[nt] à la fois des palmiers, des sapins, des tigres à droite, un lion à gauche, des minarets tartares à l'horizon, au premier plan des ruines romaines, puis des chameaux accroupis; – le tout encadré d'une forêt vierge bien nettoyée, et avec un grand rayon de soleil perpendiculaire tremblotant dans l'eau, où se détachent en écorchures blanches, sur un fond d'acier gris, de loin en loin, des cygnes qui nagent (40).[10]

However mocking the juxtapositions of Indian and African animals, European and Asian architecture, Flaubert also suggests the lyrical attraction of these images through his sharp awareness of the artistic structure and of the ways in which the quality of light on water is conveyed. This is surely the ironic intertext we are meant to perceive in the seduction scene with Rodolphe, where the surrounding nature is so implacably prosaic:

Il l'entraîna plus loin, autour d'un petit étang, où des lentilles d'eau faisaient une verdure sur les ondes. Des nénuphars flétris se tenaient immobiles entre les joncs. Au bruit de leurs pas dans l'herbe, des grenouilles sautaient pour se cacher (165).[11]

The green slime on the pond, the withered reeds, the frogs, all subvert the landscapes of the keepsakes. Even more evidently anti-Romantic is the description of Emma's garden at Tostes:

On n'entendait pas d'oiseaux, tout semblait dormir, l'espalier couvert de paille et la vigne comme un grand serpent malade sous le chaperon du mur, où l'on voyait, en s'approchant, se trainer des cloportes à pattes nombreuses (66).[12]   *wood lice*

The exotic beauty of the scenery and animals depicted in those works that have shaped Emma's vision of the world seems to have no correspondence with the reality in which she finds herself exiled.

Yet Flaubert avoids the simplistic dichotomy between dream world and the quotidian by revealing the beauty of the countryside around Emma, to which she is blinded by the landscapes she constantly seeks. There is loveliness even in her own garden, where 'la rosée avait laissée sur les choux des guipures d'argent avec de longs fils clairs qui s'étendaient de l'un à l'autre' (66).[13] When the rays of the setting sun illuminate the parallel lines of trees in the countryside near Tostes in such a way as to suggest a colonnade against a golden backcloth, Emma is seized by fear (47), and when she and Léon walk along a path bordered with flowers or by a brook sparkling in the sun, the description of the natural beauty is so alien to either character that the narrative voice speaking to us signals that distance by referring to the couple as 'la jeune femme et son compagnon' (97).[14] A similar effect is created when the beauty of the countryside in April is conveyed partly in the present tense, as something timeless, and partly through the indeterminate 'on':

> on était au commencement d'avril, quand les primevères sont écloses; un vent tiède se roule sur les plates-bandes labourées, et les jardins, comme des femmes, semblent faire leur toilette pour les fêtes de l'été. Par les barreaux de la tonnelle et au delà tout alentour, on voyait la rivière dans la prairie, où elle dessinait sur l'herbe des sinuosités vagabondes (112–13).[15]

It is, therefore, not the landscapes which surround her and to whose beauty she is blind, but those of literature that furnish Emma's imaginary space, those backdrops to scenes of adventure or passion which are so essential to the action that they are often the only thing Emma can conjure up with any clarity. So convinced is she that 'certains lieux sur la terre devaient produire du bonheur, comme une plante particulière au sol et qui pousse mal tout autre part' (42),[16] that the background she prepares for her dreams of happiness is almost always that of an exotic southern land, a parodic version of the Romantic north's yearning for the land where the lemon tree blossoms, which at times invades even the narrative voice's generalizations: 'les bonheurs futurs, comme les rivages des tropiques, projettent sur l'immensité qui les précède leurs mollesses natales, une brise parfumée, et l'on s'assoupit dans cet enivrement' (98).[17] The space opened up by Emma's reveries is always synonymous with happiness: indeed, the text suggests that these landscapes are metonymic evocations of happiness, for once Emma and Rodolphe reach that 'maison basse, à toit plat, ombragée d'un palmier, au fond d'un golfe, au bord de la mer', then 'leur existence serait facile et large comme leurs vêtements de soie, toute chaude et étoilée comme les nuits douces qu'ils contempleraient' (201).[18] As the 'comme' suggests, Emma perceives a direct correspondence between a particular landscape and a state of mind, the former being merely a means of clarifying her image of the latter.

To the landscapes that create the diegetic space and those that represent visions of happiness, Flaubert adds the emotional landscapes that give physical form to despair or boredom. Emma's melancholy at Tostes is in part produced by, in part productive of, the following scene:

> quelque chat sur les toits, marchant lentement, bombait son dos aux rayons pâles du soleil. Le vent, sur la grande route, soufflait des traînées de poussière. Au loin, parfois, un chien hurlait; et la cloche, à temps égaux, continuait sa sonnerie monotone qui se perdait dans la campagne (65).[19]

While none of this is likely to be the product of Emma's imagination, which, as we have seen, deals in more exotic material, it is her melancholy imagination that selects, rejects and combines. The watery sun, the dusty road, the sounds of monotony or suffering combine to epitomize the physical weight of a sense of *ennui* all the more pervasive and inescapable in that it has no identifiable and rational cause.

As this last quotation suggests, much of the power of these landscapes, whether imaginary, emotional or part of the diegetic space of the novel, derives from three aspects: the angle from which they are perceived, the quality of the light that falls on them, and the sounds associated with them.

J. Rousset insists that 'fenêtres et perspectives plongeantes, ouvertures sur le lointain et rêveries dans l'espace, [sont] autant de points névralgiques du récit, de nœuds où le cours narratif s'arrête'.[20] Both Charles and Emma frequently appear looking down from windows. It is from a window that Charles, in his student days, gazes down on Rouen, that Emma sees both Léon and Rodolphe, that she gazes into the darkness for much of what remains of the night after the ball, that she and Rodolphe watch and listen to the agricultural show, and, in a passage Flaubert decided to leave out of the final

version, he places the child Emma at a window to read
her stories of 'actions et . . . personnages sensibles'.[21] We
should not, of course, exaggerate the importance of these
references: the narrative voice offers here the explanation
that in the provinces the window takes the place of theatres
and promenades (130). Indeed, it is difficult to imagine sighted
people not gazing frequently from windows, as any schoolchild
or academic knows. Nevertheless, throughout *Madame Bovary,*
characters, particularly Emma, look down on the world around
them, and this privileged viewpoint is frequently associated with
happiness. In creating an emotional landscape corresponding
to joy Emma specifically depicts herself high above her daily
existence: 'une immensité bleuâtre l'entourait, les sommets du
sentiment étincelaient sous sa pensée, et l'existence ordinaire
n'apparaissait qu'au loin, tout en bas, dans l'ombre, entre
les intervalles de ces hauteurs' (167).[22] (The fact that light
is associated with the 'sommets du sentiment' and shadow
with everyday existence is also characteristic, as we shall see.)
Obviously one of the reasons for this relegation of ordinary
existence is to reduce the sense of guilt and responsibility. It
is as if the window and the view from on high, by framing
and thus controlling the external world, allow it selective
access into the character's imaginary landscape. Above all,
of course, the references to the window both highlight the
importance of perception in the novel and act as images of
the text itself, allowing us to penetrate into the lives and minds
of the characters.

At several points in the novel, however, the window has more
sinister associations. After receiving Rodolphe's letter breaking
off their love affair, Emma rushes up to the attic and, gazing
down through the window on to the ground below, is seized
by the desire to kill herself. (We shall return to this passage in
exploring the importance of light and sound.) Secondly, towards
the end of the novel, when Emma's sense of self is disintegrating,
almost as if a form of suicide were taking place even before she
swallows the arsenic, she herself is perceived through a window
by two of the townswomen. The effect of this extraordinary
passage is to create an almost tangible barrier between the reader
and Emma, a barrier created at the level of the narrative by the
window itself and at the level of the narration by the refusal to

convey her thoughts in any form of *style indirect libre*. What is most important here, however, is less the window image than the switch in narrative focus, the interest in how this episode can best be conveyed to the reader. The window, therefore, can also be perceived as a barrier, alienating those beyond it. Further examples of such alienation occur in the scene at the Vaubyessard ball, when the peasants can be seen gazing in at the celebrations, and in a metaphorical usage when Charles's mother contemplates her son's wedded bliss 'comme quelqu'un de ruiné qui regarde à travers les carreaux, des gens attablés dans son ancienne maison' (44).[23]

Important, too, are the references to mirrors. Emma is frequently depicted gazing at herself in the mirror, as if she needs assurance that she does indeed exist, and such moments tend to be charged with erotic significance: at the ball, Emma's preparations in front of the mirror arouse Charles's desire; after yielding to Rodolphe it is by gazing in the mirror that Emma convinces herself of the reality of what has just happened; and in the hotel room where Léon declares his love for her, Emma's head is again reflected in a mirror. To some extent, the mirror is also a means of suggesting repetition: it is, in addition, an aid to hypocrisy, part of the series of references to pretence, to masks, to the gap between reality and illusion.[24] A. Fairlie speaks suggestively of 'the mirror of inherited preconceptions'.[25] Thus, when Emma, in the early stages of her relationship with Léon, lacks the courage to transform longing into action, she attempts instead to convince both others and herself of her virtue: 'puis l'orgueil, la joie de se dire: "Je suis vertueuse", et de se regarder dans la glace en prenant des poses résignées, la consolait un peu du sacrifice qu'elle croyait faire' (111).[26] Emma is not alone in this narcissistic need to reflect herself: on the evening of the agricultural fair Rodolphe finds that Emma's image floats before his eyes like a magic mirror: 'sa figure, comme en un miroir magique, brillait sur la plaque des shakos' (156).[27] N. Segal, in her stimulating study of women in the French récit,[28] argues that the heroes of the confessional novels seek as lovers doubles of themselves, silent mirror reflections. Rodolphe in this scene, Baudelaire's poet in 'Les Yeux des pauvres' gazing into his beloved's eyes 'pour y lire *ma* pensée'[29] as he says, merely continue this tradition. Emma, floating in Rodolphe's

magic mirror, or echoing for Léon the initial letter of his name
('le vague "elle" de tous les volumes de vers')[30] has already
been deprived of her individuality by the men who profess to
desire her, a situation reflected in her self-destruction through
the taking of arsenic, a word whose literal meaning is 'male'.

Images of the window or mirror combine with images of the
world seen from above. The passage from reluctantly virtuous
wife to joyous adulteress takes place at an altitude from which
Yonville is reduced to the status of a toy town, just as Rouen,
when Emma arrives for her illicit days with Léon, is seen from
above, with the result that 'le paysage tout entier avait l'air
immobile comme une peinture' (268).[31] Even in the fantasy
world Emma imagines inhabiting with Rodolphe, the 'cité
splendide' is first seen from the summit of a mountain (201).
In all these cases, perception is limited and controlled, the real
world kept at bay so that the world of revery and illusion can
dominate.

PLACE AND THE SENSES

Whether we are dealing with the world of the characters'
imagination or the world of the space created by the narrative,
its texture is created above all by light and by sounds. The
role of smell is slighter, predictably enough, given the far more
restricted range of vocabulary to convey it.

Flaubert seems fascinated with light, exploring the way in
which it plays on surfaces, is reflected or refracted, the way in
which it is associated with mood, and above all he clearly relishes
the challenge of expressing this in language. Indeed, the sense of
chatoiement, as J. P. Richard has pointed out,[32] is essential to his
vision and frequently associated with the erotic and with death:
'renvoyant la conscience d'objet en objet, le chatoiement met
la nature en contradiction avec elle-même, l'amène à procéder
à son propre anéantissement'.[33] Much of Charles's excitement
in his early meetings with Emma is conveyed by the flickering
reflection of the fire on the *batterie de cuisine* or the trembling
patches of light that fall on her face through the sunshade as she
bids him farewell, while for Emma herself the enchantment of
the Vaubyessard château is in part a product of the light playing
on the silver and the crystal. High points in Emma's relationship

with Léon in her early days at Yonville are also associated with sparkling light when 'les toits d'ardoises, qui reluisaient sous la lumière âpre du ciel bleu, semblaient à la crête de leurs pignons faire pétiller des étincelles' (93).[34] Flaubert's fascination with slate, its changing shades and its ability to reflect light is a recurring feature in his writing. Similarly, Emma and Rodolphe pass their final night together watching the moon glitter on the water, like a 'monstrueux candélabre, d'où ruisselaient, tout du long, des gouttes de diamant en fusion' (203).[35] Indeed, the treatment of light is one of the means by which Flaubert creates the links between eroticism and death, as in the passage when Emma, having received Rodolphe's farewell letter, gazes out, in deep shock, from the attic window:

> En bas, sous elle, la place du village était vide; les cailloux du trottoir scintillaient, les girouettes des maisons se tenaient immobiles . . . Le rayon lumineux qui montait d'en bas directement tirait vers l'abîme le poids de son corps . . . Le bleu du ciel l'envahissait, l'air circulait dans sa tête creuse, elle n'avait qu'à céder, qu'à se laisser prendre (210–11).[36]

The evocation of heat, of a stiflingly hot afternoon with the sun beating down on the ground, is conveyed in this passage in terms that are identical with those expressing carnal attraction: there is the same kind of imagery, both as regards the treatment of light and as regards Emma's desire to lose herself, to yield to the other, whether that other be a lover or death. In both cases, the way in which light is reflected off the surface of objects has not only set Flaubert a linguistic challenge, and one to which he returns again and again in his novels, but also suggests his delight in the beauty of the world. If that indication of beauty were absent, Emma's desire to escape would lose the power of irony that is central to *Madame Bovary*.

Different forms of light can also be an essential element of the emotional landscapes. Charles's image of domestic bliss is intimately connected with the glow produced by the porcelain night-light, which is itself transposed into the imagined space he creates, in the form of the lamplight by which an adolescent Berthe embroiders him a pair of slippers. Similarly, Emma's sense of sexual frustration is as much conveyed as produced by the 'jour blanchâtre' and the way in which the furniture disappears 'dans l'ombre comme dans un océan ténébreux' (118).[37]

Just as Flaubert clearly enjoys the challenge of conveying light through language, so his treatment of sound shows him responding to a similar challenge, for he is intensely aware of the manipulative and evocative effects of sounds. Indeed, in a letter to Louise Colet he gave the following comment on the portrayal of the *comices agricoles*: 'si jamais les effets d'une symphonie ont été reportés dans un livre, ce sera là. *Il faut que ça hurle par l'ensemble,* qu'on entende à la fois des beuglements des taureaux, des soupirs d'amour et des phrases d'administrateurs'. (original emphasis)[38] Again there are two sides to this, the stress on the evocation of individual sounds, and the emphasis on the emotional effects of the whole. The sense of the relationship between sound and emotion is conveyed on numerous occasions: the noise of Charles's own blood pounding in his head as he desires Emma from a distance, the echo of footsteps on the marble floor of the Vaubyessard chateau, the irritating squeak of the wigmaker's sign, the thump of Hippolyte's wooden leg, the crunch of the cemetery gate and the rustling of Emma's dress as she and Léon walk to the wet-nurse's house are all part not only of what Roland Barthes has called 'l'effet de réel'[39] but also and, perhaps, more importantly of the emotional fabric of the text. There are numerous examples within the novel of the ways in which emotion can be suggested through sounds. Emma's sense of boredom and alienation at Tostes, for instance, is conveyed not by a passage of psychological analysis, but rather through a description of the sounds around her: 'les joncs sifflaient à ras de terre, et les feuilles des hêtres bruissaient en un frisson rapide, tandis que les cimes, se balançant toujours, continuaient leur grand murmure' (47).[40] Similarly, the full truth of Emma's death is brought home to Charles by the contrast between her silence and the noises of life: 'l'horloge de l'église sonna deux heures. On entendait le gros murmure de la rivière qui coulait dans les ténèbres, au pied de la terrasse. M. Bournisien, de temps à autre, se mouchait bruyamment, et Homais faisait grincer sa plume sur le papier'. (336)[41] Perhaps the clearest example of this technique, however, is provided in the scene where Emma first contemplates killing herself and in which to the intensity of light and heat is added the noise of Binet's lathe, 'une sorte de ronflement à modulations stridentes' (210).[42] As Emma's desire for annihilation increases, so too does the sound of the lathe, transforming itself into an angry voice summoning her to her death. Here, too, the choice of vocabulary – 'ronflement', 'modulation', 'stridente' – and the suggestion of the difficulty of finding precise terms, conveyed in the phrase 'une sorte de', shows Flaubert's interest both in the psychological analysis of what one notices in moments of great tension and in the technical side of the experiment.

Sounds are also central to the imaginary lands Emma conjures up, in which, for example, 'on entendait sonner des cloches, hennir les mulets, avec le murmure des guitares et le bruit des fontaines' (201),[43] or where one listens to 'la chanson du postillon, qui se répète dans la montagne avec les clochettes des chèvres et le bruit sourd de la cascade' (41–2).[44] Noticeably absent here is any reference to the voice of the beloved: the text indeed specifies that in all this sound, the lovers do not speak. The reader is left to decide whether the intensity of emotion makes speech impossible or whether they simply have nothing to say to one another.

Music, in particular, links Emma's daily existence with the world inhabited by her imagination. The barrel-organ, for instance, reproduces the songs and dance-tunes of Paris, 'échos du monde qui arrivaient jusqu'à Emma', and allows her to escape into reveries articulated through a suitably extravagant comparison based both on the contemporary craze for things Egyptian and on Flaubert's own experiences with an Egyptian prostitute:

> des sarabandes à n'en plus finir se déroulaient dans sa tête, et, comme une bayadère sur les fleurs d'un tapis, sa pensée bondissait avec les notes, se balançait de rêve en rêve, de tristesse en tristesse (67).[45]

Musical imagery is associated with both eroticism and death, one of the means by which the text locks the two inextricably together. After making love with Rodolphe for the first time, Emma 'entendit tout au loin, au delà du bois, sur les autres collines, un cri vague et prolongé, une voix qui se traînait, et elle l'écoutait silencieusement, se mêlant comme une musique

aux dernières vibrations de ses nerfs émus' (165–6).[46] Emma as
musical instrument, available and willing to be played on, is
only one of a series of images of availability that runs through
the novel, and it recurs at the beginning of her affair with Léon,
when, listening to the opera, 'elle se laissait aller au bercement
des mélodies et se sentait elle-même vibrer de tout son être
comme si les archets des violons se fussent promenés sur ses
nerfs' (228).[47] Yet again, we should avoid the tendency merely
to mock such a reaction: Donizetti's music at this point of the
opera is indeed singularly beautiful, and a full reading of the text
demands a complex response, a form of enlightened sympathy.
The sheer physicality of these descriptions of sounds is taken up
again when Emma scours Yonville in search of a loan that will
save her from bankruptcy: the sound of the blood pounding in
her arteries appears to her to be like deafening music filling the
countryside (319).

   Significantly, the early stages of Emma's death agony bring a
moment of calm, a crepuscular, silent world in which the only
earthly sound she hears is 'l'intermittente lamentation de ce
pauvre cœur, douce et indistincte, comme le dernier écho d'une
symphonie qui s'éloigne' (324).[48] But the unforgiving irony of
the narrative sweeps away this quiet to put in its stead Charles's
strangled sobs, the mumble of Latin prayers, the tinkling bell
and, finally, the thump of heavy boots heralding the harsh voice
 of the blind beggar singing his vulgar song and precipitating
Emma's laughter, 'un rire atroce, frénétique, désespéré' (332).[49]
Emma's inability to transform the world into the object of her
desire, these images suggest, has as its counterpart her own
transformation into the infinitely manipulable object of desire.

   Just as the importance of light is not merely to create a
'realistic' representation of the world in which Emma finds
herself but also to suggest emotion, so the sounds described
offer further insight into the minds and emotions of the central
characters. While *Madame Bovary* conjures up in the reader's
imagination a recognizable universe, rich in colours, sounds
and smells, it is also clear that the device of *style indirect libre*
forces us to perceive this universe in emotional or symbolic
terms, to accept, to some extent, the overlay of interpretable
meaning that the characters place upon it. Only on the rare
occasions when the narrative voice presents the descriptions

without mediating them through the mind of a character do we see that universe as merely a work of imagination. Roland Barthes has pointed out that the description of Rouen in Part III, chapter 5 is constructed with the aim of making the city appear to be a painting: as a result, Barthes argues, Flaubert, like Binet, imitates something that is already the simulation of an essence.[50] Yet, the sense of place in *Madame Bovary*, with its movement from physical to imaginary and emotional place, and its sense of constriction intensified by the infinite expansion of the desired space, is such as to suggest that one of the novel's central interests is in the structures of the world it represents.

WATER

The way in which the creation of space in *Madame Bovary*, whether that of the diegetic world, that of imagination or that of emotion depends on a constant oscillation between descriptive and metaphorical modes, can best be illustrated by focusing on one motif, that of water.[51] The disintegration of Emma's existence, and the way in which she is pulled along by forces over which she seems to have no control, are often indicated by images of water, closely linked to the rainswept landscapes or to the silent, fast-flowing river near Yonville. The effect on Emma of her attendance at the Vaubyessard ball is conveyed, for instance, through the following image: 'son voyage à la Vaubyessard avait fait un trou dans sa vie, à la manière de ces grandes crevasses qu'un orage, en une seule nuit, creuse quelquefois dans les montagnes' (58).[52] The space of this image is Emma's imagination: the mountain scenery, the suddenness with which things happen, the image of rapid and unexpected change, all belong to her vision. This water imagery continues to be closely associated with sexual desire and to assume more sinister implications when Emma gradually realizes that her affair with Rodolphe is grinding to a halt: 'leur grand amour, où elle vivait plongée, parut se diminuer sous elle, comme l'eau d'un fleuve qui s'absorberait dans son lit, et elle aperçut la vase' (175).[53] Finally, most sinister of all, when Rodolphe confesses himself unable to lend her the money she so desperately needs, her whole existence seems as unstable as that mud: 'le sol sous ses pieds était plus mou qu'une onde, et les

sillons lui parurent d'immenses vagues brunes, qui déferlaient'
(319).[54] Even Guillaumin's voice, when Emma tries to borrow
money, recalls a flowing stream (309). The extent to which the
river of the diegetic space invades the metaphorical space is one
of the aspects which guarantees the unity of the work.[55]

Yet the movement between the apparent 'effet de réel' and
metaphor, a movement that is often mediated by the device
of *style indirect libre*, is not of course restricted to a single motif,
however prevalent. The way in which the two domains are
interwoven can be illustrated by a quotation conveying a
moment of deep peace in the relationship between Emma and
Rodolphe, but a moment that Rodolphe knows is to be followed
by his bringing their affair to a close:

> La tendresse des anciens jours leur revenait au cœur,
> abondante et silencieuse comme la rivière qui coulait, avec
> autant de mollesse qu'en apportait le parfum des seringas,
> et projetait dans leur souvenir des ombres plus démesurées
> et plus mélancoliques que celles des saules immobiles qui
> s'allongeaient sur l'herbe (204).[56]

It is as though both domains, the mimetic and the metaphorical, were infinitely interchangeable, vast paradigms affording
innumerable substitutions, the river for tenderness, the softness
created by memory and that produced by the smell of mock-
orange and so forth. And it is, of course, that suggestion that
makes the sentence following on from those I have just quoted
all the more disturbing, for here no substitutions are made, the
decoding is left entirely to the reader: 'souvent quelque bête
nocturne, hérisson ou belette, se mettant en chasse, dérangeait
les feuilles, ou bien on entendait par moments une pêche
mûre qui tombait toute seule de l'espalier' (204).[57] Rodolphe
as hunter, Emma as ripe fruit, inner and outer worlds as endlessly
interpenetrable: what this constant substitution suggests is that
our perception of independent entities in a fixed universe
may be merely self-delusion produced by constantly changing
emotions.

OBJECTS

The oscillation between the apparent everyday realism of the
world it creates and the sense of hallucination and vertigo it

frequently presents is characteristic of *Madame Bovary*. Partly
a product of the play of light on reflecting surfaces, of the
multiplicity of voices and the associated shifting viewpoints,
partly created by the repetitions and echoes set in train by
the varying time scales, this oscillation is also the result of a
description of objects, people and gestures so meticulous as to
imply that they have meaning while at the same time suggesting
that any attempt at interpretation will be, as J. Culler puts it,
'made possible only by codes constructed of social clichés and
empty imaginative syntheses'.[58] Embedded in the novel, after
all, are three major responses to the data of the senses: Emma
and Léon, in accordance with the Romantics' privileging of
the individual, impose on everything a code of preconceived
and self-centred notions drawn from their reading; Homais
transforms everything into statistics (merely a different code
from that initially given); and Binet, like Rodolphe, simply
reduces it all to the endless repetition of the same. A. Levin's conviction that realism is 'iconoclastic', undermining any
symbols it may seem to build up,[59] provides a helpful approach,
as does J. Pontalis's more psycho-analytical reading: 'ce qui le
[i.e. Flaubert] fascine, c'est la pâte des choses, leur présence
envoûtante et leur pourrissement, ce sens tout imprégné de
matière qui fait les couleurs, les parfums, les rêveries'.[60] Above
all, of course, it is not the objects themselves – although the
delight with which Flaubert describes the wedding cake, for
instance, indicates that they can exercise a particular fascination
or repulsion for him – so much as the effect they exert on the
novel's characters that Flaubert is most eager to convey.

The novel offers us an image of the collector of apparently
meaningful objects in the scene where Rodolphe opens the
biscuit tin of sentimental memorabilia collected in his numerous
love affairs. Blood-spotted handkerchief bearing traces of a
nose-bleed Emma had suffered, miniature painting, letters
begging for love or money, bouquets, hairpins, locks of hair:
most may momentarily jog his memory, reminding of what he
had forgotten, although some evoke nothing at all, but the result
is that all these objects, kept in the first instance for what they
signified, are revealed to signify, at least for Rodolphe, nothing
but a 'tas de blagues' (207), an inner graveyard. Yet Flaubert's
irony is such that we can never be certain that Rodolphe's

reading, already thrown into question on at least one occasion by the specific intervention of a judging narrational comment (196), is appropriate, let alone definitive.

Throughout the novel can be found objects that seem imbued with some kind of meaning, given the context in which they are placed. The plaster curé reading his breviary, yet another of the images of reading in the text, is first seen when Emma, newly married, inspects her new home and finds him in the garden. The passing of time, which brings with it the disillusionment with marriage in general and her husband in particular, also brings the gradual decay of the statue, whose right foot falls off and whose face is disfigured as frost eats away at the plaster. Finally he is smashed to smithereens when the couple move to Yonville. Symbol of a decaying marriage, indicative of the powerlessness of the church to help its parishioners, prediction of the club-foot of Hippolyte and the disfigurement of the blind beggar, or merely plaster figure, empty of any meaning and therefore susceptible of all meanings? The barometer that crashes to the floor as Emma storms out of a room in fury or the cactus plants that Emma and Léon cultivate because a book has made them fashionable, and that die during the winter, can also be read as symbols measuring and giving concrete form to emotions, but the corrosive irony of the text is always there to remind us that emotions themselves, in the world of *Madame Bovary*, are expressed and shaped and perhaps even created by convention and, therefore, as mere signifiers of the individual's willingness to accept cliché, can lend no meaning to anything else. More important, perhaps, for their significance within the novel itself are the other moments at which these objects appear. The barometer, for example, is one of the objects that surround Emma at the moment when, having let her languish for six weeks after the agricultural fair, Rodolphe reappears to press home his advantage: 'la dorure du baromètre, sur qui frappait un rayon de soleil, étalait des feux dans la glace' (159).[61] The play of light, the reflection in the mirror, the association with passion, the indication of social status: these are what give contextual meaning to the object here. Equally, the cactus plants, presented by Léon and Emma as symbols of their first passion for each other, reappear to offer an ironic and unperceived prediction when Emma rushes to the notary's house in search of money(307). The phrenological head Charles receives as a present from Léon and which, ironically enough, he is allowed to keep when the Bovarys' possessions are seized, since this is one of those objects society expects a doctor to own, forces itself on our attention as a means by which the physical suggests the psychological, bumps on the skull revealing tendencies of the mind, yet itself subverts that message by giving Charles no inkling of the nature of the relationship between the giver and his own wife, no way of perceiving the cuckold's bumps on his own head. Balzac's affirmation of the interrelationship between milieu and individual, between possession and possessor, between Mme Vauquer and the building in which she runs her boarding-house, carries no weight in Flaubert's depiction of reality.

Yet these objects do seize our attention as readers, teasing us to find a meaning behind them: it cannot be merely arbitrariness or playfulness, for instance, that produces the stag's head on the wall behind Rodolphe when he sits down to write his farewell note to Emma. Our habits of reading are such that it is extremely difficult not to see it as predicting that Léon will cuckold him, or that Emma, like the stag, is a mere trophy on Rodolphe's belt, or, in accordance with M. Lowe's allegorical and mythological reading, that Rodolphe Boulanger, whose surname is a translation of one of Jupiter's appellations, is here indulging in one of the many transformations characteristic of that most adulterous of gods.[62] Here we seem to have one of the few survivors of the many private jokes inscribed in the first drafts and subsequently removed, as Flaubert turned from the more obvious to the more suggestive.

Certainly some of the most closely described objects are there primarily to reveal the fetishism that is so characteristic of eroticism in all Flaubert's novels. Typical of this is the cigar case picked up after the Vaubyessard ball that Emma so determinedly attaches to the Vicomte who danced with her and which she invests with so many of her own sexual fantasies: 'un souffle d'amour avait passé parmi les mailles du canevas; chaque coup d'aiguille avait fixé là une espérance ou un souvenir, et tous ces fils de soie entrelacés n'étaient que la continuité de la même passion silencieuse' (58).[63] Since this is part of the paraphernalia society expects of lovers, Emma's reading has taught her to make the easy shift between objects and humans: Flaubert's writing both questions such a link, through his depiction of Rodolphe and the biscuit tin, and reveals how fascinated he himself is in its possibilities. The image of the 'passion silencieuse' finding physical form in these silken threads cannot lightly be dismissed as mere parody, however much the speed with which Emma leaps to conclusions about the case's origins may suggest mockery. There is much in this expression that points forward to Flaubert's exploration of Félicité's tendency to invest objects with meaning in *Un cœur simple*.

The apparent symbolism of certain events or juxtapositions is similarly open to question. When Charles first enters the Rouault farm his horse shies, and critics seeking a realistic depiction of life have attacked this event in the novel as too evidently symbolic, too close to the Romantic novels apparently under attack. Yet, once again, it could be argued that here we are in the domain of parody, where the apparent heavy-handedness of the device, in a work of such remarkable technical sophistication, is in itself a warning that the shying of his horse is as empty of meaning as the other events in Charles's life. On the other hand, however, since at that time few novelists had in fact begun exploring the possibilities of symbolism, the device itself was not so familiar at the time as it is now.

The mere juxtaposition of objects can also offer oblique commentaries. An indication of the nature and sources of contemporary religious feeling is elliptically suggested by the fact that, in Yonville's church, the confessional is placed directly opposite a wonderfully pagan statue of the Virgin, 'vêtue d'une robe de satin, coiffée d'un voile de tulle semé d'étoiles d'argent, et tout empourprée aux pommettes comme une idole des îles Sandwich' (73).[64] The Romantics' dual image of woman, at once angelic and destructive, is evoked with similar concision in the two paintings adorning Guillaumin's dining-room, one representing Hugo's depiction of fidelity to an idolized beloved, Esméralda, the other providing a Biblical image of female betrayal of men, Potiphar's wife (307).[65]

Indeed, one of the ways in which Flaubert conveys the absurdity of existence is by supplying the reader throughout with a multiplicity of details, while providing little suggestion of a hierarchy of importance. Certainly, this feeling of being bombarded with indiscriminate detail is one of the ways in which the novel most approaches a representation of the real. The description of Yonville in the opening pages of the second part of the novel provides a case in point. Here the narrator depicts for us the typical local farmhouse:

> sur le mur de plâtre que traversent en diagonale des lambourdes noires, s'accroche parfois quelque maigre poirier, et les rez-de-chaussée ont à leur porte une petite barrière tournante pour les défendre des poussins, qui viennent picorer, sur le seuil, des miettes de pain bis trempé de cidre (72–3).[66]

The principle at issue here seems more one of accretion than of meaningful selection, a desire to convey everyday existence rather than to impose any suggestion of symbolic significance: why are we given this sudden, sharp picture of the chickens and the Normandy habit of feeding them with bread soaked in cider? Why, for that matter, mention the broomstick with its bundle of ferns (73), which swings to and fro beneath a window? This seems to me a different issue from the need for documentation in the episode of the club foot or the description of the beggar, where the density of details suggests that neither Charles nor Homais can ever assimilate them sufficiently to cure the condition involved, but where we remain convinced that other minds may well be capable of doing so. Flaubert certainly indicates such a possibility when he introduces the clear-sighted, no-nonsense Dr Larivière, to whom he devotes a paragraph of closely argued psychological analysis. The careful balance of the sentences, the fine-shading of the portrait, and above all the stress on his ability to see to the heart of the matter all indicate that intelligence can discover certain elements of truth:

> Dédaigneux des croix, des titres et des académies, hospitalier, libéral, paternel avec les pauvres et pratiquant la vertu sans y croire, il eût presque passé pour un saint si la finesse de son esprit ne l'eût fait craindre comme un démon. Son regard, plus tranchant que ses bistouris, vous descendait droit dans l'âme et désarticulait tout mensonge à travers les allégations et les pudeurs (327).[67]

In the case of the chickens or the broom, which are only two
examples chosen from among many in the text, the reader is
faced with a world on which no simplistic meaning can be
imposed, and as a result shown why the novel's characters
so often seek a means of focus and selection – the window,
the mirror, the painting, the book – but at the same time
the presence of Larivière seems to insist on the possibility
of extracting meaning by setting aside the lies and habits of
stereotypes and clichés.

TIME

As G. Poulet argues, Flaubert abandons unilinear and
monocentric images of the novel to construct *Madame Bovary*
'comme une série de foyers à partir desquels, en avant, en
arrière, de tous côtés, il y a un déploiement d'objets et un
rayonnement à la fois temporel et spatial'.[68] The image of
dispersal that dominates the sense of place in *Madame Bovary*
is also very much of the essence in the presentation of time.

The sense of dispersal is partly a product of the gap between
the time of the story (*erzählte Zeit*) and the time of the narration
(*Erzählzeit*),[69] suggested not only by the use of the first person
in the opening chapters, which presupposes a narrator who is a
contemporary of Charles speaking after the events related, but
also by the description in the present tense of Yonville with its
traditional and perhaps parodic tag – 'depuis les événements que
l'on va raconter, rien, en effet, n'a changé à Yonville' (75)[70] – and
the famous concluding paragraphs, which sketch in the fates of
Emma's family after her death and report the award of the *croix
d'honneur* to Homais, using the present tense.

The temporal fluctuations in the novel's opening chapters
anticipate in many ways the techniques of Proust in *A la recherche
du temps perdu*, for the narration proceeds through a series of false
starts, opening with the specific memory of the day on which
Charles first began attending the school, before reverting to
the boy's early childhood (where the evocation of his parent's
marriage reminds us of the social conventions of an age when
marriages were often matters of financial convenience rather
than love, and already predicts the unhappiness of Emma's
marriage, thus opening up yet another dialogue between past

and future). There is then a brief prolepsis,[71] which precipitates us into the *Erzählzeit* of the narrator's present and which also predicts the findings of the inquest on Charles's body: just as the narrator affirms: 'il serait maintenant impossible à aucun de nous de se rien rappeler de lui' (9)[72] so Canivet's autopsy found nothing ('ne trouva rien' (356)). The narration then follows Charles's progress as a student and a medical officer in descriptions that are clearly iterative, that is, where something frequently repeated is recounted a single time, before focusing sharply on the day on which Charles first visits Les Bertaux and meets Emma. Similar fluctuations occur throughout the first book. The chapter evoking the wedding scene, for instance, closes with Emma's father's memory of his own wedding and his evocation of a hypothesized present in which a son who had died in infancy is now thirty years old. The responses of both Charles and Emma to their marriage introduce a brief summary of Charles's emotional life so far, before turning to explore Emma's dissatisfaction and to trace the cause of it in her childhood and adolescence. And, too, Emma's boredom sparks off images of alternative existences, a rewriting of her life and a recasting of her partner, which leads in turn to memories of the past: 'il aurait pu être beau, spirituel, distingué, attirant, tels qu'ils étaient sans doute, ceux qu'avaient épousés ses anciennes camarades de couvent. Que faisaient-elles maintenant?' (46).[73] The visit to the Vaubyessard castle opens up further periods of time, both historic and imaginary, and creates a date whose anniversary is registered in the future as one of the devices, which, like the development of Emma's child, are used to force upon us the awareness of passing time.

The nesting technique, whereby Emma's story is framed by that of Charles, and which inserts into these main stories a variety of briefer narratives, is only one of the means Flaubert uses to create an image of fragmented time, an image that intensifies the suggestion that existence is purposeless and directionless. Although there are moments when generalizations, often couched in the form of maxims, convey a sense of timeless and universal validity,[74] most of the text is rooted in a specific sense of time. It is this sense of time continuing, however fragmentary may be the perception the characters have of it, that makes Emma's death so permanent: instead of closing with her death, as though life around her had also ceased, the narrator continues through her funeral and beyond to the death of Charles and the triumph of Homais. That sense of time's unstoppable progress is also a product of the frequent occasions on which the end of one chapter points forward to the events narrated in the following chapter: this is the case, for instance, with the transition between Charles's falling in love with Emma and the wedding, where Book I, chapter 3 ends with a pithy summary of the celebrations that are explored at such length in the next chapter. The sense of endless repetition of the same, reflected in the very fact that on the following day the celebrations began all over again, is also a product of this temporal stammer.[75] Yet, of course, this image draws very strongly on contemporary social practice, reflecting an age and a class for which weddings provided a relatively rare and eagerly seized opportunity for extended celebrations.

Equally important in this regard is the use of such anticipations as Emma's gothic and Piranesi-like image of the future as a black corridor ending in a firmly closed door (65), or Rodolphe's cynical comment after he has seen Emma for the first time and considers seducing her: 'mais comment s'en débarrasser ensuite?',[76] ironically echoed by Emma and Léon as their relationship stutters to a halt.

The narrative swings between suggestions of a particular time – 'un soir que la fenêtre était ouverte' (112), 'ce fut un dimanche de février, une après-midi qu'il neigeait' (103)[77] – and iteration – 'il en fut de même les jour suivants' (109), 'c'était le jeudi. Elle se levait, et elle s'habillait silencieusement' (267), 'tous les jours, à la même heure' (66).[78] Even when the time does seem to be specific, however, it is clear that Flaubert is not interested in a precise and carefully orchestrated chronology, often preferring to introduce dates that have a private value for him rather than bother, for instance, with counting the months of Emma's pregnancy. Our awareness of repetition is heightened by the use of such phrases as 'on certain days' (69), or the apparent dichotomy of sometimes/at other times (e.g. 294–5) where surface variation only lightly masks essential repetition. The feeling of being trapped in an ever-repeating continuum is increased by the allusion to anniversaries, such as that of the Vaubyessard ball or père Rouault's recovery from his broken leg, celebrated by the inevitable turkey. But these anniversaries also indicate the slow and certain progress of time, marked in addition by the realization that Charles has spent four years at Tostes, or the assertion that Emma has been waiting and suffering for four years, as well as by the decay of objects around them, the plaster curé who loses his right foot or Homais's collection of foetuses which 'se pourrissent de plus en plus dans leur alcool bourbeux' (75).[79] That sense of inexorable forward movement is also implied in such statements as 'jamais Mme Bovary ne fut aussi belle qu'à cette époque' (199),[80] where the use of the past historic pinpoints this as a passing phase. ——

At points the text introduces a sense that time has all but ceased, its viscous flow halted into inescapable sluggishness. The detailed evocation of the cathedral at Rouen, for example, and the description of the town when Emma arrives for one of her illicit meetings with Léon, are both means of halting the normal speed of the narration, manipulating time to suggest that, just as in Emma's reveries about knights galloping towards her, nothing will happen, or that happiness itself will by its very nature leech the intensity out of experience: 'cependant, sur l'immensité de cet avenir qu'elle se faisait apparaître, rien de particulier ne surgissait: les jours, tous magnifiques, se ressemblaient comme des flots'(201).[81]

To the actual time of the narrative is added the fictional time of the characters' reveries, the interminable series of conditionals and futures, the what might have been and the what could still be. The passage contrasting Charles's dreams of future domestic bliss, as he and Emma slowly grow old in the company of their daughter, with Emma's contemporaneous dreams of escape with Rodolphe is, of course, created around a central void, since neither vision of the future anticipates what actually happens: but what the novel reveals is that this void is present also at the heart of the time they experience in their everyday existence. Thus, Emma's past and with it her very identity are destroyed by the images of the Vaubyessard ball, with all its suggestions of the dance of death (53), so that there remains henceforth 'un trou dans sa vie' (58).[82] The sense of time circling around a void is also present in the scene of Emma's death, where not only the lapidary evocation of moments in her past but even the conflation of secular and profane love recall Emma's lifelong

inability to distinguish between the real and imaginary, and to
discover the values of language.

DEATH

Arising from Flaubert's treatment of time in the novel is his
exploitation of one of the central topoi of European literature
and art, the dance of death, where humanity, seeking to blind
itself to mortality through sensual enjoyment, symbolized by the
dance, is led in its wild celebrations by the figure of Death itself.
All Emma's dreams of permanence and perfection founder as
they encounter the transience and putrefaction of matter. G.
Finney even goes so far as to claim, in her study of the garden
as pastoral *locus amœnus* transformed by the industrialism of the
nineteenth century, that the leisure traditionally associated with
the garden becomes in *Madame Bovary* a 'paralytic torpor', which
makes eroticism merely a step away from death.[83] Ironically
enough, however, this yoking of passion and death is one of
the areas where the text is at its most Romantic, and we might
well argue that Finney is only partly right when she points out,
in reference to Lestiboudois's location of the vegetable plot
in the graveyard, that 'by associating Christianity and passion
with decay and death, Flaubert unmasks Romanticism's illusory
idealization of love and religion in the same glorified language
– the source of Emma's affliction'.[84] Romanticism in the form
of Gautier or Borel had already made this association, prepared,
moreover, by Hugo's revaluation of the grotesque. Of course
the main function of this passage is, much more pragmatically,
to reveal the profiteering of Lestiboudois.

As Baudelaire pointed out in an article published in 1851, 'Les
Drames et les romans honnêtes', 'il y a une cohue de poètes
abrutis par la volupté païenne, et qui emploient sans cesse les
mots de *saint, sainte, extase, prière*, etc., pour qualifier des choses et
des êtres qui n'ont rien de saint ni d'extatique, bien au contraire'
(original emphasis).[85] The degree to which such terminology had
invaded the language is evident not merely from *Les Fleurs du
mal*, but even from a letter, which seems to have been written
within months of the review itself, in which Baudelaire begs
his correspondent: 'soyez mon ange gardien, ma Muse et ma
Madone, et conduisez-moi dans la route du Beau'.[86] Nerval's

Sylvie reflects a similar tendency in its evocation of the 'époque étrange': 'nous étions ivres de poésie et d'amour. Amour, hélas! des formes vagues, des teintes roses et bleues, des fantômes métaphysiques! Vue de près la femme réelle révoltait notre ingénuité; il fallait qu'elle apparût reine ou déesse, et surtout n'en pas approcher.'[87] The translation of religious experience into secular code, which creates such a fertile space for the imagination to play with the ambiguities of language, is instilled in Emma from her convent days, when the comparisons based on the words 'fiancé', 'husband', 'celestial lover' and 'eternal marriage', which constantly recur in sermons, awaken in her heart unexpected delights (37). The sensual pleasure of the priest's murmuring voice, the perfumes of the altar, the glow of the candles and the coolness of the font all combine to make her abandon herself to a sense of mystical languor (37). Yet, since the sacred is articulated here to a secular code, the terms apparently denoting the sacred – 'soul', 'mystical' – instantly deconstruct into sensuality and eroticism. That initial deconstruction is reinforced by the parallels between these initiatory moments of sensuality in Emma's formation and both the waltz scene and the seduction scenes with Rodolphe and Léon, while the lack of satisfaction she experiences in her marriage is predicted for us by a scrupulous absence of any such terminology. The sense of languor experienced in the church is a staple diet in Emma's erotic reveries, becomes 'torpeur' when she waltzes at the Vaubyessard château, and deprives both Emma and Léon of the energy needed to turn their relationship into a love affair when they walk through the unseen paradise of rural Yonville on their way back from the wet-nurse's house. Rodolphe's manipulation of the code – 'vous êtes dans mon âme comme une madone sur un piédestal, à une place haute, solide et immaculée' – instantly creates the same languour, so that even when the words are so obviously subverted by the action – 'il allongeait son bras et lui en entourait la taille' – Emma tries only 'mollement' to free herself, before abandoning herself, 'défaillante' (165).[88] For Emma at this stage, eroticism involves, therefore, a sense of languorous abandonment to a stronger being, leading to a *petite mort* from which she recovers as if born anew.

When Rodolphe breaks off the affair, offering her, instead of the garden of Eden her dreams had conjured up, merely the

bitter fruit of knowledge, she falls into an illness so serious that at
one point she asks for Holy Communion, oscillating once more
from the secular to the sacred. Again what she experiences is a
languor in which she feels that 'son être, montant vers Dieu,
allait s'anéantir dans cet amour come un encens allumé qui
se dissipe en vapeur' (218).[89] And the narrative voice adds,
moving between the spiritual and the physical and picking
up echoes from the time she first gave herself to Rodolphe,
'ce fut en défaillant d'une joie céleste qu'elle avança les lèvres
pour accepter le corps du Sauveur qui se présentait' (218).[90] But
the vision of eternal joy is as short lived as her experience
of earthly pleasure, and the subsequent desire to relive and
eternalize a sensation perceived as being granted only on the
point of death is doomed to exactly the same kind of failure
as her longing to find in adultery a permanence of intensity.
There are further parallels, too, in that just as when Emma has
yielded to Rodolphe she sees herself as part of a great sisterhood
of adulteresses, so in the pride of her religious devotion, as
the narrative voice rather cruelly depicts it, Emma compared
herself to those great ladies of days gone by, whose glory she
had dreamed of as she gazed at a portrait of La Vallière (220).
However much Emma may discover in adultery the platitudes
of marriage, however short-lived her phases of religiosity, the
pattern is so permanently established that as soon as she enters
Rouen cathedral all her willpower leaves her:

> Emma priait, ou plutôt s'efforçait de prier, espérant qu'il
> allait lui descendre du ciel quelque résolution subite; et,
> pour attirer le secours divin, elle s'emplissait les yeux
> des splendeurs du tabernacle, elle aspirait le parfum des
> juliennes blanches épanouies dans les grands vases, et
> prêtait l'oreille au silence de l'église (246).[91]

But as these are precisely the original sources of her sensuality
it is small wonder that all this merely increases the tumult in
her heart. Part of the irony of this erotic experience, of course,
is that it coincides with the younger Emma's vision of passion
riding roughshod over willpower, apparently confirming the
Romantic presentation of love. What the text seems to be
suggesting here, however, is that Emma wills this failure of
will, rejecting the learning of experience in favour of what she

knows to be the lies of her education and her reading. And what gives a particularly sharp edge to Flaubert's irony here is that it is precisely this choice that determines the peculiar heroism of Don Quixote.

The inextricable linking of secular and sacred culminates in Emma's dying moments, when the administration of the last rites evokes a litany of unequivocally sensual and erotic import:

> [le prêtre] trempa son pouce droit dans l'huile et commença les onctions: d'abord sur les yeux, qui avaient tant convoité toutes les somptuosités terrestres; puis sur les narines, friandes de brises tièdes et de senteurs amoureuses; puis sur la bouche, qui s'était ouverte pour le mensonge, qui avait gémi d'orgueil et crié dans la luxure; puis sur les mains, qui se délectaient aux contacts suaves, et enfin sur la plante des pieds, si rapides autrefois quand elle courait à l'assouvissement de ses désirs, et qui maintenant ne marcheraient plus (331).[92]

The unforgiving compression of Emma's desires into these brief and weighty clauses, and the unrelenting rhythm leading inescapably to that abrupt final statement make this Flaubert's most merciless unmasking of Romantic etherealism. But it owes much of its force to another network of associations, which is itself part of the Romanticism of a Byron, a Gautier or a Borel, the insistence on the skull behind the flesh, the decay only briefly robed by beauty, a motif epitomised by the Frau Welt figures that, like the Dance of Death, are also a legacy of medieval Christianity. Indeed, that network of associations is also part of the earthy representation of death that is central to the novel's mimetic endeavour.

As in many still lifes, which present a bowl of apparently perfect fruit that on closer inspection all prove to be rotting, or which show the insects and worms that infest the flowers,[93] *Madame Bovary* offers a firmly realistic vision of decay. Even if it tells us nothing else, the plaster priest in the garden at Tostes speaks of disintegration, a curiously ironic snake in this deliberately un-Edenic garden. Emma's attempts to escape the eternal garden and the dusty road (45) and to replace it with the archetypal Romantic symbol of the ruin, in this case an abandoned house, lead only to images of rankness and decay: 'elle retrouvait . . . les bouquets d'orties entourant les gros cailloux, et les plaques de lichen le long des trois fenêtres, dont les volets toujours clos s'égrenaient de pourriture, sur leurs barres de fer rouillées' (45).[94] Nowhere is the putrefaction of the flesh that awaits Emma more forcibly thrust before her than in the débâcle of the operation on Hippolyte, as a result of which 'l'invincible pourriture allait montant toujours des extrémités vers le ventre' (186).[95] Small wonder that Charles, unwilling cause of this 'pourriture', should find it invading his dreams after Emma's death, when he reaches out to touch her and she becomes a putrefying mass in his arms. Such is the intensity with which Emma's dreams are invariably destroyed that even she cannot remain blind to the reality that crushes them: 'd'où venait donc cette insuffisance de la vie, cette pourriture instantanée des choses où elle s'appuyait? . . . '(289).[96] There is a sort of mad heroism, a Camusian revolt against the absurd, in Emma's refusal to accept the lesson of experience: yet here, too, torpor takes over from heroism, for nothing seems worth the bother of seeking it out. It is perhaps this realization more than anything else which marks the beginnings of Emma's death throes.

References to death abound in the novel. The abrupt death of Charles's first wife precipitates in père Rouault reminiscences about the time when his wife had just died and he himself wished he was 'comme les taupes, que je voyais aux branches, qui avaient des vers leur grouillant dans le ventre, crevé enfin' (21).[97] The earthy realism of this statement, reinforced by the register of *crevé*, provides an implicit commentary on Emma's reaction to the same death, expressed in a change of register using the euphemism of 'the departed' ('la défunte') (40). Already the creation of the 'tableau funèbre' with her dead mother's hair suggests the fetishism that attempts to find permanence in flux and does indeed find an ironic echo in Charles's desire for a lock of Emma's hair after her death. Scattered through the text are further references to monuments to the dead, which recall this early attempt to counterfeit intense emotion and its conclusion in boredom and 'apaisement'. The château records its dead through portraits barely perceived in the gloom, releasing a message of fragmentation: 'de tous ces grands carrés noirs bordés d'or sortaient, çà et là, quelque portion plus claire de la peinture,

un front pâle, deux yeux qui vous regardaient, des perruques . . .
ou bien la boucle d'une jarretière au haut d'un mollet rebondi'
(49).[98] The pattern of a reminder of death leading to moments
of eroticism established in this scene recurs in Rouen cathedral,
when the love-making is preceded by a description of tombs,
one in particular extracting from the guide praise for offering a
perfect representation of death (247). Emma, taking her lorgnon
the better to see this *momento mori* is, inevitably, confronted with
a depiction of the dead man's wife, 'Diane de Poitiers, comtesse
de Brézé, duchesse de Valentinois, née en 1499, morte en 1566'
(247), as the guide narrates, carefully eliding the expected
reference to her position as king's mistress. The link between
death and eroticism is tightened when Emma, summoned to
Homais's pharmacy, finds the uproar caused by Justin's crime
of taking a jar from the *capharnaüm*, and being caught with a
copy of *L'Amour conjugal*. Homais, faced with this double threat
to his family's physical and moral wellbeing, forgets that his
purpose in summoning Emma is to break to her gently the
news he so abruptly conveys, that her father-in-law has died.
Here the connection between death and sexuality is also tied
to the information that Homais keeps arsenic in his laboratory,
the information that determines, of course, Emma's mode of
suicide. The final link to the chain is forged, appropriately, by
Lheureux, who, when Emma begs for more time to repay him,
accuses her of trying to seduce him, comments on her theft of
Charles's earnings – 'personne, après tout, n'en est mort'[99] –
and then adds, 'd'une façon si perspicace et si terrible, qu'elle
en frissonna jusqu'aux entrailles' : 'Ah bah! quand on a comme
vous des amis' (300).[100]

The rigorous interweaving of passion, decay and death offers
a nexus where the text's apparent realism is revealed as a version
of gothic Romanticism, finding its most sultry echo in Flaubert's
Salammbô but already revealed in *Madame Bovary* by Emma's
own summary of what she now perceives to be the truth about
life: 'chaque sourire cachait un bâillement d'ennui, chaque joie
une malédiction, tout plaisir son dégoût, et les meilleurs baisers
ne vous laissaient sur la lèvre qu'une irréalisable envie d'une
volupté plus haute' (290).[101] The desire to desire is coupled
unalterably in Emma, as it will be in Frédéric Moreau, with
the languor that deprives the individual of the strength to

transform desire into act.[102] As a result, the ultimate object of Emma's desire, the promise of an intensity that cannot fade in the individual's consciousness, simply because the individual's consciousness will no longer register, is death itself, the ultimate *volupté* because it is also the ultimate torpor. But Flaubert insists through the very structures of his narrative on the falsity of such a conclusion: not only is Emma's death no slow fading into unconsciousness, rather a moment precipitated by the galvanized convulsion and manic laughter occasioned by the Blind Man's song, but it is also not the final moment of the novel, which, like life itself, grinds on inexorably.

NOTES: CHAPTER 6

1 'She bought herself a map of Paris, and with the tip of her finger, on the map, she went on errands in the capital. She walked along the boulevards, stopping at each corner, between the lines of the streets, in front of the white squares which represent the houses ... Paris, vaguer than the Ocean, glittered therefore in Emma's eyes in a rosy haze. The mass of people moving in this tumult was, however, divided into groups, classed in distinct tableaux. Emma perceived only two or three of them, and these hid from her all the others and represented on their own all humanity.'

2 'as for the rest of the world, it was lost, it had no particular place, it seemed not to exist. Moreover, the closer things were to her, the more her mind turned away from them. Everything in her immediate vicinity, the boring countryside, the imbecile lower middle classes, the mediocrity of existence, struck her as an exception in the world, a specific fate in which she found herself trapped, while beyond there extended as far as the eye could see an immense landscape of bliss and passion.'

3 'after an indeterminate distance, there was always a blurred area where her dream died away'.

4 *Les Métamorphoses du cercle* (Paris: Plon, 1961), p. 389: 'what Flaubert wanted to show in *Madame Bovary* is an existence which sometimes folds in on itself, and sometimes fans out'.

5 'the flat countryside extended as far as the eye could see, and at long intervals, the clumps of trees around the farms made dark purple patches against this vast grey surface which dissolved at the horizon into the drab tones of the sky'.

6 'a bastard land where the language lacks accentuation as the countryside lacks character'.

7 'existences where the heart dilates and the senses blossom'.

8 'enclosed within those high walls'; 'the universe, for him, did not go beyond the silken sweep of her skirt'.

9 'seemed small, precisely in order to bring them closer together in their solitude'.

10 'pale landscapes in dithyrambic climes, which often show us at one and the same time palm trees, pines, tigers on the right, a lion on the left, Turkish minarets on the horizon, in the foreground Roman ruins, then

some kneeling camels; – all of this framed by a perfectly tidy virgin forest, with a great beam of sunlight falling perpendicularly to tremble on the water, on which stand out, here and there, in white scratches against a steel-grey background, flotillas of swans'.

11 'He drew her further on, around a small pond, where duckweed turned the waves green. Wilted water lilies stood motionless among the reeds. At the sound of their footsteps in the grass, frogs leapt to hide themselves.'

12 'No birds could be heard, everything seemed to be asleep, the espalier covered with straw and the vine like a great sick snake under the cladding on the wall, in which could be seen, if one went closer, wood lice dragging themselves along on their numerous legs.'

13 'the dew had left on the cabbages silver lace with long light threads stretching from one cabbage to the next'.

14 'the young woman and her companion'.

This is just one of the counter-examples to Genette's claim that 'la plupart du temps, et même dans les pages descriptives d'une certaine ampleur, le mouvement général du texte est commandé par la démarche ou le regard d'un (ou plusieurs) personnage(s)' (Genette, *Figures III,* (Paris: Editions du Seuil, 1972) p. 135) for here neither character is capable of seeing in the way the passage is described.

Indeed, what is more often the case is that a dual perspective operates, the character's vision and that of the narrator.

15 'It was at the beginning of April, when the primroses are open; a warm wind rolls over flower beds ready for planting out, and the gardens, like women, seem to be preparing their toilet for the summer celebrations. Through the bars of the arbour and all around beyond it could be seen the river in the meadow, drawing its roving meanders on the grass.'

16 'certain places on earth must produce happiness, as if it were a plant requiring a specific soil and which grew poorly anywhere else'.

17 'future moments of happiness, like the shores of tropical climes, project over the immense spaces that precede them their native softness, a perfumed breeze, and one grows drowsy in their intoxication'.

18 'low house, with its flat roof, in the shade of a palm tree, at the top of a gulf, beside the sea': 'their lives would be as easy and comfortable as their silken clothes, all warm and starry like the mild nights they would gaze on'.

19 'a cat, on the roofs, walked slowly along, arching its back under the pale sunbeams. The wind, on the highway, blew trails of dust. In the distance, from time to time, a dog howled; and the bell, in its even tempo, continued its monotonous tolling which drifted out into the countryside.'

20 J. Rousset, *Forme et signification* (Paris: Corti, 1962), p. 127: 'windows and plunging views, openings on to distant vistas and dreams in space, each is a neuralgic point of the story, nodes where the narrative flow ceases'.

21 Ebauches, I, 147: 'adventures and sensitive characters'.

22 'a vast bluish expanse surrounded her, pinnacles of sentiment sparkled far beneath her thoughts, and ordinary existence receded into the distance, far below her, in the shade, between the intervals of these summits'.

23 'like a person who has been ruined and who looks through the window-panes at people sitting at table in the house he used to own'.

24 See Flaubert's *Souvenirs* (Paris: Buchet/Chastel, 1965), p. 104: 'on se regarde au miroir mais votre visage est renversé, bref il est impossible de dire vrai quand on l'écrit': 'you look in the mirror, but your image is reversed; in a word, it is impossible to tell the truth when you write it'.

25 A. Fairlie, *Flaubert: Madame Bovary* (London: Edward Arnold, 1962), p. 43.

26 'then the pride, the joy of saying to oneself: "I am virtuous", and of gazing at oneself in the mirror while assuming resigned poses, consoled her a little for the sacrifice she believed herself to be making'.

27 'her face, as in a magic mirror, gleamed on the surface of the shakos'.

28 N. Segal, *Narcissus and Echo*, (Manchester: Manchester University Press, 1988) in particular chapter 7, pp. 202-23.

29 'to read *my* thought'.

30 'the vague "she" of all volumes of poetry'. On this subject see N. Wing, *The Limits of Narrative*, (Cambridge: Cambridge University Press, 1986) p. 70, who points to the pun on 'elle' (she) and the letter L.

31 'the entire countryside looked motionless, like a painting'.

32 *Littérature et sensation* (Paris: Editions du Seuil, 1954), p. 176: see also D. L. Demorest, *L'Expression figurée et symbolique* (Geneva: Slatkine, 1967).

33 ibid, p. 177: 'sending our consciousness on from one object to another, shimmering makes nature contradict herself, leads her to proceed to her own annihilation'.

34 'the tiled roofs, which glittered under the harsh light of the blue sky, seemed to be making sparks fly from the crests of their gables'.

35 'a monstrous chandelier, from the entire length of which flowed down drops of molten diamonds'.

36 'Directly below her, the village square was empty; the pebbles of the footpath glittered, the weathercocks on the houses were motionless ... The ray of light which came directly up from below her drew down to the abyss the weight of her body ... The blue of the sky invaded her, air blew round in her empty head, she had only to yield, to let herself go.'

37 'whitish light': 'into the shadows as if into a shadowy ocean'.

38 Corr, II, 449: 'if ever the effects of a symphony have been translated into a book, it will be there. *The whole thing must howl.* The reader must hear at the same time the bellowing of the bulls, the sighs of love and the sentences of the administrators.'

39 'L'Effet de réel', in *Littérature et Réalité* (Paris: Editions du Seuil, 1982), pp. 81-90.

40 'the reeds whistled at ground level, and the beech leaves rustled as they trembled rapidly together, while the tree tops, still swaying, continued to make their great murmuring'.

41 'the church clock sounded two o'clock. They could hear the loud murmur of the river which flowed in the dark, at the foot of the terrace. From time to time, M. Bournisien blew his nose noisily, and Homais made his pen squeak on the paper.'

42 'a sort of humming with strident modulations'.

43 'one could hear bells ringing, mules neighing, together with the murmur of guitars and the sound of fountains'.

44 'the postillion's song, which echoes through the mountain together with the bells of the goats and the murmur of the waterfall'.

45 'echoes of the world which reached right to Emma'; 'endless sarabands unrolled in her head and like an oriental dancing-girl on the flowers of a carpet, her thoughts leapt with the notes, swayed from dream to dream, from sorrow to sorrow'.

46 'heard far away, beyond the wood, on the hills opposite, a vague, prolonged cry, a lingering voice that mingled like music with the last vibrations of her trembling nerves'.

47 'she abandoned herself to the movement of the melodies and felt her entire being vibrating as if the violin bows were moving across her nerves'.

48 'the intermittent lamentation of that poor heart, soft and indistinct, like the last echo of a symphony fading away'.

49 'a laugh that was atrocious, frenetic, despairing'.

50 op. cit. p. 85. See M. Bal, *Narratologie* (Paris: Editions Klincksieck, 1977) for a different reading.

51 On the theme of fluidity see D. Demorest, and on that of droplets seen as part of desire and death, J. P. Richard.

52 'her trip to La Vaubyessard had made a hole in her life, like those great crevasses that a storm can sometimes dig out in the course of a single night, in the mountains'.

53 'their great love, in which she had been immersed, seemed to be diminishing beneath her, as the water of a river is absorbed into its bed, and she caught sight of the mud'.

54 'beneath her feet the earth seemed softer than a wave and the furrows appeared to her like immense brown combers, on the point of breaking'.

55 For a study of these grouped images see M. Hardt, *Das Bild in der Dichtung* (Munich: Wilhelm Fink Verlag, 1966), pp. 140-88.

56 'The tenderness of days gone by returned to their hearts, as abundant and silent as the river which flowed by, with as much softness as that which the perfume of the mock-orange wafted to them, and it projected into their memories shadows more vast and more melancholy than those of the motionless willows spreading out on the grass.'

57 'often some nocturnal animal, a hedgehog or a weasel, launching itself after its prey, stirred the leaves, or they could hear, from time to time, a ripe peach falling untouched from the espalier'.

58 J. Culler, *Flaubert* (London: Elek, 1974), p. 100.

59 H. Levin, *The Gates of Horn* (New York: Oxford University Press, 1966), p. 62.

60 Pontalis J., 'La Maladie de Flaubert', *Après Freud* (Paris: Julliard, 1965), p. 311: 'what fascinates Flaubert is the substance of things, their bewitching presence and their decay, that sense entirely impregnated with matter which makes colours, smells, reveries'. See also his comments on fetishism, pp. 321-2. For other stimulating studies of the role of objects see G. Bollème, *La Leçon de Flaubert* (Paris: Julliard, 1964) and C. Duchet, 'Roman et Objets', *Europe,* 1969, pp. 172-201.

61 'the gilding of the barometer, struck by a ray of sunlight, displayed its fire in the mirror'.

62 M. Lowe, *Towards the Real Flaubert* (Oxford: Clarendon Press, 1984), p. 56.

63 'a breath of love had passed over the stitches in the canvas; each stitch the needle had made had fixed there a hope or a memory, and all the interwoven silk threads were merely the continuation of the same silent passion'.

64 'clad in a satin dress, wearing on her head a tulle veil studded with silver stars, and as brightly rouged on her cheeks as an idol from the Sandwich islands'.

65 Flaubert's original plan here had been to provide Esméralda with the counterpart of Judith, but since the latter's betrayal of the man stems from fidelity to her race, the irredeemable Potiphar's wife is chosen instead. An indication of the importance of this theme in Romantic, or rather frenetic, literature is provided by P. Borel's *Madame Putiphar.*

66 'on the plaster wall diagonally crossed by black joists can sometimes be

seen clinging a scanty pear tree, and the ground-floor rooms have a little
swinging gate at their doors, to prevent the chickens coming in as they
peck on the threshold at crumbs of brown bread steeped in cider'.

67 'Disdainful of crosses, titles and learned bodies, hospitable, generous,
paternal with the poor and practising virtue without believing in it,
he would almost have passed for a saint, were it not that the finesse
of his mind made him as feared as a demon. His glance, sharper than his
scalpels, went straight into your soul, and tore apart every lie through your
allegations and your shame.'

68 *Les Métamorphoses du cercle* (Paris: Plon, 1961), p. 390: 'like a series of focal
points from which fan out, forwards, backwards and on all sides, a series
of objects and a network that is at once temporal and spatial'.

69 See G. Müller, 'Erzählzeit und erzählte Zeit', in *Morphologische Poetik*
(Darmstadt: Wissenschaftliche Buchgesellschaft, 1968), pp. 269–86.

70 'since the events that are about to be related, nothing, indeed, has changed
in Yonville'.

71 See G. Genette, *Figures III* (Paris: Editions du Seuil, 1972), p. 105. On the
time scales in *Madame Bovary* see also M. Vargas Llosa, *The Perpetual Orgy*
(London: Faber, 1978), pp. 163 ff., and C. Gothot-Mersch, 'Aspects de
la temporalité dans les romans de Flaubert', in *Flaubert, la dimension du
texte*, ed. P. M. Wetherill (Manchester: Manchester University Press, 1982)
pp. 6–55.

72 'today it would be impossible for any of us to remember anything
about him'.

73 'he could have been handsome, witty, distinguished and attractive, like,
no doubt, those whom her former convent classmates had married. What
were they doing now?'

74 For example, the opening sentence of Part III, chapter 9.

75 See also G. Genette, *Figures III* (Paris: Edition du Seuil, 1972), p. 111, and
chapter 4, 'Transitions', p. 51 ff.

76 'but how will I get rid of her afterwards?'

77 'one evening when the window was open'; 'it was a Sunday in February,
an afternoon when it was snowing'.

78 'the same thing happened on the following days'; 'it was a Thursday. She
would rise and dress silently'; 'every day, at the same time'.

79 'grow more and more rotten in their cloudy alcohol'.

80 'never was Mme Bovary more beautiful than at that period'.

81 'nevertheless, in the immensity of that future she produced for herself,
nothing stood out: the days, each magnificent, were as alike as waves
in the sea'.

82 'a hole in her life'.

83 G. Finney, *The Counterfeit Idyll* (Tübingen: Max Neimeyer Verlag, 1984),
p. 42.

84 ibid, p. 43.

85 Baudelaire, *Œuvres complètes* (Paris: Pléiade, 1976), II, p. 40: 'there is a
cohort of poets besotted by pagan pleasure, who constantly use the terms
saint, ecstasy, prayer, etc., to qualify things and beings that have nothing
saintly or ecstatic about them, indeed the contrary would be true'.

86 Baudelaire, *Correspondance* (Paris: Pléiade, 1973), I, p. 182: 'be my guardian
angel, my Muse and my Madonna, and lead me in the path of Beauty'.

87 Nerval, *Œuvres* (Paris: Pléiade, 1974), p. 242: 'we were intoxicated with
poetry and love. Love, alas! of vague shapes, of blue and pink shades,
of metaphysical phantoms! Seen from close up real women offended our

ingenuity; they had to appear as queens or goddesses, and above all you had to refrain from going near them.'

88 'in my soul you are like a Madonna on a pedestal, in a lofty, solid and immaculate place'; 'he stretched out his arm and put it round her waist'; 'lethargically'; 'swooning'.

89 'her being, flying towards God, was going to annihilate itself in this love, as burning incense turns into vapour'.

90 'swooning with celestial joy she moved her lips to accept the Saviour's body as it was offered to her'.

91 'Emma was praying, or rather endeavouring to pray, hoping that a sudden decision would descend from heaven; and, to summon divine aid, she filled her eyes with the splendours of the tabernacle, breathed in the perfume of the white rocket flowers in their large vases, and listened to the silence of the church.'

92 '[the priest] dipped his right thumb in the oil and began the unctions: first, on her eyes, which had so deeply desired the sumptuous delights of the earth; then on her nostrils, which had been so fond of warm breezes and the smells of love; then on her mouth, which had opened for lies, groaned with pride and screamed in lust; then on her hands, which had delighted in soft contacts, and finally on the soles of her feet, which had in the past run so quickly to satisfy her desires and which now would never walk again'.

93 Although it has been argued that such portrayals merely represent the reality of a time when insecticides did not exist, the metaphorical reading is still, I believe, both explicit and unavoidable.

94 'she found . . . the same clumps of nettles around large pebbles, the patches of lichen along the three windows, whose shutters were always closed and were falling apart with rot, over their rusty iron bars'.

95 'the unconquerable decay climbed continuously from his limbs towards his stomach'.

96 'where did it come from, this insufficiency of life, this instant decay of the things she relied on? . . .'

97 'like the moles I could see in the branches, their stomachs full of worms, croaked, in a word'.

98 'from all those great black squares with their gold borders emerged, here and there, a lighter area of the painting, a pale brow, two eyes which looked at you, wigs . . . or a garter buckle above a well-moulded calf'.

99 'no one, after all, has died as a result of this'.

100 'so perspicaciously and so terrifyingly that she trembled to the very centre of her being': 'Well, so what! when someone has friends as you do.'

101 'every smile hid a yawn of boredom, every joy a curse, every pleasure its disgust, and the best kisses left on your lips only the unachievable longing for a higher pleasure'.

102 For a slightly different reading see F. Jameson, *The Political Unconscious*, p.184.

CHAPTER 7

The spur of style

Ma mère me dit que la rage des mots m'a desseché le cœur
(Flaubert)

The constant desire to create beauty, with the insistence on the importance of style, posed Flaubert major problems in a novel in which the apparently hackneyed nature of the subject matter, and the banality of the sentiments, hardly made for the stuff of which fine style is traditionally created. Convinced that what was most beautiful and rare in prose was the purity of the sound[1] and that the reader's initial response is based on auditory responses, physical rather than intellectual or moral, he worked with almost manic intensity to banish infelicities of sound or rhythm. The physical intensity of his response can be gauged by such statements as the following: 'le style, qui est une chose que je prends à cœur, m'agite les nerfs horriblement, je me dépite, je me ronge. Il y a des jours où j'en suis malade et la nuit j'en ai la fièvre.'[2] Frequently his letters contain complaints of days spent avoiding unintended assonances, of discovering in every sentence words that had to be changed. Concatenations of 'qui' and 'que', for instance, are ruthlessly mocked in his letters, and excised from his novel. The proliferation of drafts bears eloquent testimony to his refusal to rush over a sentence with which he was not yet satisfied, and reflects very clearly his search for a sonorous and rhythmical style, together with both a desire for rigorously correct metaphors and the sense that, as he puts it in an exuberant pastiche of Rabelais written to his friend Louis Bouilhet in December 1852:

toutes sortes grouillantes de papulles, acymes, phurunques et carbons (allégories innombrables et métaphores incongrues, ie veux dire) tousiours poussoyent emmy mes phrases, contaminant par leur luxuriance intempestive, la nice contexture d'icelles.[3]

Like a painter studying hands or expressions, Flaubert frequently tries out sentences or images, worrying away at them until either they reach his exacting standards or he abandons them completely.

In describing Charles's joy in the early days of his marriage to Emma, for instance, Flaubert struggled with a sentence for which he wrote at least ten separate versions before finally rejecting it. G. Leleu's edition of the drafts and fragments gives the various forms of this sentence under the rubric 'étude de phrase'. Certain aspects of Charles's new wife, Flaubert writes, in yet another image lending concrete form to emotions by a parallel with buildings, 'distillaient des voluptés muettes de toutes les parois de sa vie'. This then becomes: 'distillaient silencieusement des voluptés muettes filtrant de toutes les parois de sa vie', as Flaubert struggles with the rhythm, and works to make the image itself more convincing. The slightly awkward long adverb is replaced by an adverbial phrase and the participle exchanged for full verbs in a third version which, also extends the image: 'distillaient en silence quantité de voluptés muettes qui tombaient, qui filtraient de toutes les parois de sa vie, comme les gouttelettes régulières qui tombent sans s'arrêter du haut des stalactites'. Yet this creates a cacophony of 'quantité' and 'volupté', as well as the assonances of 'distillaient', 'tombaient' and 'filtraient', not to mention the repetition of the verb 'tomber'. Flaubert's fourth version of the sentence, therefore, reads as follows: 'distillaient [sur tout lui], sur son cœur, quantité de joies silencieuses qui tombaient, qui filtraient de toutes les parois de sa vie, comme tombent dans une grotte les gouttelettes régulières qui pendent aux stalactites'.[4] Still dissatisfied with this version, he produced several more before reaching this one: 'lui distillaient de toutes les parois de son existence quantité de voluptés silencieuses sur le cœur, comme tombent dans une grotte les gouttelettes des stalactites sur la nappe d'eau qui n'est ridée que par elles seules'.[5] Yet even this finely honed version is eventually rejected, perhaps because the complexity of the image, coming so hard on the heels of the famous comparison between Charles ruminating his happiness and those savouring the taste of the truffles they have just eaten, would have seemed more than a little baroque. Moreover, while the comparison with food is clearly close to Charles' own experience, the more unusual evocation of stalactites and subterranean pools would be difficult to attribute to his consciousness rather than to an external narrative voice.

Indeed, several suppressions seem to result from an awareness that a particular image runs counter to the psychological truth of the character concerned. Emma's musings over what might have been had she not married Charles initially provoked a comparison that does not accord with the depiction of her as more sentimental than artistic: 'comme un poète qui combine, elle cherchait à trouver, dans sa tête, des aventures non survenues'.[6] The reference to the poet is of course absent from the final text.

A further example of this desire both for stylistic perfection and for appropriateness in the choice of image is provided by the passage exploring Emma's longing to confide in a sympathetic mind her sense of disappointment in her marriage. Emma's problem here is not merely the social one of having no one of her own class and age available in the small community of Tostes, but also the linguistic difficulty of pinning down vague and fleeting emotions. An early version has the following formulation:

> Conter ses songes, c'est en jouir davantage et se consoler de leur mensonge. Mais comment s'y prendre pour exposer en détail le tourment confus, qui gît on ne sait où, qui change de forme, un désir qui change de but, un regret de ce qu'on n'a pas eu? C'est fixer la nuée qui passe, la pensée qui fuit. Les mots lui manquaient, l'occasion, la hardiesse.[7]

The first sentence of this passage was suppressed at an early stage, perhaps because it states, rather flatly, an obvious truism, or perhaps because it recalls too closely the kind of authorial intervention common to the novels of Balzac or Stendhal, but rejected by Flaubert's desire for narrational impersonality. 'Tourment confus' was replaced by the more euphonious and forceful 'insaisissable malaise', and the final sentence was rendered more rhythmical by the insertion of 'donc' after 'manquaient'. Most important, the rather dull initial comparison between the sense of dissatisfaction and the fleeting clouds is strengthened by a reference to the rapidity with which clouds change their form and by the addition of a second, more forceful analogy: 'qui tourbillonne comme le vent' (43), 'which swirl around like the wind'.

A further preoccupation revealed by the drafts as well as by statements in his letters is the value Flaubert places on concision, a belief he frequently attempts to impose on the prolix Louise Colet. A passage describing Charles's boredom in the early days at Yonville shows how ruthlessly Flaubert rejected phrases and images not essential to the psychological or dramatic needs of the novel. An early draft of this passage ran as follows:

> Cependant Charles paraissait triste ou préoccupé du moins: la clientèle n'arrivait pas. Depuis le temps que son prédécesseur était parti, les gens d'Yonville avaient pris l'habitude d'un médecin des environs et il fallait du temps pour se faire un nom, comme disait le pharmacien. . . Les journées donc lui semblaient longues et les soirs surtout, où, ne lisant pas, il restait assis auprès du feu, les bras croisés, l'œil béant et ne disant mot; il s'employa d'abord comme homme de peine dans la maison, il rangea le bois, nettoya le jardin.[8]

The published version is far shorter, excising the explanation of why it needed time to attract patients, and removing the unnecessary nuances of the opening sentence. The image of Charles staring into emptiness is replaced, perhaps because it suggests a capacity for dream, by a depiction of him either sleeping or watching Emma sew, alternatives which evoke both a lack of inner reserves and his love for his wife: 'Charles était triste: la clientèle n'arrivait pas. Il demeurait assis pendant de longues heures, sans parler, allait dormir dans son cabinet ou regardait coudre sa femme. Pour se distraire, il s'employa chez lui comme homme de peine.'(90)[9]

This desire for concision may well lie behind the suppression of various passages where the intensity of imagination or the irruption of comedy may leave the reader regretting their absence from the final version. One thinks in particular of the episode with the coloured glass after the Vaubyessard ball, where Emma, looking through different colours at the surrounding countryside, explores the effects on her emotions of these transformations. Perhaps the image seemed too obvious, too laboured for Flaubert's purposes: nevertheless the description is not without a certain charm, and it points forward interestingly to Huysmans's experimentations in *A rebours*:

> A travers les bleus, tout semblait triste. Une buée d'azur, répandue dans l'air, allongeait la prairie et reculait les collines. Le sommet des verdures était velouté doucement par une poussière marron pâle, floconnée sur le dessus, comme s'il fût tombé de la neige. En face, dans un champ, bien loin, un feu d'herbes sèches, qui brûlait, avait des flammes d'esprit de vin. Mais par les vitres jaunes, les feuilles des arbres étaient plus petites, le gazon plus clair et le paysage en entier comme découpé dans du métal; on eût dit l'atmosphère illuminée. C'était joyeux; il faisait chaud dans cette grande couleur topaze, délayée d'émeraude.
>
> Elle mit son œil au carreau vert, et tout fut vert: le sable, l'eau, les fleurs, la terre elle-même se confondant avec les gazons. Puis, sous le reflet de pourpre qui dévorait tout de sa couleur, la verdure était grise, la rivière coulait comme un fleuve rose, les plates-bandes de terreau semblaient des mares de sang caillé, le ciel immense amoncelait des incendies. Elle eut peur. Alors, par la fenêtre aux verres blancs, tout à coup, le jour ordinaire reparut.[10]

However much one may regret the suppression of this passage, elsewhere the desire for compactness has led to the removal of comparisons whose lengthy unfolding would have slowed down the inexorable forward progress of the final draft. Léon's musings on Emma as archetypal mistress are so dense and taut in the final version that they lay bare the paucity of his imagination and the clichéd nature of his love, based on his knowledge of novels, plays and poetry, and on the stereotypes of contemporary painting (271). In previous drafts, a more prolix presentation ran the risk of letting the reader participate too much in the vision created to allow the intervention of irony. An introductory sentence was excised at an early stage, perhaps because it simply sums up what is to come, and is too heavy-handed in its analysis, rather than leaving the reader to draw the conclusions: 'Emma réalisait pour l'apprenti procureur quantité de ces types vagues que les adolescents plus ou moins rêvent dans les livres et qui leur sortent ensuite de la cervelle, par défaut de mémoire ou d'imagination.'[11] The teasing out of the reference to books is also unnecessarily detailed, offering a close parallel to the description of Emma's convent reading, and the vignettes she gazed at, without adding much to what the reader already knows about the sources of Léon's erotic imagination:

> Elle valait bien la fiancée de toutes les romances, l'héroïne de tous les drames, le vague *elle* des volumes de vers. Il retrouvait sur ses épaules la splendeur de l'Odalisque au bain qu'il avait convoitée jadis d'après une lithographie montrant une femme nue au bord de l'eau sous un platane. Elle avait la taille allongée et mince des châtelaines féodales et elle ressemblait aussi (parce qu'alors c'était la mode), à la femme pâle aux baisers muets, qui porte des mitaines noires jusqu'au coude et soupire sur les balcons. Ainsi tour à tour ou à la fois sultane, senora, princesse, Elvire, mais elle était par-dessus tout l'Ange.[12]

Significant, too, is the decision to replace 'valait bien', which suggests an equivalence, with 'était', which proposes an personality, and more precisely shows Léon stripping Emma of her own identity to impose instead a tamed and manageable stereotype.

Other suppressions seem motivated above all by an eagerness to reject authorial comment. Emma's desire for a son is clarified in the drafts by somewhat unsubtle irony, which the final version leaves to the reader's own percipience:

> Car elle croyait, précisément parce que le seul homme qu'elle connaissait n'était pas ainsi, que les hommes sont énergiques. Chaque sexe ainsi, par ignorance de l'autre, lui suppose des qualités qu'il n'a pas, comme les siècles supposent aux siècles précédents, des énergies que la distance seule leur donne.[13]

The comparison with past ages here clearly does little to further the meaning of the text, and the reference to energy may well have struck Flaubert as smacking too much of Stendhal or Balzac. A further suppression which seems to have been determined by the belief in an impersonal narrative, occurs when Emma, at an early stage of her marriage, attempts to make herself fall in love with Charles. Here the comparison between early and final versions reveals not only the removal of authorial comment, but also the value of concision, for whereas the published text has: 'd'après des théories qu'elle croyait bonnes, elle voulut se donner de l'amour' (45),[14] Flaubert had originally written: 'elle essaya (facticement, et d'après des théories qui, du moment qu'elles étaient théories, étaient fausses, anti-naturelles), de l'exciter et de s'exciter'.[15]

Although, as the novel proceeds, authorial intervention in the drafts becomes less frequent, suppressions from later chapters continue to reveal the intensity with which the ideal is pursued. The exploration of Emma's emotions in the hours after she has first made love with Rodolphe initially included an anticipatory warning: 'elle ne pensait pas à l'avenir; elle ne cherchait pas si Rodolphe l'aimerait'.[16] This rather obvious wink of complicity from writer to reader is removed from later versions. One final example of such suppressions indicates that Flaubert also excised authorial generalisations drawing too closely on his own experiences. Léon, for instance, is shown gradually recovering from his first, platonic love for Emma while still remaining irrevocably altered by it, in a passage which closely echoes Flaubert's own comments on the way in which his adolescent love for Mme Schlésinger coloured his subsequent emotional development. Having asserted that 'l'impression de la première femme est longue à s'effacer', Flaubert went on to write: 'Le désir que l'on en garde se tourne en habitude en une fonction normale et continue, puis il s'attache à vous et pénètre l'âme entière, comme ces maladies qui à force d'être portées finissent par devenir quelque chose de votre tempérament.'[17] Here, too, the reference to illness recalls Flaubert's own apparently epileptic condition.

This Proust-like comparison between love and illness is only one of many images suppressed or polished beyond recognition during the long process of writing *Madame Bovary*. An exploration of such images in the early drafts shows how much Flaubert was aware of what later critics were to perceive as a weakness in his narrative skills. Indeed, in his wonderfully dense and suggestive study of Flaubert's style, Proust, for his

part, admits that if Flaubert's novels are not among his favourite
works it is because 'pour des raisons qui seraient trop longues
à développer ici, je crois que la métaphore seule peut donner
une sorte d'éternité au style, et il n'y a peut-être pas dans tout
Flaubert une seule belle métaphore'.[18] Flaubert's own position
as regards metaphor may well have been somewhat different, as
a sentence in a letter to Louise Colet implies: 'j'avais à faire un
passage psychologico-nerveux des plus déliés, et je me perdais
continuellement dans les métaphores, au lieu de préciser les
faits'.[19]

The first paragraph of chapter 10 in the second book, whether
or not it is the passage 'psychologico-nerveux' referred to in
Flaubert's letter, reveals the extent to which the finished text
acquires greater concision through the removal of metaphors.
The long explanation of why Emma feels so enervated on
returning from La Huchette and the associated comparison
suggesting that all her energy had been left behind on her
lover's bed[20] are replaced in the final version by a simple
presentation of her actions, with the reader left to draw any
necessary conclusions. The assertion that the sounds she hears
distress her because they seem to be calling her name is also left
to the reader's imagination. The principle here seems to be to
'faire rêver', to leave the drawing of conclusions to the reader
rather than supplement a passive reading by a series of explicit
comparisons and substitutions.

The draft versions, therefore, not only reveal the extent to
which Flaubert worked and reworked certain of his metaphors,
but also reinforce the artistic judgements expressed more
theoretically in his letters. Exploring Emma's feelings when
she begins to realize that she does not love Charles, or at
least that what she feels for him bears little relationship to
what her reading has led her to conceive as love, Flaubert
initially produced a somewhat complex and clumsy metaphor
for which he subsequently produced numerous alternatives:
Emma believes that had Charles shown any sympathy for her
plight 'une abondance de sentiment se serait alors épanchée
de son cœur, comme la chute d'un moulin, quand on casse
la glace au-dessus de l'écluse'.[21] In a long series of try-outs,
Flaubert substituted 'vanne' for 'écluse' and 'canal' for 'moulin',
removed the reference to ice and varied the verbs before trying

an image drawn from a quite different area: 'une abondance subite se serait détachée de son cœur, comme la récolte mûre d'un poirier, quand on secoue son feuillage'.[22] The reference to a specific fruit and the somewhat violent verb 'secouer' were then replaced by 'la récolte mûre d'un espalier, quand on touche au treillage' with the final clause eventually being transformed into 'quand on y porte les mains' (42).[23] It is interesting that both the initial image of water and the final one of fruit are very much part of the series of metaphors that recur in the novel and provide such an important element of its structure.

One final example of a series of experiments with possible images shows Flaubert moving between the exotic and the everyday in an attempt to find a visual analogue for Léon's sense of melancholy:

> étaient-ce seulement les perplexités d'une volonté trop timide ou [bien] cette tristesse particulière à toutes les passions profondes, et qui s'exhale d'elle [incessament],
>> comme fait la fumée des volcans?
>> comme la fumée des volcans se perd dans le vague des cieux, en spirales continues?
>> comme la fumée lente des vésuves endormis perd incessament au vent sa spirale continue?
>> comme une fumée de volcan pousse incessament dans le vague des vents sa spirale continue?
>> ...
>> comme la fraîcheur subtile des appartements fermés?
>> comme fait le froid dans les souterrains fermés?
>> comme fait le froid dans les appartements ténébreux?
>> comme une émanation naturelle?
>> comme la buée d'un gouffre?[24]

The initial symbol of the volcano, however much it might participate in the general imagery of Léon's imagination, recalling the description of Etna in Chateaubriand's *René*, or the tumultuous visit to the volcano in *Corinne,* nevertheless suggests too much energy to evoke accurately this indecisive young man. Obviously the reference to the spiral appealed through its evocation of the circle and its suggestion of patterns of repetition. But the image of melancholy linked to cold or mist and above all, perhaps, associated with the more familiar physical referent of cellars or appartments, fits more closely into the general pattern of imagery in the novel and creates an interesting comparison with the stalactites' image Flaubert had contemplated using for Charles. Perhaps the decision to omit this image altogether reflects yet again a desire to suggest rather than explain, to indicate Léon's melancholy without having recourse to the generalising voice of an external narrator. Certainly the dogged repetition and revision of images and sentences reveals the extent to which Flaubert believed in the comment he made to Louise Colet in 1852: 'dans un bouquin comme celui-là, une déviation d'une ligne peut complètement m'écarter du but, me le faire rater tout à fait'.[25] And he adds, in a remark which shows how much he shared the convictions of Baudelaire and Poe about the total effect of a work of art: 'au point où j'en suis, la phrase la plus simple a pour le reste une portée infinie. De là tout le temps que j'y mets.'[26]

Flaubert's manipulation of what he terms the anatomy of style[27] is evident not just in the choice of image and metaphor but also in the sound patterns created. The obsessive repetition of desire is paralleled and underpinned by obsessive sound patterning, particularly around such words as 'pourriture' 'passant' and 'poussière'.[28] One example of the many suggestions he draws from such phonetic devices is provided by the description of Emma's creation of a funeral monument to her mother. The whipping up of emotions according to a pre-established pattern – 'elle se laissa donc glisser dans les méandres lamartiniens, écouta les harpes sur les lacs, tous les chants de cygnes mourants, toutes les chutes de feuilles' (40)[29] – indicates through the very sound patterns of the sentence not merely repetition (the assonances of the nasals, the alliteration of sybillants) but also an unambiguous echo of the despised 'cœurs médiocres' taken up in the repeated hard *c* and the *mé* of *méandres*. A further example, again drawing on the repetition of the *p* and the sybillants, comes at the point where Emma, with more pusillanimity than virtue, repulses Léon's advances and the text reveals through the sounds used the degree of bottled-up anger her frustrated desires arouse in her:

Ce qui la retenait, sans doute, c'était la paresse ou l'épouvante, et la pudeur aussi. Elle songeait qu'elle

l'avait repoussé trop loin, qu'il n'était plus temps, que
tout était perdu. Puis l'orgueil, la joie de se dire: "Je suis
vertueuse", et de se regarder dans la glace en prenant des
poses résignées, la consolait un peu du sacrifice qu'elle
croyait faire (111).[30]

The psychological analysis here, with its subtle nuances and
careful discriminations, is supported by the memories set in train
by the alliteration. But it is also a product of a further aspect
central to Flaubert's endeavour, rhythm; and although a detailed
study of the effects he derives from the various rhythms he uses
exceeds the bounds and purposes of this book, some indication
should be given of what he achieves.[31] The extent to which
Flaubert uses the balances of his sentences to suggest further
layers of meaning or to intensify the surface meaning is revealed
by the passage just quoted, exploring Emma's frustration when
she is unable to transform her desire for Léon into action: 'ce
qui la retenait, sans doute, c'était la paresse et l'épouvante, et
la pudeur aussi. Elle songeait qu'elle l'avait repoussé trop loin,
qu'il n'était plus temps, que tout était perdu.' (111)[32] In the first
of these sentences, the way in which the phrases are broken up,
with the intervention of 'sans doute' and the tacking on of 'et
la pudeur aussi', suggests the lax structures of Emma's own
thought patterns, contrasting sharply and deliberately with the
narrative voice's own more firmly welded constructions. The
tripartite balance of the second sentence, though typical of the
novel's rhythmical patterns, is more evocative in this context of
the obsessive repetitions of a spoken complaint. Those ternary
balances, while frequent in French literary writing, are very
much part of the narrative voice's language, often allowing a
sense of the psychological complexity of a character or situation,
as in the following evocation of Emma: 'alors, les appétits de la
chair, les convoitises d'argent et les mélancolies de la passion,
tout se confondit dans une même souffrance' (111),[33] or in
this ironic depiction of her through the eyes of others: 'les
bourgeoises admiraient son économie, les clients sa politesse, les
pauvres sa charité', mocked both semantically and rhythmically
in the sentence which immediately follows: 'mais elle était pleine
de convoitises, de rage, de haine' (110).[34]

Indeed, the awareness that the meaning of a phrase or sentence is in part a product of the rhythms created by the words dominated many of Flaubert's stylistic struggles. Lieuvain's rhythmic blunder in his evocation of the hen, where the long and rounded clauses fall abruptly into bathos with 'et des œufs' (149) and the apparently self-generating phrases evoking the possibilities of disaster in days gone by – 'le temps n'est plus . . . où la discorde civile ensanglantait nos places publiques, où le propriétaire, le négociant, l'ouvrier lui-même, en s'endormant le soir d'un sommeil paisible, tremblaient de se voir réveillés tout à coup au bruit des tocsins incendiaires, où les maximes les plus subversives sapaient audacieusement les bases. . .' (146)[35] as well as his marvellously ridiculous mixed metaphor of the chariot of state being guided by a firm hand in the perils of a stormy sea, all signpost pitfalls for those who seek to manipulate language. Equally, Larivière's pun at Homais's expense – Mme Homais's fears that her husband thickens his blood by falling asleep after dinner provoke from the learned doctor the comment: 'Oh! ce n'est pas le *sens* qui le gêne' (329)[36] – shows Flaubert using direct dialogue to reveal some of the problems encountered by him as writer in creating his novel.

Dominant in the rhythmical nature of *Madame Bovary* is the frequent use of the imperfect tense, which, more than either the more variable present or past historic, invests the text with a degree of heaviness, a sense of unchanging repetition. Thus, Emma's sense of boredom and inescapable monotony is conveyed to us as much by the rhythms as by the surface meaning in a passage describing their time at Tostes and in particular Charles's return from work each night:

> il disait les uns après les autres tous les gens qu'il avait rencontrés, les villages où il avait été, les ordonnances qu'il avait écrites, et satisfait de lui-même, il mangeait le reste du miroton, épluchait son fromage, croquait une pomme, vidait sa carafe, puis s'allait mettre au lit, se couchait sur le dos et ronflait (43).[37]

Here the insistent rhythms determined by the imperfect endings and by the way in which the accumulated weight of the sentence descends on 'ronflait' reveals the unbridgeable gap between, on the one hand, Charles's sense of satisfaction and his pleasure in the meal, which is what is conveyed by the surface meaning, and, on the other, Emma's feelings of repugnance, implied by the sentence's structure.

However much the rhythms, the sound patterns, the rejection of over-explicit narrational comments and the search for concision may seem to indicate an approach to writing based on intellect and rationality, however much Flaubert's stylistics serves the purposes of his psychology, there are also moments in the novel in which he conveys a sense of pure, almost physical joy in the act of writing and in particular in the possibility of description. This is not to suggest that such passages do not also serve other purposes, but rather to counter the image of Flaubert as uniquely intellectual. His own insistence on the physical nature of language, and his desire to make the reader experience organically what is described, are illustrated throughout the novel, particularly, perhaps, in those passages of description which, while they unquestionably set a mood, are not reducible to the evocation of physical correlatives for states of mind. One such example is the description already quoted of the Normandy cakes; another creates a landscape into which Emma stares, unseeing and unhearing:

> une rafale de vent fit se courber les peupliers, et tout à coup la pluie tomba; elle crépitait sur les feuilles vertes. Puis le soleil reparut, les poules chantèrent, des moineaux battaient des ailes dans les buissons humides, et les flaques d'eau sur le sable emportaient en s'écoulant les fleurs roses d'un acacia (124).[38]

None of this is appreciated by Emma, and the joyous celebration of the return of the sun is not shared by her, for her thoughts are solely with Léon.

However much, in his letters, Flaubert might give the impression of a writer struggling with a difficult and unrewarding task, *Madame Bovary* owes much of its pleasure to the constant tension it reflects between struggle and spontaneity, mental disgust and physical delight.

NOTES: CHAPTER 7

1 Corr, II, 137.
2 Corr, I, 475: 'style, which is something I take to heart, sets my nerves

horribly on edge. I fret and fly into rages. There are days when it makes me ill and the following night it puts me into a fever.'

3 Corr, II, 215: 'a whole teeming host of papules, boils, furuncles and pustules (countless allegories and incongruous metaphors, I mean) are always bursting up in my sentences, contaminating by their untimely luxuriance the neat structure of the latter'.

4 Ebauches, I, p. 137-8: 'distilled mute pleasure from all the walls of his life'; 'silently distilled mute pleasures filtering through all the walls of his life'; 'distilled in silence numerous mute pleasures that dropped and filtered from all the walls of his life like the regular drops that fall unceasingly from the tip of stalactites'; 'distilled [over his whole being] over his heart, numerous silent joys which dropped and filtered from all the walls of his life as there fall in a cave the regular droplets hanging from the stalactites'.

5 ibid., p. 139: 'distilled into his heart from all the walls of his existence numerous silent pleasures, as, in a cave, the droplets fall from the stalactites on the sheet of water that they alone disturb'.

6 Ebauches, I, p. 194: 'like a poet combining possibilities, she tried to discover in her imagination adventures that had not taken place'.

7 ibid., p. 169: 'to tell one's dreams is to take further delight from them, and to console oneself for the fact that they are a lie. But how can one set about explaining in detail a confused turmoil, whose centre lies one knows not where, which changes shape, a desire whose object alters, a regret for what one has not had? It would be like fixing the passing cloud, the fleeting thought. Words failed her, she lacked the opportunity and the courage.'

8 ibid., pp. 339-40: 'meanwhile Charles seemed sad, or at least preoccupied: the patients weren't coming. Since the departure of his predecessor, the people at Yonville had grown used to a doctor who worked in the vicinity and it took time to make a name for oneself, as the apothecary used to say ... So the days seemed long to him and the evenings even more so, for then, he would sit by the fire, not reading, arms folded, gazing into space and not saying a word; at first he did the tasks around the house, stacking the wood and tidying the garden.'

9 'Charles was sad: the patients weren't coming. He would sit for long hours, not speaking, would go and sleep in his study or watch his wife sew. To give himself something to do, he did the heavy tasks around the house.'

10 Ebauches I, pp. 235-6: 'through the blues everything seemed sad. An azure haze, floating in the air, made the meadow seem longer and the hills further away. The crowns of the trees took on a soft velvet texture with a cover of pale brown dust which had fallen on top of them as if snow had been falling. Opposite, in a far-off field, a fire of dry grass burnt with flames the colour of spirits of wine. But through the yellow panes, the leaves of the trees were smaller, the grass brighter and the whole countryside seemed made of metal; the atmosphere seemed illuminated. It was a joyous sight; it was warm in that great topaz glow, tinged with emerald.

She put her eye to the green pane, and everything was green: the sand, the water, the flowers, the very earth blended into the lawns. Then, under the purple reflection that devoured everything with its own colour, the greenery turned grey, the stream flowed like a pink river, the flower beds seemed lakes of clotted blood, the vast sky piled fire on fire. She was afraid. Then through the window with white panes there suddenly appeared the ordinary light of day.'

11 Ebauches, II, p. 364: 'for the trainee prosecutor, Emma gave form to a

host of those vague images adolescents dream up, more or less, from their
reading and which then leave their minds through lack of memory or of
imagination.'

12 ibid, pp. 364–5: 'she was certainly as good as the betrothed in all the
romances, the heroine of all the plays, the vague 'she' of volumes of
poetry. He rediscovered on her shoulders the splendour of the bathing
odalisque whom he had desired in the past as he gazed at a lithograph
showing a naked woman beside a river under a plane tree. She had the
long, slim waistline of feudal chatelaines and she also resembled (since it
was at that time fashionable to do so) the pale woman of the silent kisses,
who wears black gloves reaching to her elbows and sighs on balconies. Thus
she was, by turns and simultaneously, sultana, señora, princess, Elvira, but
above all she was the Angel.'

13 Ebauches, I, p. 347: 'for she believed, precisely because the one man she
knew was not like that, that men are energetic. Thus each sex, through
ignorance, assumes the other has qualities it does not possess, as each
century supposes that preceding centuries had energies that distance alone
grants them.'

14 'according to theories she believed to be valid, she wanted to make herself
fall in love'.

15 Ebauches, I, p. 190: 'she attempted (artificially and on the basis of theories
which, given that they were theories, were false and anti-natural) to excite
both Charles and herself'.

16 Ebauches, II, p. 22: 'she gave no thought to the future; she did not seek to
know whether Rodolphe would love her'.

17 ibid, p. 257: 'the impression of the first woman is slow to fade'; 'the desire
one continues to feel becomes a habit, a normal and continuous function,
then it clings to you and penetrates your entire soul, like those illnesses
which you suffer from for so long that they end by becoming a part of
your own nature.'

18 'A propos du "style" de Flaubert', in *Contre Sainte-Beuve* (Paris: Gallimard,
1971), p. 586: 'for reasons I have not the space to develop here, I believe
that metaphor alone can give a form of eternity to style, and there may well
not be in all Flaubert's works a single beautiful metaphor'.

19 Corr, II, p. 514: 'I had to write a really slender psychologico-nervous
passage, and I was continually getting lost in the metaphors instead of
pulling my facts into focus.'
J. Bruneau suggests that this may be the passage at the beginning of Part
II, chapter 10, where Rodolphe's fears of detection begin to affect Emma.

20 Ebauches, II, p. 38.

21 Ebauches, I, pp. 169–70: 'an overflow of feeling would then have flooded
from her heart, like the water-fall in a mill when the ice above the lock is
broken'.

22 ibid, p. 171: 'a sudden abundance of feeling would have fallen from her
heart, like the ripe harvest of a pear-tree, when its leaves are shaken'.

23 'the ripe harvest of an espalier, when you touch the trellis'; 'when you touch
it with your hands'.

24 Ebauches, I, pp. 388–9: 'was it simply the perplexities of a willpower which
was too weak, or [else] that sorrow which is characteristic of all profound
passions and which [constantly] emanates from them, as smoke does from
volcanoes?
as smoke from volcanoes disappears into the far horizons, in continuous
spirals?

as the slow smoke from dormant Etnas ceaselessly loses its continuous spiral in the wind?

as the smoke of a volcano ceaselessly pumps into the formless winds its continuous spiral?

. . .

like the subtle coolness of closed apartments?

as the cold air does in closed basements?

as the cold air does in dark apartments?

like a natural emanation?

like the mist over an abyss?'

25 Corr, II, 156: 'in a book like this, a deviation of a single line can lead me entirely off course, and make me miss my goal completely'.

26 ibid: 'at the point I've reached, the simplest sentence has an incalculable bearing on the rest. Hence all the time I'm putting into it.'

27 Corr, II, 427.

28 This aspect has been explored by my PhD student, Adam Piette, in his Cambridge University thesis *Memory and Rhyme in the Prose of Proust, Joyce and Beckett.*

29 'so she allowed herself to glide along Lamartinian meanders, she listened to harps on lakes, all the songs of dying swans, all the falling leaves'.

30 'What held her back, in all probability, was laziness or horror, and shame, too. She thought she had driven him too far off, that the time had passed, that all was lost. Then the pride, the joy of saying to herself: "I am virtuous", and of looking at herself in the mirror as she assumed resigned poses, consoled her a little for the sacrifice she believed she was making.'

31 For a more detailed study of this aspect see G. Bollème, *La Leçon de Flaubert.*

32 'what held her back, no doubt, was laziness and horror, and modesty, too. She used to think she had driven him too far off, that the time was no longer ripe, that all was lost.'

33 'then, the appetites of the flesh, the lust for money, and the melancholy of passion, all blended in a single sense of suffering'.

34 'the housewives admired her economy, the patients her politeness, the poor her charity': 'but she was full of lust, rage, hatred'.

35 'Those days are gone when civil discord stained with blood our public squares, when the proprietor, the merchant, even the worker, falling peacefully asleep at night trembled to find themselves awakened suddenly by the sound of fire alarms, when the most subversive maxims audaciously undermined the foundations . . .'

36 The pun on 'sang' (blood) and 'sens' (sense) can perhaps best be rendered in English by: 'It's not his blood that's thick'.

37 'he would recount one after the other all the people he had met, the villages where he had been, the prescriptions he had written, and satisfied with himself, he would eat the remains of the boiled beef, peel his cheese, empty his carafe, then go off to bed, lie flat on his back and snore'.

38 'a gust of wind bent the poplars, and suddenly the rain fell; it drummed on the green leaves. Then the sun reappeared, the hens cackled, sparrows fluttered in the damp bushes, and puddles on the sand carried with them as they flowed away the pink flowers of an acacia.'

CHAPTER 8

The critical response

Triste chose que la critique
(Flaubert)

The publication of *Madame Bovary* and the notoriety it received as a result of the trial provoked a flood of critical reviews in the periodical press, not merely in France, but also in Belgium and in North America.[1] For political as well as aesthetic reasons many of these were unmitigatedly hostile and were expressed with the unabashed virulence common at the time. For the majority of critics Flaubert's choice of subject matter would not have been seen as scandalous had Emma not only repented of her adulteries but also died as a direct result of them, rather than in reaction against the horrors of bankruptcy. As P. Moreau puts it, 'assurément, l'adultère, de part et d'autre, est en pratique et même en faveur, mais à condition que les apparences soient sauves'.[2] There were two further sins to be laid at Flaubert's door: first, and most centrally, his refusal to offer a direct judgement on the behaviour and fate of his protagonists; and, secondly, his decision to focus on characters who were seen as unrelievedly ordinary. Cuvillier-Fleury, a right-wing critic who was a regular contributor to the pro-government *Journal des débats*, is typical of many of his contemporaries in complaining that 'Flaubert y met du sien le moins qu'il peut: ni imagination, ni émotion, ni morale'.[3] Flaubert's refusal to offer an easily identifiable authorial viewpoint was seen as an abnegation of his duties as writer and led to his depiction by caricaturists as a cold-hearted surgeon dissecting his characters as though they were lifeless cadavers. Lemot's caricature on this theme, dating from as late as 1869, appears on the cover of the Garnier edition of *Madame Bovary*. Flaubert himself, however, had insisted as early as 1853 that 'il faut faire de la critique comme on fait de l'histoire naturelle, *avec absence de morale*'(original emphasis).[4] Sainte-Beuve, the doyen of French literary critics,[5] was torn between admiration for Flaubert's analysis and disquiet at his refusal to offer moral guidelines: 'est-ce moral', he asks, 'est-ce consolant? L'auteur ne semble pas s'être posé la question; il ne s'est demandé qu'une chose: Est-ce vrai?'[6] The Catholic novelist and critic Barbey d'Aurevilly, despite his disapproval of the subject matter, acknowledged his admiration for the language in which it was written, describing it as 'colorée, brillante, étincelante et d'une précision presque scientifique',[7] an opinion endorsed by the most perceptive of Flaubert's contemporaries, Baudelaire, who referred to the style as 'nerveux, pittoresque, subtil, exact'[8] and who recognized that in *Madame Bovary* was indeed revealed a new creative method.

Part of that new creative method lay in the depiction of the central character, seen by Sainte-Beuve as the archetypal woman, by Baudelaire as a blend of masculine and feminine traits, and by Barbey d'Aurevilly as a representation of the author himself: 'M. Flaubert est la Madame Bovary de son livre'. Baudelaire's insistence on what he defines as masculine tendencies in Emma – her lively imagination, her sudden bursts of energy, her love of seduction, her taste for domination and her astonishing appetite for life[9] – is no doubt one of the causes of an aspect of the critical response to the novel that has continued to the present day, the curiously ambiguous and sometimes downright misogynistic reaction to a character who does not conform to sexual stereotypes.[10] Equally important to the new creative method that Baudelaire mentions is the decision to explore the human condition through characters and events that appear irredeemably banal. For Baudelaire this was not only a brilliant piece of innovation but also the result of an intellectual wager: he imagines Flaubert deciding that society's love of the mediocre forced him to choose a trivial subject, to focus on an outworn theme, that of adultery, and thus to lock the most passionate of feelings into the most ordinary of adventures.[11] When Baudelaire presents this as Flaubert's greatest triumph, he is of course responding to the great weight of critical opinion according to which the characters and subject matter of *Madame Bovary* were unworthy of artistic attention. It was, however, some time before Baudelaire's judgement was accepted as a critical commonplace: as is well known, even so perceptive a critic as Henry James laments that Flaubert chose as 'special conduits of the life he proposed to depict, such inferior . . . human species'.[12]

The balance of critical opinion at the time of publication found in Flaubert's favour where his style was concerned and with regard to his observation both of external details and of the psychology of his characters. Where critics were antagonistic, they based their attacks on what they saw as an excessive number of descriptive passages and on the moral implications of authorial impassivity. The journalist Merlet, in an article written in 1860, complained, for example, that Flaubert was so possessed by the demon of the picturesque that his characters were mere descriptive machines,[13] while Monpont, in a monograph on adultery in contemporary literature, accused him of being neither a writer, nor a thinker, nor a profound observer, but nothing more than a form of objective daguerrotype.[14]

After Flaubert's death, the *succès de scandale* associated with the trial was forgotten, and critics focused less on the moral issues. Instead, two major critical approaches can be detected: that which, taking for granted the realism of the novels, attempted to find the sources of his inspiration in historical or literary documents or in the geographical characteristics of his native Normandy; and that which focused above all on his stylistic achievements.

To present-day readers and critics there is something mildly disturbing about the approach of a critic such as R. Dumesnil, who was so convinced that *Madame Bovary* was a novel 'calqué sur la réalité'[15] that he affirmed that all the characters had actually lived and set out to discover them. Other critics argued over whether Yonville was to be identified with Ry or with Forge-les-Eaux.[16] A generation familiar with, if not necessarily convinced by, the argument that language can have no external referent may find it both alien and amusing to explore such affirmations and the debates sparked off among citizens of other towns eager to claim the after all dubious privilege of being the model for Yonville. Studies devoted to what the novel owes to Louise Pradier's journals or to Louise Colet[17] have more to offer, but only in so far as they chart the immense gulf between what may have been Flaubert's raw material and the use he made of it.

The other major direction taken by Flaubert studies during the first fifty years after his death was the exploration of novelistic techniques, with Flaubert only gradually coming to be acknowledged as a master of the form not merely by critics but also – and often more cogently – by a wide range of creative writers.[18] Modern readers may well be surprised at the mealy-mouthed and grudging way in which many early critics assessed what he had achieved and the eagerness with which they point out what could be seen as stylistic or grammatical weaknesses. Indeed, contemporary habits were such that it was often left to creative writers rather than journalistic or academic critics to indicate the areas and the extent of Flaubert's innovations. Maupassant, whose own stylistic mastery owes a great deal to Flaubert, was one of the first to analyse the creative method revealed by the text: 'il imaginait d'abord des types; et, procédant par déduction, il faisait accomplir à ces êtres les actions caractéristiques qu'ils devaient fatalement accomplir avec une logique absolue, suivant leurs tempéraments'.[19] Zola was also adamant about Flaubert's importance in the formation of the novel, depicting him as a forester bringing light into the inextricably dense forest left by Balzac. Zola's interest, however, focuses uniquely on the subject matter, leaving aside the creative artistry: 'le premier caractère du roman naturaliste, dont *Madame Bovary* est le type, est la reproduction exacte de la vie, l'absence de tout élément romanesque'.[20]

Around the centenary of Flaubert's birth, three writers produced studies of Flaubert whose insight, complexity and originality ushered in a new era in appreciations of his work. In November 1919 the distinguished critic Thibaudet published in *La Nouvelle Revue française* an article entitled 'Une querelle littéraire sur le style de Flaubert', in which he asserted that Flaubert was not a great stylist, arguing that full verbal mastery was not one of Flaubert's natural gifts. In the following January Proust published in the same review his own richly suggestive refutation of Thibaudet's assertion, under the title 'A propos du "style" de Flaubert'. The critic's reply was published in March of that year and in 1922 appeared his influential full-length study, *Gustave Flaubert. 1821-1880. Sa vie, ses romans, son style*. The same

year saw the publication of Charles Du Bos's innovative article
'Sur le milieu intérieur dans Flaubert' in a collection of his essays,
Approximations I.

Proust's greatest contribution to Flaubert studies is argu-
ably his suggestion that what, until Flaubert's time, had been
expressed in terms of action could now be conveyed in terms
of impressions, and his forthright judgement of the novelist as:

> un homme qui par l'usage entièrement nouveau et person-
> nel qu'il a fait du passé défini, du passé indéfini, du participe
> présent, de certains prénoms et de certaines prépositions,
> a renouvelé presque autant notre vision des choses que
> Kant, avec ses Catégories, les théories de la Connaissance
> et la Réalité du monde extérieur.[21]

Proust's profound insight into the close relationship between
language and perception in the novel enters into Flaubert's
experiment with far more sympathy and originality than many
far lengthier and more apparently complex studies, and it should
be read by any serious student of *Madame Bovary*.

Thibaudet's exploration of Flaubert's creative writing is a
detailed and sympathetic attempt to trace the development of
his thought and of his techniques from his early to his final
works. Although he follows Sainte-Beuve's methods by drawing
very much on the novelist's biography in the conviction that the
cast of his mind was created above all by the family atmosphere,
Thibaudet also pays close attention to the novels as creative
artefacts, stressing above all the degree to which Flaubert
belongs to what he calls the race of the great creators of
images, and his ability to convey delicate and complex feelings
through physical correspondences.[22] Although, despite Proust's
riposte, he remains unrepentant about what he perceives as
stylistic flaws, Thibaudet nevertheless acknowledges Flaubert
as a master of psychological observation. His study is an urbane
and easily accessible introduction to the novel, although we may
feel that the biographical bias is at times more restrictive than
productive.

Du Bos, for his part, sets out to recreate and understand the
writer's consciousness by exploring, through a close reading not
only of the text but also of the correspondence, his perception
of the three great categories of beauty, truth and life. Very

much aware of the extent to which Flaubert represents what Du Bos terms the artistic rather than the bourgeois morality, the critic sets aside moral polemics to concentrate on what the physiologist Claude Bernard termed the *milieu intérieur* from which *Madame Bovary* derives. While Du Bos considers that *L'Education sentimentale* is Flaubert's masterpiece, his analysis of *Madame Bovary* reveals with sensitivity and subtlety the reasons why, as he puts it, the novel remains the artistic museum all aspiring novelists need to study and from which they derive continual sustenance. This intelligent and sympathetic response to the text deserves to be better known to modern readers.

Here it is worth abandonning briefly the chronological order followed so far in this survey, for Dubos's study was to prove a source of inspiration in terms of method for several critics who explored the evolution of certain themes and metaphors in Flaubert's writing with the aim of discovering his response to such central phenomena as space and time. Among the first of these was D. L. Demorest, whose *L'Expression figurée et symbolique dans l'œuvre de Gustave Flaubert*, first published in 1931, sets out to explore the symbolic dimension not merely of certain images, but also of characters like the wet-nurse and the blind man, of objects like the cactus Léon gives Emma, and of names such as Mlle Lebœuf, Lestiboudois and Hippolyte. J. P. Richard, in an imaginative and stimulating essay first published in 1954 as part of the collection *Littérature et Sensation*, revealed the precarious balance that exists in *Madame Bovary* between the individual's desire to incorporate the external world, conveyed for example in terms of food (the opening sentence of Richard's study, 'On mange beaucoup dans les romans de Flaubert' (there is a great deal of eating in the novels of Flaubert) has become a *locus classicus*) and the individual's tendency to become subsumed by that external world, a danger expressed above all in *Madame Bovary* through water imagery. A further turn of this method's screw is revealed by J. Pontalis, who by subjecting such networks of images to a psychoanalytical reading seeks to reveal the degree of fetishism Flaubert and his characters show in regard to objects. This leads him to the conclusion that 'quant à l'évolution catastrophique du destin de son héroïne, Flaubert la manifeste toujours comme si la corruption venait des choses plutôt que de la faillite des désirs'.[23] These very close readings of the text, although running the risk of forcing it into an alien grid, whether phenomenological or psychoanalytical, nevertheless uncover patterns that, although they may not have been consciously intended, are nevertheless revelatory.

In 1946 Erich Auerbach's epoch-making exploration of the ways in which Western literature tried to capture and represent the individual's awareness of reality[24] suggested further possible methods for the analysis of *Madame Bovary*. Auerbach's greatest contribution may well lie in his insistence on the mechanisms through which the interpretation of any scene in the novel is contained in its description rather than being the product of authorial interventions. As he puts it:

> in a series of pure pictures – pictures transforming the nothingness of listless and uniform days into an oppressive condition of repugnance, boredom, false hopes, paralyzing disappointments, and piteous fears – a gray and random human destiny moves towards its end.[25]

Despite the brevity of Auerbach's study of *Madame Bovary*, to which, given the ambitious scope of his work, he can allot only a few pages, his insights into Flaubert's ability to explore his characters' psychologies while remaining apparently detached from them remains both influential and pertinent.

Drawing on, and extending, these studies of the representation of forms of reality, G. Poulet, in his analysis of the literary depiction of space and time, and J. Rousset, in his examination of the interplay of form and meaning in a novel, both explored networks of metaphors running through Flaubert's work. Through his reading, and in particular through the attention he pays to intercutting circles, Poulet concludes that 'Flaubert est le premier qui . . . construise son roman comme une série de foyers à partir desquels, en avant, en arrière, de tous côtés, il y a un déploiement d'objets et un rayonnement à la fois temporel et spatial.'[26] Rousset, for his part, illuminates the devices Flaubert employs to reveal to us the inner consciousness of his characters, asserting that 'l'originalité de Flaubert sera dans la combinaison du point de vue de l'auteur et du point de vue de l'héroïne, leur alternance et leurs interférences, et surtout dans la prédominance accordée à la vision subjective du personnage en perspective.'[27] That vision, Rousset points out, is conveyed above all through a network of images based on windows, scenes viewed from on high and reveries stimulated by the sight of wide-open spaces.

Rousset's approach draws on both the analysis of metaphor and a further thread uniting a series of Flaubertian critics, the study of what Henry James called the 'point of view'. James's remarks were developed by P. Lubbock, whose assertion that 'the most obvious point of method is no doubt the difficult question of centre of vision'[28] needs to be seen in conjunction with a range of studies refining the concept of *style indirect libre*. The devices that enable Flaubert to convey the thoughts and speech of his characters by expressing them as part of the narrative discourse attracted the attention of linguistic critics from an early stage, notably M. Lips, S. Ulmann and A. Banfield, and more recently that of narratologists, especially F. K. Stanzel and D. Cohn.[29] While Lips's study, first published in 1926, deserves attention for its originality, Cohn's elegant, witty and thorough exploration of the topic offers an excellent starting point for any reader interested in seeing Flaubert's experiments as part of a broader pattern.

While some source studies may offer little more than anecdotal interest, a far more important and informative area of study, present from an early stage in the critical response to the text, has been the literary parallels, first between Flaubert and other writers, and secondly between his earlier and later works. Jean Bruneau has enriched our understanding of the novelist's early preparation in his study entitled *Les Débuts littéraires de Gustave Flaubert*, by drawing attention to the vast number of works read during the writing of *Madame Bovary*. This vast reading programme, indicated by the correspondence, ranges from Apuleius, Juvenal and Plutarch, through Shakespeare, Dante and Rabelais to contemporaries such as Hugo, Balzac and Champfleury. Above them all, however, towers Cervantes, whose direct influence on Flaubert, although explored by various critics,[30] could still be further analysed. Thanks to the existence of very detailed notes and manuscripts, *Madame Bovary*'s evolution from initial plan to finished work can be charted in minute detail and has attracted the scrutiny of numerous genetic critics: on the basis of the editions of these manuscripts compiled by the critic J. Pommier and the Rouen

librarian G. Leleu, the intellectual history of the work has been
closely explored, notably by C. Gothot-Mersch, M. J. Durry and
Geneviève Bollème.[31]

Several more general studies of the novel were published
in the 1960s and 1970s. Three of these, written mainly for
an undergraduate audience, combine elegance of exposition
with an unshaken conviction that Flaubert is indeed a master
of his craft. While V. Brombert and R. Sherrington both
enable the student of *Madame Bovary* to set the novel into
the broader context of Flaubert's novelistic production, A.
Fairlie's monograph remains a uniquely sensitive and concisely
suggestive statement, fully deserving its reputation as the best
introduction for readers of English.

Given the growing conviction of Flaubert's status as one
of the world's greatest novelists, it is hardly remarkable that
biographical studies of him have continued to appear. Enid
Starkie's *Flaubert, The Making of the Master*, for all the vindictive
hammering it receives from Julian Barnes in *Flaubert's Parrot*,
provides a workmanlike and sensible background study for those
who wish to see the development of the novelist's talent within
a biographical and social framework. By far the most detailed
study based on biographical and literary sources, however, is
Sartre's immense but unfinished *L'Idiot de la famille*, three
volumes of which appeared in 1970–71. Sartre's initial question,
one which remains central to his whole endeavour, is: 'what can
one know about a man?', in this instance, at least ostensibly,
of course, Gustave Flaubert. Through a highly imaginative
manipulation of the information at his disposal and using the
grid of an existentialist psychoanalysis, Sartre sets out to reveal
the forces and choices that made Flaubert the man and the writer
that he was. Whatever disagreements we may have, however
unconvinced we may be that the person under the microscope
is Flaubert rather than, say, Sartre himself, there is no denying
the excitement and originality of the study. Ian Collas's study of
the novel, using the psychoanalytical methods of both Freud and
Sartre,[32] is based on the curious, although not original premiss,[33]
that the financial mess is not enough to provoke suicide (the
experience of the Wall Street crash notwithstanding) and that
since so many images are derived from food, the real cause of
Emma's death can be traced back to her mother's failure to love

her as a child. While raising interesting points, such a thesis fails to convince partly through its refusal to set the whole question in historical context, partly because it draws rather naively on the already crude Freudian view of women, and partly because it constantly conflates Flaubert's Emma and Sartre's Flaubert.

The way in which Flaubert, through such devices as 'style indirect libre', apparently abnegates authorial responsibility and thereby forces the reader into accepting a more active pact with the writer, has attracted to him the attention of a further group, the *nouveaux romanciers*, particularly Robbe-Grillet and Nathalie Sarraute. Sarraute ushered in a new era in Flaubert criticism with her insistence on Flaubert as precursor of the new novel, particularly in what she sees as his use of language to reveal language's inability to refer to anything but itself, and in his vision of the novel as performing a more important and disruptive function than mere entertainment. As a result, D. La Capra claims, in his stimulating, if not always entirely convincing, study, *Madame Bovary on Trial*, 'the conviction that Flaubert's project in writing was a formalistic quest for pure art has by now unseated earlier views of him as a realist or as a frustrated romantic'.[34] Two critics in particular, J. Culler and T. Tanner, have drawn on these suggestions. Culler, in exploring what he suggestively terms the 'uses of uncertainty' in Flaubert's novels, affirms that 'the strategies of reading and interpretation must be understood as attempts to avoid boredom'[35] and argues that:

> in Flaubert not only is the production of meaning delayed or arrested, but the ironic distancing repeatedly suggests that such interpretative operations are made possible only by codes constructed of social clichés and empty imaginative syntheses.[36]

Culler also puts forward the suggestion that our sense of Emma's tragic destiny is a result not of any external or psychological force, but rather a product of the novel's style: 'Emma', he argues, 'is fated to be destroyed by the irony of Flaubert's prose.'[37] Yet this, surely, is to ignore Flaubert's frequently reiterated interest in portraying both social and psychological forces. T. Tanner, in a wide-ranging exploration of the theme of adultery in the European novel, points out how often the adulterous act itself is not described, but merely inscribed into the text as a nexus of silence. He argues that as a result of this 'the invisible, inaudible deed becomes a silence and an absence in the text that gradually spreads, effectively negating what *is* made audible and present'.[38] Here, too, the argument is vitiated by a failure to recall the historical context in which the novel was written: Flaubert had enough difficulties with the censors as it was, and the absence of any description of the act of adultery is far less likely to be a textual than a pragmatic strategy. According to Tanner, the silence surrounding the adulterous act is exacerbated by the way in which language can create objects – Tanner's example is Charles's schoolboy cap – that are *lisibles* but not *visibles*: 'such an object, and all that it implies, instead of making for a clarification and enrichment of consciousness, works to produce its confusion and obfuscation'.[39] I shall return in my conclusion to the question of whether or not Charles's cap cannot be visualized.

In recent years, however, there can be detected a movement away from this assertion of the non-representational function of Flaubert's text, and a return to the exploration of the mimetic.[40] Equally, questions concerning his use of myth and his exploration of the spoken language continue to attract attention.[41] Perhaps the greatest gap in studies devoted to *Madame Bovary* at present is in the field of feminist responses. L. Czyba's evaluation of women in Flaubert's novels lays some of the essential ground lines, but a gendered reading might begin to unravel many of the male-centred minsinterpretations that have grown up around the novel ever since Baudelaire depicted as masculine all Emma's positive and active attributes.

Whatever direction Flaubert criticism may take in the future, the degree to which his novels have been seen as exemplary and the way in which they have been used as the basis of a wide range of critical methods indicates not only their importance but also their enigmatic suggestiveness. Certainly no study of *Madame Bovary* can avoid the challenge of responding both to Flaubert's fascination (in both the positive and negative meaning of the word) with the external world and the questions he raises about the possibility of using language to convey either reality or truth.

NOTES: CHAPTER 8

1 For a detailed bibliography of contemporary articles see my *Baudelaire's Literary Criticism* (Cambridge: Cambridge University Press, 1981), pp. 318–19.

See also B. Weinberg, *French Realism* (New York: Modern Language Association, 1973) and, for a handy compendium of critical responses from George Sand to Michel Foucault, R. Debray-Genette's *Flaubert: miroir de la critique* (Paris: Firmin-Didot et Didier, 1970).

2 *Amours romantiques* (Paris: Hachette, 1963), p. 47: 'assuredly, adultery, by both parties, is both practised and popular, but on the condition that appearances are kept up'.

3 *Journal des débats*, 26 May 1857: 'Flaubert gives as little of himself as possible: there is neither imagination nor emotion nor morality'.

4 Corr, II, 451: 'literary criticism should be carried out as one carries out natural history, *morality should be completely absent*'.

5 Referred to on one occasion by Flaubert as 'ce lymphatique coco' (Corr, II, 45).

6 First published in a government paper, *Le Moniteur universel*, on 4 May 1857, reprinted in *Causeries du lundi*, XIII, pp. 346-63: 'is it moral? is it consoling? The author does not seem to have asked himself that question; he has asked himself but one thing: is it true?'

7 *Le Pays*, 6 October 1857: 'coloured, brilliant, sparkling and all but scientific in its precision'.

8 *Œuvres complètes* (Paris: Pléiade, 1976), II, 80: 'tense, picturesque, subtle, exact'.

9 Baudelaire, *Œuvres complètes*, II, 82-3.

10 See, for instance, A. de Lattre, *La Bêtise d'Emma Bovary*. Sartre, for his part, constantly stresses what he sees as the androgynous nature of Flaubert.

11 Baudelaire, *Œuvres complètes*, II, 80.

12 *The Art of Fiction* (New York: Oxford University Press, 1948), p. 135.

13 'Le Roman physiologique', *Revue européenne*, VIII, p. 718.

14 Monpont, *Les Chantres de l'adultère* (Paris: Ledoyen, 1859), p. 31.

15 *Gustave Flaubert: l'homme et l'œuvre* (Paris: Desclée de Brouwer, 1947), p. 7: 'copied from reality'.

16 See, for instance, G. Dubosc, 'La véritable Madame Bovary', *Journal de Rouen*, 22 November 1890, and R. Herval, *Les Véritables Origines de Madame Bovary* (Paris: Nizet, 1957).

17 See Chapter 2, p. 15.

18 One of the most exciting studies of *Madame Bovary* is that of Vargas Llosa, *The Perpetual Orgy*.

19 Maupassant's judgement appeared in his 'Etude sur Gustave Flaubert', published as the preface to *Lettres de G. Flaubert à G. Sand* (Paris: Charpentier, 1884): 'he would begin by imagining types; and, proceeding by deduction, he would make these beings carry out the characteristic actions which they were fated to carry out with complete logicality, according to their temperaments'.

20 Zola, 'Romanciers naturalistes: Flaubert', p. 126: 'the first characteristic of the naturalist novel, of which *Madame Bovary* is the archetype, is the exact reproduction of life, the absence of every novelistic element'.

21 *Contre Sainte-Beuve* (Paris: Pléiade, 1971), p. 586. G. Bollème, in *La Leçon de Flaubert* (Paris: Julliard, 1964) explores in detail the points Proust touches on here: 'a man who, by the entirely new and personal use he made of the past historic, the imperfect, the present participle, certain pronouns and certain prepositions, has renewed our vision of things almost as much as Kant, with his Categories, changed our theories of the knowledge and reality of the external world'.

22 *Gustave Flaubert* (Paris: Librairie Plon, 1922), p. 227.

23 J. Pontalis, 'La Maladie de Flaubert', *Après Freud* (Paris: Julliard, 1965),

p. 324: 'as for the catastrophic evolution of his heroine's destiny, Flaubert always reveals it as if the corruption came from objects rather than from the bankruptcy of desires'.

24 *Mimesis: The Representation of Reality in Western Literature* (New York: Double day, 1957: first published 1946). Translated by W. Trask.

25 *Mimesis*, p. 431.

26 Poulet, *Les Métamorphoses du cercle* (Paris: Plon, 1961), p. 390: 'Flaubert is the first to construct his novel like a series of focal points, from which, backwards and forwards, on all sides, there is a spreading out of objects and both a temporal and spatial radiation.'

27 Rousset, *Forme et Signification* (Paris: Corti, 1962), pp. 117–18: 'Flaubert's originality lies in the combination of the author's point of view and that of the heroine, their alternation and their interferences, and above all in the predominance granted to the subjective vision of the character in perspective.'

28 Lubbock, *The Craft of Fiction* (London: Jonathan Cape, 1926: first published 1921), p. 73.

29 See Chapter 5, pp. 80–4.

30 H. Hatzfeld, 'Don Quijote und Madame Bovary', *Jahrbuch für Philologie*, II (1927), pp. 54–70, 116–31; Levin, H., *The Gates of Horn* (New York: Oxford University Press, 1966), pp. 246–69; H. Hatzfeld, 'Le Réalisme moderne dans *Don Quichotte* et *Madame Bovary*', in C. Carlut (ed.), *Essais sur Flaubert*, pp. 271–84; A. J. Cascardi, *The Bounds of Reason* (New York: Columbia University Press, 1986).

31 For excellent studies in this area see D. L. Demorest, *L'Expression figurée et symbolique dans l'œuvre de Flaubert* (Geneva: Slatkine, 1967), C. Gothot-Mersch, *La Genèse de Madame Bovary*, (Paris: Corti, 1966) M. J. Durry, *Flaubert et ses projets inédits* (Paris: Nizet, 1950) and G. Bollème, *La Leçon de Flaubert* (Paris: Julliard, 1964). See also the more theoretical study of R. Debray-Genette, 'Génétique et Poétique: le cas Flaubert', in *Essais de critique génétique* (Paris: Flammarion, 1979), pp. 21–68, and her 'La Chimère et le sphinx: *Madame Bovary*' in *Métamorphoses du récit* (Paris: Seuil, 1988), pp. 49–70.

32 *Madame Bovary. A Psychoanalytical Reading* (Geneva: Droz, 1985).

33 See E. Starkie's response to this judgement, op. cit., pp. 302–3.

34 *Madame Bovary on Trial* (Ithaca, NY, and London: Cornell University Press, 1982), p. 65.

35 *Flaubert: The Uses of Uncertainty* (London: Paul Elek, 1974, p. 19.

36 ibid, p. 100.

37 ibid, p. 144.

38 *Adultery in the Novel* (London: Johns Hopkins University Press, 1979), p. 13.

39 ibid., p. 240.

40 See for a particularly clear statement of this view in a recent work D. Knight, *Flaubert's Characters: The Language of Illusion* (Cambridge: Cambridge University Press, 1985), p. 6.

41 See M. Lowe, *Towards the Real Flaubert* (Oxford: Clarendon Press, 1984) and S. Haig, *Flaubert and the Gift of Speech* (Cambridge: Cambridge University Press, 1986).

CHAPTER 9

Towards a conclusion

L'ineptie consiste à vouloir conclure
(Flaubert)

If *Madame Bovary* makes such an impact on the reader, if it has influenced so many writers from Henry James to Vargas Llosa, from Proust to Kafka, and if it has inspired so many critical theories, the reasons lie very much in the tensions it maintains between irony and sympathy, between pessimism and optimism, between the disappointments of life and the promises of life. Although all these oppositions are in part linguistic products, to limit them to such a narrow area, to argue in other words that the novel is merely self-referential, is to deprive it of much of its force and almost all its brutality. Flaubert's realism is no simple reproduction of external realities, even if such a thing were possible: it operates by intertwining images of the mind and the responses of the senses, by constantly drawing attention to the deceptive power of language and the eagerness with which the mind allows language to deceive it. For Flaubert, too, realism both subsumes the classical myths and creates its own myths, so that even so minor a character as the blind beggar, for instance, can simultaneously offer a sharply etched image of a debased Tireisias and a suggestion of an image of the connections between sexuality and physical decay that is much more firmly rooted in the nineteenth century. Charles's cap provokes both a mocking description of a contemporary reality and a symbol of the kind of unnecessary complexity with which so many of the characters invest their existences. Those critics, mainly Anglo-Saxon, who have asserted that it is *lisible* but not *visible* seem, for the purposes of theoretical arguments, to ignore the obvious fact that here, as in numerous other depictions (that of the wedding cake or Binet's wooden copy of an ivory ornament, for instance), part of Flaubert's purpose and pleasure lies in facing the challenge of rendering in language the bad taste of an age devoted to materialism and not yet enjoying the easy simplicity of mass production.

The sense of challenge that colours so much of the novel, and which this study has attempted to emphasize, is also what makes this such a brutal novel, one that constantly throws down the gauntlet to the reader. Do we respond to Charles with the patronising condescension suggested by the opening passages' first-person narrator? Do we accept the blandly expressed assertion by the second book's narrative voice that Emma's death has changed nothing, and allow ourselves to regard her existence merely with irony, disregarding the constant murmur of sympathy that runs through the work? Do we mock Emma for her lack of intelligence and discrimination when the only character in the novel who is granted intelligence rather than mere cunning, Larivière, is shown to be powerless when confronted with the unalterable reality of death? Above all, Flaubert raises questions about the nature of desire, particularly about the desire to make the world, or ourselves, different from what it is and we are. What he reveals is that the more Emma desires something, the further away it seems, as is the case with Paris, for instance. The more she thinks of something the less clear it becomes, so that her image of an ideal lover loses all clarity behind the layers of expectation, building up like the attributes of a god until finally all she perceives is the accumulation of attributes rather than any individual. The more she explores language, the less meaning the words seem to possess. Yet what gives the work its particular bite is that Flaubert does not set himself apart from Emma in this: on the contrary, he implacably inscribes the same failure into his own desire to describe and capture reality. Moreover, we as readers are enmeshed in Flaubert's web of irony, for if we read *Madame Bovary*, we probably do so either through escapist longings, as Emma reads her novels, or because we believe that literature has something to reveal to us, also as Emma does. We may convince ourselves that our reading is more complex and subtle than hers, but that is in itself a commonplace of Romanticism. We may dismiss her as an inadequate vehicle, and find ourselves in good company by doing so, but Flaubert's guffaw would remind us of his conviction that there are no adequate vehicles, or more precisely that for the message he is conveying all vehicles are equal. Above all, through the interactions of his characters, the structures of the narrative and the patterns of the metaphors, he forces us to acknowledge that while Emma's aspirations, interpretations and responses may leave her open to ridicule and despair, and may mark her as anachronistic in comparison with Homais, without them she might have been as unobjectionable as Charles, as placid as Mme Homais, and as contented as Rodolphe, but she would have remained as empty as they.

Bibliography

1 *EDITIONS*

Madame Bovary, ed. C. Gothot-Mersch (Paris: Garnier Frères, 1971).
Madame Bovary, *Ebauches et Fragments inédits*, 2 vols (Paris: Louis Conard, 1936).
Madame Bovary, *nouvelle version*, ed. J. Pommier and G. Leleu (Paris: José Corti, 1949).

2 *OTHER WORKS BY FLAUBERT QUOTED IN THIS STUDY*

Bibliomanie et autres textes 1836–1839 (Paris: Jean-Cyrille Godefroy, 1982).
Correspondance, 5 vols (Paris: Conard, 1926–29).
Correspondance, 2 vols (Paris: Pléiade, 1973, 1980).
L'Education sentimentale, first version (Paris: Garnier-Flammarion, 1980) (also contains *Passion et Vertu*).
Souvenirs, Notes et Pensées intimes (Paris: Buchet/Chastel, 1965)

3 *SELECTED CRITICAL READING*

Abel, E. (ed.), *Writing and Sexual Difference* (Brighton: Harvester, 1972).
Amossy, R. and Rosen, E., 'Le cliché ou l'envers de la "représentation" romanesque: *Madame Bovary*', in Amossy and Rosen, *Les Discours du cliché* (Paris: CDU et SEDES réunis, 1982) pp. 66–82.
Auerbach, E., *Mimesis*, translated by W. Trask (New York: Doubleday Anchor Books, 1957).
Badinter, E., *L'Amour en plus* (Paris: Livre de poche, 1980).
Bakhtin, M., *The Dialogic Imagination* (Austin: University of Texas Press, 1981).
Bal, M., *Narratologie* (Paris: Editions Klincksieck, 1977).
Bancquart, M.-C., editor, *Flaubert, la femme, la ville* (Paris: Presses universitaires de France, 1982).
Banfield, A., *Unspeakable Sentences* (London: Routledge and Kegan Paul, 1982).
Bart, B., *Flaubert's Landscape Descriptions* (Ann Arbor, Mich.: University of Michigan Press, 1956).
Béguin, A., 'En relisant *Madame Bovary*', *La Table ronde*, 27 March 1950, pp. 160–4.

Bersani, L., 'Emma Bovary's dangerous fictions', *Novel*, vol. 8, no. 1 (Fall, 1974), pp. 16–28.

Bollème, G., *La Leçon de Flaubert* (Paris: Julliard, 1964).

Bonwit, M., 'Gustave Flaubert et le principe d'impassibilité', *University of California Publications in Modern Philology*, vol. XXXIII, no.4 (1950), pp. 263–420.

Booth, W., *The Rhetoric of Fiction* (Chicago: Chicago University Press, 1961).

Bopp, L., *Commentaire sur 'Madame Bovary'* (Neuchâtel: A la Baconnière, 1951).

Brombert, V., *The Novels of Flaubert* (Princeton, NJ: Princeton University Press, 1966).

Bruneau, J., *Les Débuts littéraires de Gustave Flaubert 1831–1845* (Paris: Armand Colin, 1962).

Butor, M., 'L'Espace du roman', *Répertoire*, II (Paris: Editions de minuit, 1964), pp. 42–50.

Carlut, C., *La Correspondance de Flaubert: étude et répertoire critique* (Columbus, Ohio: Ohio State University Press, 1968).

Cohn, D., *Transparent Minds* (Princeton, NJ: Princeton University Press, 1978).

Collas, I. K., *Madame Bovary. A Psychoanalytical Reading* (Geneva: Droz, 1985).

Crouzet, M., 'Le Style épique dans *Madame Bovary*', *Europe*, vol 47 (September–October–November 1969), pp. 151–72.

Culler, J., *Flaubert: the uses of uncertainty* (London: Paul Elek, 1974).

Czyba, L., *La Femme dans les romans de Flaubert* (Lyon: Presses de l'université de Lyon, 1983).

Danger, P., *Sensations et objets dans le roman de Flaubert* (Paris: Armand Colin, 1973).

Debray-Genette, R., *Flaubert, mirroir de la critique* (Paris: Firmin-Didot et Didier, 1970).

Debray-Genette, R., 'Génétique et Poétique: le cas Flaubert', in Debray-Genette, *Essais de critique génétique* (Paris: Flammarion, 1979), pp. 21–68.

Demorest, D. L., *L'Expression figurée et symbolique dans l'œuvre de Gustave Flaubert* (Geneva: Slatkine Reprints, 1967: first published 1931).

Descharmes, R. and Dumesnil, R., *Autour de Flaubert* (Paris: Mercure de France, 1912).

Digeon, C., *Flaubert* (Paris: Hatier, 1970).

Douchin, J.-L., *La Vie érotique de Flaubert* (Paris: Carrère, 1984)

Du Bos, C., 'Sur le milieu intérieur de Flaubert', *Approximations*, I (Paris: Plon, 1922), pp. 158–79.

Dubuc, A., 'La Première critique sur *Madame Bovary*', *Les Amis de Flaubert*, no. 46, mai 1975, pp. 41–8.

Duchet, C., 'Roman et objets: l'exemple de *Madame Bovary*', *Europe*, vol. 47 (September-October-November 1969), pp. 172–201.

Duchet, C., 'Signifiance et in-signifiance: le discours italique dans *Madame Bovary*', in C. Gothot-Mersch (ed.), *La Production du sens chez Flaubert* (Paris: Union générale d'édition, 1975), 358–94.

Dumesnil, R., *La Publication de Madame Bovary* (Amiens: Malfère, 1928).

Dumesnil, R., *Gustave Flaubert: l'homme et l'œuvre* (Paris: Desclée de Brouwer, 1947).

Durry, M. J., *Flaubert et ses projects inédits* (Paris: Nizet, 1950).

Fairlie, A., *Madame Bovary* (London: Edward Arnold, 1965).

Fairlie, A., *Imagination and Language* (Cambridge: Cambridge University Press, 1981), pp. 325–460.

Felman, S., *La Folie et la chose littéraire* (Paris: Editions du Seuil, 1978).

Finney, G., *The Counterfeit Idyll* (Tübingen: Max Niemeyer Verlag, 1984), pp. 40–6.

Furst, L., *Fictions of Romantic Irony in European Narrative 1760–1857* (London: Macmillan, 1984).

Genette, G., 'Silences de Flaubert', *Figures I* (Paris: Editions du Seuil, 1966), pp. 223–43.

Genette, G., *Figures III* (Paris: Editions du Seuil, 1972).

Genette, G, and Todorov, T. (eds), *Littérature et Réalité* (Paris: Editions du Seuil, 1982).

Gothot-Mersch, C., *La Genèse de Madame Bovary* (Paris: Corti, 1966).

Haig, S., *Flaubert and the Gift of Speech* (Cambridge: Cambridge University Press, 1986).

Holloway, J., *Narrative and Structure: Exploratory Essays* (Cambridge: Cambridge University Press, 1979).

Jameson, F., *The Political Unconscious* (London: Methuen, 1983).

Iknayan, M., *The Concave Mirror* (Saratoga, Calif.: Anma Libri, 1983).

Knight, D., *Flaubert's Characters: The Language of Illusion* (Cambridge: Cambridge University Press, 1985).

La Capra, D., '*Madame Bovary*' on Trial (Ithaca, NY, and London: Cornell University Press, 1982).

Lattre, A. de, *La Bêtise d'Emma Bovary* (Paris: Corti, 1980).

Levin, H., *The Gates of Horn* (New York: Oxford University Press, 1966).

Lips, M., *Le Style indirect libre* (Ann Arbor, Mich.: University Microfilms International, 1979: first published 1926).

Lowe, M., *Towards the Real Flaubert* (Oxford: Clarendon Press, 1984).

Lubbock, P., *The Craft of Fiction* (London: Jonathan Cape, 1926).

Lukács, G., *Essays on Realism* (London: Lawrence and Wishart, 1980).

Medina, A., *Reflection, Time and the Novel* (London: Routledge and Kegan Paul, 1979).

Moreau, P., *Amours romantiques* (Paris: Hachette, 1963).

Nadeau, M., *Gustave Flaubert, écrivain* (Paris: Les Lettres nouvelles, 1980: first published 1969).

Neefs, J., *Madame Bovary de Flaubert* (Paris: Hachette, 1972).

Pascal, R., *The Dual Voice* (Manchester: Manchester University Press, 1977).

Perruchot, C., 'Le Style indirect libre et la question du sujet dans *Madame Bovary*' in C. Gothot-Mersch, *La Production du sens chez Flaubert* (Paris: Union générale d'édition, 1975), pp. 253–85.

Pommier, J., 'Flaubert et Alfred de Dreux', *Les Amis de Flaubert*, nos: 2–3 (1951).

Pontalis J., 'La Maladie de Flaubert', in Pontalis, *Après Freud* (Paris: Julliard, 1965).

Pouillon, J., *Temps et Roman* (Paris: Gallimard, 1946).

Poulet, G., *Etudes sur le temps humain* (Paris: Plon, 1950).

Poulet, G., *Les Métamorphoses du cercle* (Paris: Plon, 1961)

Prendergast, C., 'Flaubert: Writing and negativity', *Novel*, vol 8, no 3 (Spring 1975), pp. 197–213.

Prendergast, C., *The Order of Mimesis* (Cambridge: Cambridge University Press, 1986).

Proust, M., 'A propos du "style" de Flaubert', in M. Proust, *Contre Sainte-Beuve* (Paris: Pléiade, Gallimard, 1971), pp. 586–600.

Ricœur, P., *Temps et récit*, I (Paris: Editions du Seuil, 1983).

Robert, M., *Roman des origines et origines du roman* (Paris: Gallimard, 1972).

Rousset, J., *Forme et signification* (Paris: Corti, 1962).

Sarraute, N., 'Flaubert le précurseur', *Preuves*, February 1965, pp. 3–11.

Sartre, J. P. , *L'Idiot de la famille*, 3 vols (Paris: Gallimard, 1971–72).

Schöning, U., *Literatur als Spiegel* (Heidelberg: Carl Winter Universitätsverlag, 1984).

Schor, N., 'Pour une thématique restreinte', *Littérature*, XXII (May 1976), pp. 30–46.

Segal, N., *Narcissus and Echo* (Manchester: Manchester University Press, 1988).

Sherrington, R., *Three Novels by Flaubert* (Oxford: Clarendon Press, 1970).

Stanzel, F., *A Theory of Narrative* (Cambridge: Cambridge University Press, 1984).

Starkie, E., *Flaubert: The Making of the Master* (London: Weidenfeld and Nicolson, 1967).

Steegmuller, F. *Flaubert and Madame Bovary: A Double Portrait* (London: Faber, 1968).

Stern, J. P., *On Realism* (London: Routledge and Kegan Paul, 1973).

Sternberg, M., *Expositional Modes and Temporal Ordering in Fiction* (Baltimore, Md: Johns Hopkins University Press, 1978).

Tanner, T., *Adultery in the Novel* (London: Johns Hopkins University Press, 1979).

Thibaudet, A., *Gustave Flaubert 1821–1880. Sa Vie, ses romans, son style* (Paris: Librairie Plon, 1922).

Ullmann, S., *Style in the French Novel* (Cambridge: Cambridge University Press, 1957).

Vargas Llosa, M., *L'Orgie perpétuelle* (Paris: Gallimard, 1978).

Vial, A., *Le Dictionnaire de Flaubert ou le rire d'Emma Bovary* (Paris: Nizet, 1974).

Watt, I., *The Rise of the Novel* (Harmondsworth: Penguin, 1979: first published 1958).

Weinberg, B., *French Realism: The Critical Reaction 1830–1870* (New York: Modern Language Association, 1973).

Wetherill, P. M. (ed), *Flaubert: la dimension du texte* (Manchester: University Press, 1982).

Wing, N., *The Limits of Narrative* (Cambridge: Cambridge University Press, 1986).

Wright, A., *The Formal Principle in the Novel* (Ithaca, N. Y.: Cornell University Press, 1982).

Zeldin, T., *France 1848–1945* (Oxford: Oxford University Press, 1973).

Zola, E., *Romanciers naturalistes* (Paris: Charpentier, 1903).

4   FLAUBERT'S MAIN WORKS

1857   *Madame Bovary*
The best edition in French is that of Mme Gothot-Mersch (see section 1, p. 254).
Readers seeking a good English translation with a selection of critical responses are recommended to use Paul De Man's version published in the Norton Critical Editions series (New York: W. W. Norton and Co., 1965).

1862   *Salammbô*
Recommended edition is that of E. Maynial in the Classiques Garnier series. Translated by A. J. Krailsheimer (Penguin, 1977).

1869   *L'Education sentimentale*
Recommended edition is that of C. Gothot-Mersch (Garnier-Flammarion, 1986). Translated by R. Baldick (Penguin, 1979).

1874   *La Tentation de Saint-Antoine*
Recommended edition is that of J. Suffel (Garnier-Flammarion). Translated by Kitty Mrosovsky (Ithaca, NY: Cornell University Press, 1980).

1877   *Trois Contes*
Recommended edition is that of J. Suffel (Garnier-Flammarion). Translated by R. Baldick (Penguin, 1969).

1880   *Bouvard et Pécuchet*
Unfinished on Flaubert's death, this eccentric comic novel was first published in serial form in *La Nouvelle Revue*, from December 1880. Recommended edition by E. Maynial in the Classiques Garnier series. Translated by A. J. Krailsheimer (Penguin, 1978).

INDEX